OP
EICHM

OPERATION EICHMANN

PURSUIT AND CAPTURE

ZVI AHARONI AND **WILHELM DIETL**

CASSELL

Cassell Military Paperbacks

Cassell & Co
Wellington House, 125 Strand
London WC2R 0BB

First published in English by Arms and Armour 1997
This Cassell Military Paperbacks edition 1999

British Library Cataloguing-in-Publication Data
A catalogue record for this book is available from the British Library

ISBN 0-304-35201-2

Edited and designed by DAG Publications Ltd.
Edited by John Gilbert; designed by David Gibbons

Printed and bound in Great Britain by
Cox & Wyman Ltd., Reading, Berks.

Contents

Foreword

BY GENERAL (RES.) MEIR AMIT

Director of *Mossad* 1963–1968

The operation to capture Eichmann in Argentina was regarded by the Israeli intelligence community with mixed feelings. Some of the intelligence community heads (mainly from among the military intelligence, responsible for the national security evaluation in Israel) felt at the time that *Mossad* was not fulfilling its proper role: the true enemies of Israel were the Arab armed forces, and the ongoing struggle against hostile neighbours demanded a constant supply of information on the current situation and events. There was no doubt that for many months, largely as a result of Operation Eichmann, the main efforts of *Mossad* were diverted from its prime target, and this fact angered a section of the military intelligence.

In the event, it became clear that Operation Eichmann was justified, not just because its objective was of major national importance – capturing the man who was responsible, almost directly, for the operation of the Nazi extermination machinery and for causing the deaths of millions of Jews. But, in addition, the successful planning of this operation, the unfailing determination to see it through, the great resourcefulness shown by the operators in the field, and its clean execution, resulted in increased respect for the Israeli intelligence community in general, and *Mossad* in particular. There is not the slightest doubt that the immense regard for the intelligence community generated by this operation, together with recognition of the extraordinary dimensions of its operational capacity, strengthened Israeli intelligence and contributed to its subsequent success.

Operation Eichmann has been covered by a wide range of 'literature'. A considerable number of books have been written, and the events have been described by various persons at various levels and from various angles of observation. However, in all the books written so far there have been certain constraints which have meant that the writers were not able to present a full and correct picture of what actually happened. This book by Zvi Aharoni describes the operation in a level-headed and objective manner. The reason for this is simple: he was the major factor in the operation, from its beginning to its end. He spent many weeks without despairing and without letting go of the target until the objective was reached. An experienced investigator, with a long-standing record (he served with the British FSS during the Second World War), Zvi Aharoni is an obstinate and honest person who, with endless patience examined the facts and pursued the leads that eventually resulted in the capture of Eichmann. One of the *Mossad* 'old-timers', he was involved in Operation Eichmann from its very beginning, through all the stages of finding and identifying the subject, capturing him and transporting him to Israel.

Zvi Aharoni, who served under me for many years, is known in *Mossad* as a trustworthy person; he climbed through the ranks of *Mossad* and attained one of its highest positions. One could always trust in his evaluation of the situation and his correct action. He was not one to leave loose ends, and he persisted in any objective until the outcome (usually with success). He is a good team member, and here gives full credit to everyone who brought this complex operation to a successful conclusion.

There is no doubt that this book represents an objective and authentic addition to the tale of heroism that led to the capture of Eichmann and his standing trial in Israel. Without Zvi Aharoni and his friends we would never have achieved what we did.

General (Res.) Meir Amit

CHAPTER 1
How It All Began

'The intermingling of blood and the resulting decline in the racial standards is the sole cause of the downfall of all cultures, because people are not destroyed by losing wars, but by the loss of that power of resistance that is vested only in pure blood.'

Adolf Hitler in *Mein Kampf*

The Aronheim family left Germany only a few short weeks before the so-called *Reichskristallnacht*. Hermann Zvi recalls: 'Our train rolled towards Amsterdam and I sat in a compartment in the first class. My mother and my brother were sharing a berth in the sleeper. I had decided in favour of the compartment, because I did not fancy sleeping in the same room with some stranger. The train was fairly empty and I was therefore able to have the compartment to myself. I could stretch out and sleep. We reached the Dutch border at about two o'clock in the morning. The sliding door to my compartment was opened with a crash. Someone turned on the light. I was blinded. Two Germans in civilian clothes came in.

'"Passport, please!"

'It did not sound like a request, but more like an order. I handed them my passport which had the word "Jew" prominently stamped on the front page. The taller of the two leafed through the passport. "Well then, young man, and where are you going?" I explained that I was leaving Germany and emigrating to Palestine. The reaction was not long in coming.

' "Is that so, to Palestine? Well, that's where you all belong."

'The two men looked at each other. Then the shorter one, clearly the one with the higher rank, came to a decision: "Gather up all of your belongings and get off the train. You will be searched in our office in the station." Without waiting for my obvious next question, the taller one added: "No, you will not be able to continue on this train. We do not have sufficient time for a thorough search in the few minutes the train stops here. If everything turns out to be in order, you can continue with the next train early in the morning."

'My heart was beating so heavily that I felt the two of them must hear it. This simply could not be true. I was now so close to the long-planned escape from Nazi Germany. Only a few metres separated me from the border. And here stood these two henchmen of the Hitler regime and were threatening to ruin everything. On the other hand, maybe it actually only did mean a physical search and I might be allowed to travel on in the morning after all.

'I was seized by a feeling that is difficult to describe. I imagined that it would probably turn out for the worst. Jews from all over Germany were disappearing into concentration camps daily. Ridiculous, flimsy explanations were given as reasons for this. If they found my grandfather's gold watch on me, this would probably be enough to accuse me of attempting to smuggle valuables out of Germany. Even the slightest suspicion of a real or imagined breach of the law would be enough to have me disappear into one of their concentration camps.

'I felt panic, but forced myself to stay calm. Don't show them your true emotions and fears now. Don't give them any grounds to become suspicious. Smile. Stay cool.

'I no longer remember how I managed to suppress my panic and control my trembling knees. I got up smiling, gathered up my coat and took my case out of the baggage rack. In a matter-of-fact tone of voice I told the two "guardians of the law": "Half a minute, please. I just have to inform my mother in the sleeper. I don't want her to worry needlessly on my account."

'The two of them were just leaving my compartment, when they suddenly stopped in the door. "So, your mother is in the sleeper?" They looked at me searchingly. The taller one muttered something in the ear of his colleague, who was probably also his boss. I became aware that for the moment they were hesitant.

'Later on I often asked myself what caused them to change their minds. Was it the overly generous tip my mother had given the conductor? Maybe they would share the money with him. Was it my calm and innocent demeanour? Was it humane feelings that the shorter one disguised by his rough manner, or was it my lucky star, that was watching over me? Who knows?

'The shorter one turned back and asked me to open my case. He took a rather superficial look at the objects that were visible, but did not delve down into the depths of the case. Then he closed the case and gave me back my passport. "All right, it's OK. Have fun in Palestine." Both of them left the compartment, grinning, and made the sliding door bang closed with a shudder.

'I wiped the cold sweat off my brow and could hardly credit my luck. I put back my coat and my case and sat down. I did not know what I should do. Maybe the two men would come back. They could possibly take my mother or my brother with them. In my mind's eye, I conjured up all kinds of catastrophes.

'After several minutes which felt like an eternity, the train began to move again and I leaned back. Another stop, and this time a Dutch customs guard came into my compartment. I almost threw myself into his arms. It was now certain that I was safe and that Nazi Germany lay behind me forever.'

The marriage of Heinrich and Eugenie Aronheim was in no way different from that of millions of other Germans. The intelligent social climber Aronheim came from an old family, had once fought in the Army of the *Kaiser* and then opened up a legal practice in Frankfurt on the Oder. By 1933 his was the largest practice in the city. Many of his clients were farmers from the surrounding area. They admired him, because he was always prepared to lend them his ear. And then suddenly, overnight, the Aronheims were 'enemies of the State', because they were Jews.

From then on things went downhill. First the Nazis took away his licence as a notary public. In 1935 this was followed by his debarment from practising law. Heinrich Aronheim was arrested and badly mistreated for a whole day. The Nazis advised him to leave town with his family. At this time, policy was still to foster 'the Zionist emigration of Jews from Germany by any means'. Of the 550,000 German Jews, about 130,000 left their native land between 1933 and 1938.

The Aronheims had three sons. In 1935 Peter Michael was nine, Hermann Zvi was fourteen and Hans Josef was sixteen years old. Hermann viewed developments with great concern: 'When I entered the first form of the Frankfurt *Friedrich-Gymnasium* in 1930, I was a German. I knew nothing else. Germany was my fatherland. Beethoven and Brahms, Goethe and Kleist belonged to me. And then, in January 1933, when I was in the third form, I was suddenly no longer supposed to be a German?

'On the day Hitler seized power, I experienced my first verbal assault. Little Nazi tyrants, who were just two years my senior, had the right to push me around and there was no one I could complain to. Most of the teachers were members of the NSDAP and some openly wore the Party badge.

'The worst of all was the Latin teacher. His name was Thiede. If I gave a wrong answer, he slowly came up to my desk, stared at me for a while and then smacked me in the face without warning. He was a big, strong man. It hurt. He did not hit any other pupil in the class as hard as he did me. Worse than the pain was the sniggering of my classmates. There was no Jewish school in town, so I could not escape.

'We had to run the gauntlet endlessly. Daily we heard slogans such as "Juda, die a miserable death" and "The Jew is the enemy of our nation". I can still hear the song "When Jewish blood spurts from the knife..." ringing in my ears.'

In 1935 the Aronheims packed up and left the city on the Oder. They hoped for greater anonymity in nearby Berlin. And there was an additional reason: Heinrich Aronheim, just turned fifty-five, was gravely ill – mortally ill. The doctors diagnosed cancer, removed a kidney and prescribed radiation therapy. In May 1937, just when the family firmly believed in an imminent recovery, he died. In those days, it was not common practice to inform patients and their families about cancer.

In April 1938, the *Herrenmenschen* published special regulations on how to deal with Jewish property. Fortunes of more than five thousand marks had to be declared, as well as any silver and gold jewellery. The next order required Jewish shop-owners to write their names on their display windows in clearly visible white letters. However, the 'Jewishness' was still not always discernible. The name of the owner of the highly popular leather goods store *Alligator* in Berlin's Tauentzienstrasse, for example, was Adolph Schmidt. Later on the Nazis found a way to close this loophole. Jewish men were forced to adopt the all-inclusive name Israel and all Jewish women the name Sarah.

Eugenie Aronheim, whom everybody simply called Lotte, knew that there was no way back for herself and her sons. Hermann recalls: 'When we left our provincial town and moved to Berlin, it was already clear that we would emigrate sooner or later. Years ago, my father had bought a piece of land in Palestine and my elder brother Hans Josef had started school there in 1933. The only thing holding us back was my father's illness. He was far too weak even to consider emigration.'

On the occasion of the 300th anniversary of the *Friedrich-Gymnasium* in Frankfurt (Oder) in 1993, Hermann Aronheim was asked to give a typical example of an experience during those former days: 'It must have been in 1935, when I was in the fifth form. As fourteen- to fifteen-year-olds we already had quite a lot of instruction and exercises in military matters. One fine day, every pupil was required to fire three shots at a target in the gymnasium. Our form was one of the last to have its turn. The record thus far was held by a boy from the upper sixth who had scored thirty-three points (thirty-six, in other words three times twelve, was the maximum possible). I was one of the last to try. Most of my classmates had already finished and no one had scored better than thirty.

'My first shot was an eleven. Hardly anybody took this seriously. Then I scored a twelve. Pandemonium broke out. What! The Jew is going to be the highest scorer? That simply cannot be possible. All I needed was a ten to share the record with the sixth-former. An eleven or a twelve would put me at the top of the whole school. Therefore, all of my class began to protect the honour of the Aryans. They started to whistle, to stamp their feet, to shout, to scream. The Jew had to be distracted at all costs. They succeeded. The next shot was a seven and everything was back to rights.

'It was only six years later I was to realise that my aptitude as a marksman had not been due to pure chance. In 1941, during a similar competition in my company of the *Haganah*, the Jewish self-defence forces in Palestine, I was to achieve first place.'

Nevertheless, young Aronheim was in many ways a lucky devil and his luck was to stay with him throughout his whole life. Had he stayed in the *Reich*, he no longer would have found Jewish schools except in the major cities. Then, in the summer of 1942, these were also closed down. By now, the *Rassengesetze* (Nuremberg Race Laws) had been in force for some time. Jews who had reached age six had to wear a palm-sized yellow star on their left breast with the word 'Jew' written on it. The so-called *Wannsee-Konferenz* had also taken place, at which the systematic extermination of all Jewish life had been discussed. The greatest catastrophe in German history had begun to run its course.

Hermann Aronheim and his brother Michael escaped extermination because they had a very prudent mother: 'Only weeks after the death of our father, our mother started the ball rolling. She applied for permission to emigrate to Palestine. We were to emigrate on a so-called *Kapitalisten-Zertifikat* (capitalist certificate). This meant we had been able to prove that we owned more than one thousand pounds sterling. We were classed among those who were capable of supporting themselves. Unfortunately, the directives covering such certificates were extremely strict. Only a very few were issued each month. We therefore had to wait for more than one year before we received our certificate for the British Mandate government in Palestine.'

The exodus from Germany was well under way by then. In the end, more than half of the Jews were to succeed in escaping the Nazi criminals. Between November 1938 and September 1939 alone, 115,000 Jews were able to save their lives beyond the borders of the *Reich*.

'It was only in early September 1938, after many hectic and enervating preparations, that we were finally ready. The time had come. My mother, my little brother and I left our Berlin apartment and took a taxi to the railway station at the zoo. It was late in the evening. Due to a light rain and a strong wind, the streets were almost empty of people. At the station we met some of our relatives. They had come to say a tearful goodbye. We were leaving everything behind in order to begin a new life in a strange land.

'They wished us the best of luck. And no one dared raise the question as to who was facing the harsher fate. We were well aware that centuries of Jewish life and Jewish culture in Germany were coming to an end. But obviously no one could conjure up a detailed picture of the approaching "*Endlösung*" (Final Solution), even in his wildest fantasies. The fact was, that we were never again to see any of our relatives who had come on that late summer night. They all died in the Holocaust.'

Let us return to Hermann Zvi and his recollections of the train journey: 'There was further excitement when we reached Amsterdam in the early hours of the morning. Relatives were already waiting on the platform. As the hissing and groaning steam engine came to a stop, we discovered that my younger brother Michael was missing.

'Well past the border, we had met in my mother's sleeper and had had some coffee. Michael wanted to take a little walk through the train. That was his way of letting off steam. It took longer than we had expected. Half an hour before our arrival in Amsterdam, our mother began to worry. I tried to calm her down. "Where else can he be? He is probably on the toilet. Don't worry. Michael will be back in time."

'When my prediction did not come true, I began a systematic search for my brother. I opened the doors to all the toilets. He had disappeared. My mother was already standing on the platform, completely dissolved in tears. Her cousin vainly tried to comfort her.

'A moment later the excitement was over. A husky railway official with a moustache came over to us and explained something in Dutch. Our aunt translated immediately. At the last station, two carriages had been uncoupled and suddenly a young boy had climbed down from one of them. He would arrive with the next train in about half an hour. And that is exactly what happened. Mother embraced him as if she had not seen him for at least a year. It was a beautiful morning in Amsterdam, cool but still sunny. We felt on top of the world.

'The rest was easy. After spending a few days in Amsterdam we travelled on to London, to meet another cousin of my mother's. We wanted to make use of this opportunity to see our relatives again, possibly for the last time. We had paid for this trip with our account in Berlin. The rest of our funds, however, had been kept back in Berlin. We had grave doubts whether we would ever be able to afford such a trip from Palestine.

'From London we flew to Paris. In those days, flying was something quite exotic. Only adventurers flew. Our time was limited, because our ship was leaving from Trieste on 14 September. We therefore booked three seats on an aircraft of Imperial Airways which was then quite famous. It was a four-engined monster that flew the route from England to Indonesia. The first stop-over was Paris.

'From there we took the Orient Express to Trieste. Next morning we boarded an Italian liner. After five uneventful and restful days we had finally made it. At three o'clock in the morning I was standing on deck by myself and was the first to see the lighthouse on Mount Carmel near Haifa. I had just not been able to sleep on this final night of the three weeks of our escape. A few hours later we dropped anchor facing the beaches of Tel Aviv, in those days the only Jewish city in the world. We left the big ship in small motor launches, because there was no port for ocean-going vessels.

'We had reached the land of our dreams, our Holy Land. In Germany we had heard stories about Palestine for many years. Letters from my brother Hans Josef, stories told by visitors, films, magazines... all of this had been exciting and of great promise.

'It is rather curious: even though everything about this new country was strange to me, from the very first day I had the feeling of having come home. I knew that we belonged here. Here, being a Jew was normal. We were not an unloved minority. Here no one would shout "dirty Jew" at our backs. No one would taunt us with "Go home to Palestine". We had come home.'

Two men of a completely different kind also travelled from Berlin to Palestine towards the end of 1937: *Oberscharführer* Herbert Hagen and *Hauptscharführer* Adolf Eichmann, both members of the infamous *Sicherheitsdienst-Hauptamt* (Central Security Office) which two years later was to be renamed *Reichssicherheitshauptamt* (Central Reich Security Office, abbreviated RSHA) and was to unite both the *Sicherheitsdienst* (Security Service) of the SS and the *Gestapo* (Secret Police) under one roof. The RSHA resided at No. 102 Wilhelmstrasse in a former palace of the Hohenzollerns and was the principal secret service of the Third Reich.

This was the lair of the order with the *Totenkopf* (death's head) and the *Sieg rune*, the kraken that began with 270 men in 1929 and was to grow into a mass organisation with more than 750,000 members. Heinrich Himmler left a description of how he went about developing his team: 'Just as the seed-grower, who, being required to again purify a formerly sound strain that has been contaminated and has degenerated, begins by applying the so-called method of herbaceous selection to his field, so too did we begin by weeding out those people who, based on outward appearance alone, we believed we could not use to build up the *Schutzstaffel* (SS).'

Agents Hagen and Eichmann had survived this 'herbaceous selection' and already belonged to Department I, charged with overseeing Zionist organisations. In logical consequence, they subsequently also organised the emigration of the Jews. By a smooth transition, the phase of total extermination was to follow later.

How had it come about that both of them came to Palestine in 1937? Eichmann, who had just turned thirty-one, had met a visitor from the Levant in Berlin and had acquired information about the self-defence army *Haganah*, the *kibbutz* system and the new state, which Zionist Theodor Herzl had already envisaged. Eichmann was then invited to come and see everything on the spot. His boss Reinhard Heydrich approved the trip.

The two secret agents travelled 'under cover'. Adolf Eichmann purported to be a writer for the *Berliner Tageblatt*, Herbert Hagen went as a student. The *SD-Hauptamt* transferred £100 to the newspaper to cover travel expenses. The Eichmann/Hagen duo collected the money from the editor-in-chief. Four years previously, the paper had been taken over by the Nazis and brought into line with Party objectives. Before that, it had belonged to renowned Jewish publishers and the *Sicherheitsdienst* believed that the Nazi take-over was still not widely known outside Germany.

Eichmann recalls: 'We set off via Poland, Romania, to Constanza, boarded the steamer *Constanza*, and so we came to Haifa. After it had made fast in the harbour, we were given permission to land. I took a *droschke*, a taxi, and had myself driven up Mount Carmel.' During a two-day stay, these 'experts on the Jews' visited a *kibbutz* near Tel Aviv and the German colony of Sarona, a place of refuge for Freemasons that had been re-located.

Because the two Germans did not have an extended residence permit for the British Mandate, they next went to Egypt. They visited Alexandria and Cairo. There they met with correspondents of the *Deutsche Nachrichtenbüro* (German News Agency) and applied to the British for a visa to Palestine. This was denied them, probably because the British secret service had discovered the true identity of the SD men. One meeting did come about – with Grand Mufti Amin al-Husseini, an admirer of Hitler and the leader of the rebellious Palestinians. After two weeks, the largely unsuccessful and frustrated Eichmann and Hagen returned to Europe on an Italian steamer.

After his return, Eichmann wrote a report on the trip for Heydrich which (according to its author) was 'completely negative, factually negative'. He cited Jews living in Palestine who would prefer to move into a German

Schulungslager (education camp) rather than continue to stay in the Promised Land. One of Eichmann's muddled explanations for the Jews' longing for the German *Reich* had to do with the alleged 'economic chaos in Palestine'. The Jews were 'defrauding each other, because there was a lack of Aryans to do business with'. Eichmann goes on: 'Characteristic of the total inability of Jews to manage an orderly economy in their own country is the fact that in Jerusalem alone, there are forty Jewish banks that survive by cheating the members of their own race.'

Pseudo-scientific studies of the Jewish race were to become Eichmann's personal obsession. An insignificant recipient of orders was required to report to his superiors and he did so in exactly the vein they wanted to read. Truth did not matter, only confirmation of the prevailing racial ideology. Eichmann, who in the next seven years was to become the architect of the *Endlösung*, in his earliest days with the SS, already personified the 'banality of evil' (to quote Jewish philosopher Hannah Arendt). In her sensational court report 'Eichmann in Jerusalem', she wrote of this exterminator of the Jews: 'The wind had blown him out of a monotonous life lacking any sort of importance or standing into history, as he understood it to be, namely into a movement that constantly remained in motion and in which he – who in the eyes of his class and his family, and therefore in his own eyes, was a failure – could begin anew and still make a career.'

Publisher Gerhard Szczesny contradicts this with a well-considered objection: 'Hannah Arendt is mistaken when she speaks about the "banality of evil" and takes Eichmann for a typical German bureaucrat. Hundreds of thousands of German civil servants, who were just as capable of conducting negotiations and could organise railway movements just as perfectly, and who would also have enjoyed rapid career advancement, neither joined the SS, nor assembled railway cars for the transports to Auschwitz.'

Hannah Arendt points out that Eichmann's principal character trait was a total lack of imagination, in other words, the inability to envisage mentally the sufferings experienced by the millions of Jews sent into the gas chambers; and this lack was particularly remarkable, because when dealing directly with Jewish functionaries, Eichmann proved himself to be quite affable. The nature and dimensions of Eichmann's involvement with evil were anything but banal. Eichmann, like so many of his accomplices, was a failure. Since he had not achieved anything in normal life he became – in accordance with the times – a *Staatsterrorist* (state-employed terrorist), a term, incidentally, that did not exist in those days. If applied to himself, he would not have understood the term then, nor would he now.

Born in 1906 in Solingen as the son of Adolf Karl Eichmann and his wife Maria, née Schefferling, he grew up in the Rhineland during the first seven years of his life and later on in Linz in Upper Austria. The family moved to the banks of the Danube because Eichmann senior took up a position with the Linz Tram and Power Company.

Young Adolf attended Kaiser-Franz-Josef State Secondary School in Linz, from which his future *Führer* Adolf Hitler had already graduated some decades before. A coincidence, and yet such parallels were to influence his life time and again. In 1921, Adolf, the oldest of the five Eichmann children, graduated from secondary school and entered the Linz Higher Federal College for Electrotechnology, Engineering and Construction. After four terms, he left to join the firm of his father, who had meanwhile gone into business for himself. However, Adolf Karl senior's business ventures failed repeatedly and Adolf junior was therefore not able to profit from them.

Three months later he moved to the *Oberösterreichische Elektrobau* company, where he concentrated on selling the new wireless receivers which had just been developed. This job did not satisfy him either and so his father found him a position as 'travelling official' with the Vacuum Oil Company of Upper Austria. At age twenty-two, Adolf Eichmann, the future butcher of the Jews, was selling 'Sphinx Petrol, Petroleum and various types of Gargoyle Mobil Oil'.

For a time this job worked out all right, but then it too came to an end by mutual agreement: 'The work no longer pleased me, I didn't enjoy selling, making calls, any longer. While I did carry on with my job, when the Whitsun holidays were over in 1933, Director Blum told me that they were forced to reduce staff. Since I was the only unmarried field salesman, they had hit upon me and I was being given notice. Personally I was quite pleased that this notice had come about.'

Adolf returned to his parents' house with a settlement of five months' salary in his pocket. By now, his father had taken up trading in electrical products. His son, too, was at his wits' end and had meanwhile turned to politics, having been gathered in by the pied pipers of the *Jungfront-kämpferverband* (Young Front Fighters Organisation). At a rally of the NSDAP, he had met an old friend of the family named Ernst Kaltenbrunner, a lawyer from Linz, who had talked him into joining the SS. At the time, no one could know that Troop Leader Kaltenbrunner, a drunkard prone to violence, was to succeed Heydrich as Chief of the *Reichssicherheitshauptamt* in 1942.

In his private life, Adolf Eichmann was to be more successful than in the harsh world of gainful employment. He had met a plump, dark-haired

Czech girl named Veronika Liebl. On 15 August 1931, twenty-five-year-old Adolf became engaged to the twenty-two-year-old farmer's daughter from near Budweis. Four years later they were married. They were to have three sons, born in fairly rapid succession: Klaus in March 1936 in Berlin, Horst Adolf in January 1940 in Vienna, and Dieter Helmut in March 1942 in Prague.

On 1 April 1932 Adolf Eichmann became a member of the NSDAP with Party No. 889,895. In the SS he was registered as No. 45,326. Mentally he had long abandoned the notion of conventional employment and now merely spent his days within the narrow confines of right-wing comradeship. In June 1933, the subversive Brownshirts were banned in Austria and the whole organisation had, temporarily, to go underground. Adolf Eichmann suddenly remembered his German descent and went back 'home to the Reich':

'So one morning I started out from Linz with the blessings of my family and a German passport; also a certificate from the German consul which said that I was a member of one of the most distinguished families of the German colony in Linz and requested that all German offices give me any support I might need.' The weedy repatriate joined the Bavarian State Police in the Lechfeld camp and became a member of its 'Austrian Legion'. In October 1933, he was transferred to the 'Liaison Staff of the *Reichsführer SS* in Passau'. The SS conducted patrols along the Austrian border together with the border police. 'After Christmas 1934, the whole staff was disbanded and we all marched off to Dachau. Rank-wise I had achieved one star on my collar by then, in other words I was an *Unterscharführer* (corporal).'

Adolf Eichmann was now a member of the *Deutschland* battalion which was comprised exclusively of Austrians. He was again dissatisfied and longed for a posting to the *Sicherheitsdienst des Reichsführers SS* (Security Service of the Reich Leader SS) which had been formed in 1931. What he had in mind was a job as bodyguard, but he had his terminology confused, because the task of protecting the Party bigwigs in Berlin was assigned to the *Reichssicherheitsdienst* (Reich Security Service, RSD). Next came marching orders for Berlin and Adolf Eichmann found himself with the *Freimaurerkartei* of the *SD-Hauptamt* (Freemason File of the Central Security Office), the desk that kept watch on the activities of Freemasons. For him, this too was a strange new world.

But then the twenty-nine-year-old Eichmann was to discover another, very exotic field: The 'Jewish Department' was being established. His first assignment was to write a synoptic review for the SS of Herzl's book about the Jewish State. After this, Eichmann was put in charge of all of the specialised literature (on or by Jews). This included a newspaper called *Hajnt*, which was only published in Hebrew. With painful effort, he began to familiarise himself with the strange characters. His application to be allowed to learn Hebrew with a rabbi was turned down, even though the lessons would only have cost three marks an hour.

Eichmann was very diligent and a born underling in every respect. One of his colleagues from those days already described him as an 'extraordinarily colourless creature', as being 'pedantic, conscientious and without any specialised knowledge'. What he lacked in the way of knowledge, he attempted to make up for by extra zeal, by fanatic dedication. Slowly, the 'Jewish Department' of the *SD-Hauptamt* grew. It was given the code designation II 112. SS *Untersturmführer* Dieter Wisliceny, the twenty-six-year-old son of an estate-owner, was appointed as its head.

For Adolf Eichmann, the conscientious subaltern, 1938 was to be the year of fate. On 30 January, he was promoted to *Untersturmführer* and received official recognition for his 'broad knowledge of the organisational and ideological methods of the enemy, the Jews'. On 12 March 1938, the *Führer* ordered the annexation of his Austrian homeland. The German troops were welcomed in a holiday atmosphere. Adolf Eichmann, too, was ordered by his superiors to go to Vienna. In Prinz-Eugen-Strasse, in the confiscated palace of Jewish banker Louis von Rothschild, he established his first *Zentralstelle für jüdische Auswanderung* (Central Office for Jewish Emigration).

Here the human slave-master with the polite manners and the icy demeanour first began practising his future tactics. He ordered *Judenräte* (Jewish Councillors) and other leading functionaries of the Jewish community to his office and put them under pressure. By such means he succeeded in despoiling the richer Jews bit by bit and in creating an atmosphere, in which they later voluntarily agreed to be resettled in the East – in reality to extermination in concentration camps such as Auschwitz and Maidanek.

The very day the Germans marched into Austria, the Jews in the country had already become fair game. There were anti-Jewish pogroms. Eichmann and Hagen had the Jews arrested according to lists that had already been prepared beforehand in Berlin. The main objective was to destroy the leadership structure of the Jewish organisations and to secure documents and internal records. At this stage Eichmann had left his largely theoretical office work in Berlin behind him. He was now part of the executive, could order arrests and also have people put into concentration camps. The idea was to 'purify' Austria of the Jews.

The main effort was still directed towards emigration. In a 'justification report' to the RSHA on 21 October 1938, the newly promoted *Obersturmführer* Eichmann was able to announce a daily quota of 350 expelled Jews. By 30 September, 38,000 people of Jewish denomination had already left Austria. Eight months later, there was even talk of 99,672 Jews having 'emigrated'. The numbers were exaggerated and only served as Nazi propaganda. Nevertheless, ethnic purification had begun.

Then came 9 November 1938, a Wednesday.

Reichskristallnacht.

This was the day the relatively close season for Jews came to an end. Adolf Eichmann's career as a mass murderer began. He, and no other, was to organise the industrialised extermination of a whole race.

CHAPTER 2
Holocaust

'Only between the two of us will the battle for world supremacy be decided, between the Germans and the Jews. The rest is mere illusion.'

Adolf Hitler

Herschel Grynszpan was the seventeen-year-old son of Polish Jews living in Hanover. He himself was in Paris. There he received a letter from his father, informing him that the National Socialists were expelling the Polish Jews from Germany. Poland, on the other hand, was not allowing them in. They now had to camp in no-man's-land without food or protection from the cold autumn weather. This infuriated the young man.

Acting spontaneously, he went to the German Embassy and asked to speak to the Chief of the consular section or his deputy. Herschel Grynszpan was taken to see the Third Secretary, Ernst von Rath. Without saying a word, the young man pulled a revolver out of his pocket and let off five shots. Ernst von Rath was still alive and Herschel Grynszpan was taken away by the French police. The assassination attempt had taken place at 0930 on 7 November 1938.

The *Reich* Propaganda Ministry recognised this as a unique opportunity to stage a campaign against the Jews. Immediately, the German press was instructed to put the blame on the 'Jewish emigrant clique' and the 'international Jewish criminal scum'. The *Völkische Beobachter*, mouthpiece of the Nazi party, provided further impetus for the events of the next few days. The German nation would react to the deed committed in Paris. It was not to be permitted that thousands of Jews should dominate German shopping malls and pocket the rent money of German tenants. This hit the mark: on the following two days, the first synagogues, as well as Jewish apartments and stores, were put to the torch in Hessen, Saxony and Anhalt.

Ernst von Rath died late on the afternoon of 9 November. On that same evening, Hitler was in Munich with the old guard of his Party and was commemorating the anniversary of the *putsch* attempt in 1923. When the news reached him, he left the rally without having addressed his adherents. *Reich*

Propaganda Minister Josef Goebbels did so in his stead. In a highly emotional speech, he reported on 'measures of revenge' that had already been taken, and said that he foresaw further eruptions of 'national anger'. While he did not explicitly order this, he intimated that no one would be called to account for it.

At dawn, all hell broke loose. Young SA men fanned out and set fire to synagogues. Only a few of them wore uniforms, while most did not let themselves be recognised for what they were, because they were supposed to embody the 'spontaneous anger of the people'. The Brown hordes raged through the streets, demolished Jewish stores, broke into Jewish homes and carried off all the Jews they could lay hands on. They plundered, stole and beat people up. Many of the victims of the pogrom landed in concentration camps – Sachsenhausen, Buchenwald and Dachau. Historians agree on a total of about 30,000 people.

The anti-Jewish activities continued throughout the whole day of 10 November. Everywhere one could hear shouts of 'Down with the Jews!' and 'Kill them!' Only a very few of the so-called 'decent' Germans intervened on behalf of their Jewish neighbours. The orgy of violence was without precedent and uncontrollable. In some cities it lasted for three entire days. About one hundred Jews were murdered in their own homes. Many hundreds lost their lives in the camps during the ensuing months.

In these few days, 267 houses of prayer, 7500 Jewish stores and some Jewish cemeteries were destroyed. The extent of the damage to private property was never documented. Reports by the German media were very low-key and they tried to give the impression that only limited actions of a local nature had taken place.

In reality, it was the beginning of the state-coordinated 'organic solution to the Jewish question', as Hermann Göring called it in a little-publicised speech on 6 December 1938. Göring was addressing *Gauleiter* (District party leaders), District Presidents and *Reich* Provincial Governors.

To quote from what Göring actually said: 'And then there is the matter of setting fires, the matter of burning, so-called incendiary murder. Gentlemen, here it is also very difficult, here it is most difficult, to prosecute someone. Because here, I believe, nobody who set fires – with synagogues this is self-evident, but probably also in the case of private homes – was thinking in terms of a personal gain, but here it also took place out of rage, out of a desire for revenge against the Jews, out of bitterness against the Jews...'

Next, an absurd situation developed: insurance companies were legally required to compensate their Jewish clients for the damages sustained.

Thereupon the government of the *Reich* 'punished' the Jews and confiscated the insurance money, in total 225 million marks. In addition, all German Jews with a fortune exceeding five thousand *Reichsmarks* were ordered jointly to pay one billion marks as 'atonement' for the murder of Ernst von Rath. Since the Nazis assumed the total Jewish wealth to be five billion marks, they calculated on confiscating twenty per cent. Later on they increased the quota to twenty-five per cent.

This national pogrom was followed by further enactments against the Jews. Already on 12 November, they were banned from attending all cultural events. On 28 November, Himmler authorised the District Presidents to ban the Jews from appearing in public at certain times of day. A day later, the order came prohibiting Jews from owning carrier pigeons. Next, they had to hand in their driving permits and car registrations, and were banned from sports facilities and public as well as private swimming pools. In 1938 alone, more than 700 Jewish companies and twenty-two banks were 'aryanised', in other words, stolen.

In the meantime, Adolf Eichmann had established his 'Central Office for Jewish Emigration' in Vienna, known internally as Department II 112. Already in the spring of 1938, shortly after the *Anschluss* (annexation of Austria), the henchmen of the SS were at work. They confiscated the property of the Jewish organisations and had their leaders arrested. Several of these organisations were subsequently re-established, now, however, under the control of the SS. Eichmann involved himself personally in the most minute details and actively took part in the interrogations of Jewish functionaries. The cultural community was allowed to continue activities under Dr Josef Löwenherz, particularly in the area of Jewish emigration. Allegedly, 45,000 applications for exit permits were received by Löwenherz within a matter of only a few days.

Pale, unimpressive Eichmann worked at his new job with utmost dedication. Finally, he was in a position to make things happen, was no longer buried behind shelves of files and index cards in a Berlin office. His boss Heydrich watched him with approval and was not sparing with praise. At a conference held on the 'Jewish question' on 12 November 1938, not only Göring but Heydrich as well took part.

It has been recorded what Heydrich, Chief of the Security Service, said on this occasion: 'In Vienna, based on orders from the *Reich* Commissar, we have established a centre for Jewish emigration, through which we have brought as many as 50,000 Jews out of Austria, while during the same period, only 19,000 Jews were brought out of the *Altreich* (Old Reich, i.e. Germany proper)... The way we did it is, that we made the rich Jews who wanted to emigrate deposit a certain sum of money with the cultural community. This money, and additional foreign currency, was then used to bring the poorer Jews out. The problem was not how to get the rich Jews out, but how to get rid of the Jewish mob.'

Whoever was listening to Hitler knew no later than in 1939 where the road was leading. On 30 January, the anniversary of his seizure of power, the *Führer* threatened: 'If the international Jewish plutocracy inside and outside Europe were to succeed in again embroiling the nations in a world war, the result will not be the Bolshevisation of the earth and victory for the Jews, but rather the destruction of the Jewish race in Europe.' Hitler believed himself to be the Chosen One and he demanded an accounting: 'Only between the two of us will the battle for world supremacy be decided, between the Germans and the Jews. The rest is mere illusion.'

Hermann Aronheim had entered a different world. In Germany, being a Jew meant accepting and practising the tenets of the faith. On Jewish holy days one would go to synagogue. On Friday evening, the candles were lit. Without religion, there was no Jewishness. Those who did not believe took part in the ceremonies out of tradition. It was the only way to demonstrate solidarity and to express a feeling of wanting to belong. In addition, young Hermann had been an active member of a Zionist youth organisation. He had already started to learn Hebrew in the old country and had dreamt of a future as a farmer in the Holy Land.

'Now suddenly, I could be a Jew without ever again having to see a synagogue from the inside. We had so many things in common, the language, the history, the culture. We were all Jews. We lived with Jewish policemen, Jewish judges, Jewish bus drivers, Jewish shop-owners, Jewish street-sweepers. After two thousand years, one could again be a Jew without having to cling to meaningless religious rituals.'

Seventeen-year-old immigrant Hermann Aronheim had only one aim: to be accepted as a member of a *kibbutz*, a farmers' cooperative. He was an idealist, a convinced, even dedicated Zionist and an enthusiastic socialist. It was inconceivable for him, not to live in a *kibbutz*. Therefore he did not hesitate to build himself a new existence under primitive living conditions. Many years later, however, he regretted not having followed his mother's advice, namely to acquire a higher education.

'My elder brother Hans Josef, who was called Yochanan in Palestine, had prepared the way for me. Some months before our arrival, he had joined *kibbutz* Alonim. My brother knew my intentions and he therefore suggested

I should also come to Alonim. I accepted with delight. I registered and six months later, I was a full member. I came to a settlement without a police-man, without a jail, without money, without a house of prayer. There were no locks on any of the doors. Nobody was rich, nobody was poor. The person who cleaned the toilets had exactly the same rights and privileges as the Sec-retary General. I was happy.

'Not counting several short breaks, I lived in Alonim from 1938 to 1943, after which I volunteered for the British Army. These five years in Lower Galilee were, beyond any doubt, the most important of my life. I came to Alonim as a boy and left it as a man. In Alonim I started shaving, learned how to handle a rifle and also how to ride a horse. I learned to speak Hebrew, got married and turned my back on socialism in disappointment. On two occasions during these rough pioneering days, I almost lost my young life through attacks by Arab irregulars.'

In Hebrew *alonim* means 'oaks'. The horseshoe-shaped hills around Alonim are covered with oak forests. In those days in Palestine, this was the only spot with a natural growth of trees. As late as the beginning of the cen-tury, large parts of Palestine had still been heavily wooded. But the Turks needed wood to build and run their railways. After their withdrawal at the end of the First World War, it took more than twenty years before the origi-nal forests slowly began to recover.

'I came to Alonim full of romantic ideals and dreams of Palestine and the *kibbutz* concept. Alonim was a young *kibbutz*, lying to the north of the main highway leading to the entrance of the Yezreel valley. I was a bit sur-prised when all I found on my arrival was a number of tents, surrounded by a chest-high stone wall. This was supposed to protect us from Arab snipers. Each of the round tents contained three iron bedsteads with straw mat-tresses. I shared my tent with another boy and a girl. In those days, no one gave a thought to housing both sexes separately.

'The girls all wore very brief shorts, even those that were not exactly young or pretty. We boys ran around with peaked caps, similar to those worn by Russian farmers. At evening festivals, particularly at marriages, we danced the *hora* and sometimes the Russian *krakoviak*. The accompanying music was provided by a single accordion.'

Hermann Aronheim adapted his name to the new environment: he was now known as Zvi Aharoni. In November 1941, at the age of twenty, he mar-ried Ursula Neumann from Berlin, who was two years his senior. She had come to Alonim in 1937 with a group of young Jews. In the *kibbutz* she was in charge of the herd of goats and sheep. In Hebrew, her first name had been changed to Ge'ulah.

'Those were the darkest days of the Second World War. One got married young, because no one could be sure whether there would be a "next year".' However, the couple was to survive many more 'next years' together. Ge'ulah Aharoni died of cancer in the autumn of 1973.

Like many others in the agricultural community, young Zvi Aharoni had become a jack-of-all-trades. He had guarded the settlement at night against the Arab enemy, had helped with the harvest and built walls. In 1941, he entered the ranks of the Jewish Settlement Police, an offshoot of the Palestine Police Force. Ten members from Alonim were in the police. One of their most important assignments was to counter the Arab irregulars who kept attacking Jewish settlements or mining roads and fields in the neighbourhood.

In 1936, the Palestinian people's revolt had begun. The peaceful prelude consisted of a demand by the Arab political parties: they requested the British High Commissioner to permit a democratic government, stop Jewish immigration and ban the selling of land to Jews. Between 1932 and 1936, 200,000 Jews had come to Palestine legally and already made up thirty per cent of the population. After local disagreements and several murders, the conflict escalated.

Amin al-Husseini, The Grand Mufti of Jerusalem, proclaimed a 'holy war for the Holy Land' and the mass of his people followed him. Numerous strikes and acts of sabotage occurred, whereupon the British declared a state of emergency. A British investigating committee finally recommended a partitioning of Palestine. An Arab and a Jewish state were to be formed. The cities of Bethlehem, Nazareth and Jerusalem were to remain under British Mandate. A key sentence from the report by the Peel Commission said: 'The internationally recognised right of the Jews to return to their ancient homeland does not include the recognition of a Jewish right to rule the Arabs against their will.'

Both the League of Nations and the Arabs objected. The conflict grew. Throughout the whole of Palestine, arms were taken up. Between 1 July and 30 September 1938 alone, 640 Arabs, 160 Jews and 28 Britons were killed. In Judaea, a guerrilla organisation fought under the leadership of Abd el Kader Husseini, a popular relative of the Grand Mufti. In the north, armed bands attacked British positions, Jewish settlements and the road and railway system.

In the second half of 1938, the revolt became a national war. In the mountains, the *fedayeen* blew up railway lines and bridges and the British were forced to withdraw from several important locations. Pushed to the wall in this manner, they took drastic action, imposed collective sentences on villages friendly to the insurgents and executed almost one hundred activists.

The British government also opposed the partition plan of the Peel Commission and instead invited the representatives of the Arabs and the Jews to London for a conference on Palestine. This, too, ended without any tangible result. Among other things, the Arabs demanded complete independence for their country and an immediate stop to Jewish immigration. The opposing side also demanded a sovereign state and the British proposed compromises, among other things, partitioning Palestine into three zones.

Finally, in May 1939, the famous White Paper was issued, its most important statements being: creation of an independent State and a stop to Jewish immigration, as soon as the Jews were to number a third of the population. Selling of land to Jews was to be restricted or banned entirely, if this threatened to cause the Arabs the loss of the basis for their existence.

The Jews now speeded-up immigration. Already in 1939, for every ten Jews entering Palestine legally, eight were coming in illegally. Both the Jews and the Palestinians unanimously rejected any solution by negotiation. The result was again fighting akin to civil war. In particular, the newer settlements outside the relatively safe cities such as Tel Aviv or Haifa needed every man capable of bearing arms.

Aharoni recalls: 'I only joined the settlement-police with great reluctance. Ever since the war had started, I had intended to volunteer for the British Army. I felt it was important to contribute to the fight against Nazi Germany, my former homeland, that had treated us so completely without pity. Every time when our *kibbutz* had been requested by the Jewish Agency to send one or two volunteers for military service in accordance with the nationally established quota, I had asked them to send me. Every time I was turned down. I do not know the reason why.

'Then, towards the end of 1941, I was persuaded to join the Jewish Settlement Police. At this time, the war was going very badly for the Allies. The German *Afrika Korps* had overrun North Africa and was knocking at the gates of Egypt. All of the Balkans were in German hands and in Russia, the German *Panzer* divisions were moving towards the Caucasian Mountains. Everybody believed it to be only a matter of time before the Germans would take the eastern Mediterranean in a pincer movement and unite their forces on the Suez Canal. On their way there, they would naturally overrun strategically situated Palestine.

'The Jews in Palestine were prepared to defend themselves against this advance to the last man. We would have fought even without tanks. The

British could regroup in Iraq or in Pakistan, the Russians could withdraw to Siberia. We had no possibility of escape. We would have stood up and fought.

'The Jewish Settlement Police was regarded as an important element in the defensive network. Every policeman had a rifle, quite openly and legally, day and night. Our force was organised and trained along military lines. In those trying days, the Settlement Police was valued more highly for the defence of Palestine than were the British military units. The majority of the Jewish volunteers in the British Army were sent to Iraq or East Africa in those days, to guard ammunition dumps or similar things. They were lost to the defence of Palestine. When I realised this, I agreed to join the Settlement Police. This was in 1941.

'In March 1943, however, after El Alamein and Stalingrad, it was clear that the Germans no longer posed a threat. The German *Wehrmacht* was in retreat on all fronts. I still wanted to fight against Nazi Germany. So I left the police, in order to join the regular British Army. The leadership of the *kibbutz* still vetoed the idea. I therefore resigned as a member of Alonim and joined the British Army as a private citizen.'

In January 1939, Eichmann's 'Vienna model' was extended throughout the whole *Reich*. In the *Innenministerium* (Home Office) in Berlin, Heydrich established the '*Reich* Centre for Jewish Emigration'. This expert from the *Ostmark* (Austria) was allowed to climb one rank higher to become a *Hauptsturmführer*. After the Nazis had created their Bohemia-Moravia protectorate, Eichmann was transferred to Prague in April 1939. He was far from happy about this: 'When one has built up such an office, one does not like relinquishing it.' In exchange, he was permitted to establish a new 'Central Office' on the Moldau (Vltava River). Eichmann, recalling his time in Vienna:

'Up to the moment I was ordered to Prague, the number of Jews that had emigrated from Austria had risen to 150,000. In total, I believe I recall, the number finally reached 224,000 or 234,000.'

Prague was to be only a short stop-over for Eichmann and his experts on expulsion. In Berlin the need soon arose to establish the Jewish Section IV D 4 of the *Gestapo* at No. 8 Prinz-Albrecht-Strasse. With this, the instrument for the extermination of the Jews had been created. The first organised deportations of Jews to the East began in early autumn of 1939, after the *Wehrmacht* had overrun Poland and the Second World War had begun.

In those days, utopian plans for the resettlement of Jews in the East still existed; for example, on a reservation between the Vistula and San rivers in Galicia. In September 1939, Heydrich spoke about 'a Jewish State near Cracow under German administration'. Later on Eichmann even claimed that he had still understood the term *Endlösung* to mean the old concept of deporting the Jews to Madagascar in East Africa – a deliberate attempt to falsify historic contexts.

In any case, in October 1939, Eichmann began the *Verschickung* (sending off) of Jews to conquered eastern Poland. The orders to do so came from his superior, SS *Oberführer* Heinrich Müller, who was Chief of the *Gestapo*'s Department II, Managing Director of the '*Reich* Centre for Jewish Emigration' and Head of Department IV of the RSHA. The first transport with 900 men from Moravian-Ostrau left on 18 October. Two days later, a train from Vienna followed.

The victims were maltreated, hunted and killed. The whole operation was conducted in a very chaotic manner and was therefore subsequently discontinued. Furthermore, there was a lack of trains, because the troop transports of the *Wehrmacht* were given priority. Towards the end of 1939, Eichmann and his staff again discussed all the possible variations of an *Endlösung* – from a reservation in Poland all the way to Madagascar. This tropical island was to be secured in a peace treaty with France.

In the course of 1940, the SS leadership decided that the planned expulsion of the Jews was progressing far too slowly. After all, there were three and a quarter million Jews living in the countries under German domination. Heydrich was of the opinion that a 'territorial *Endlösung*' had to be found. In December 1940, Hitler ordered further deportations of Jews from Vienna. He decided that 'because of the housing shortage in Vienna, the deportation of the 60,000 Jews still living in the *Reichsgau* Vienna to the *Generalgouvernement* (the part of Poland not directly annexed by Germany but administered as an "independent state") is to be brought forward, in other words, is already to take place during the war'.

In early 1941, about 5000 Viennese Jews were shipped to small Polish towns. This operation, too, was only of short duration. There were again problems with transportation. Eichmann's office was now called IV B 4 ('Jewish Affairs, Evacuation Matters'). During May 1941, he was occupied with the expulsion of Slovenes from annexed territories in Yugoslavia and Austria. In France and Holland, Jews were being registered, arrested and some already deported.

The *Führer* Order on the extermination of Jews and Gypsies, 'racially inferior and anti-social elements', was only passed on to the responsible authorities in part. No one was given an order in writing. Later on, *Feldmarschall* Keitel mentioned a meeting at Hitler's headquarters during the first half of March 1941 at which Himmler was given far-reaching powers of authority, which included all required police actions.

In October 1941 in the Czernin Palace in Prague, Heydrich mentioned a 'directive from the *Führer*', containing a 'short-term objective' and an 'ultimate solution'. Heydrich applied the term *Endlösung* to the Czechs. The Bohemia-Moravia protectorate, so Heydrich said, had to become German. The Czechs 'in the final analysis, had no further business being in this territory'.

Historians maintain that Hitler's order to murder the European Jews must have been issued in the summer of 1941. On 3 January 1946, Dieter Wisliceny, Eichmann's former boss, who was later to become his subordinate, testified at the Nuremberg war crimes trials. He reported on a meeting with Eichmann in the summer of 1942 at No. 116 Kurfürstenstrasse in Berlin. At this meeting Eichmann had stated that his assignment to exterminate the Jews was based on an order from Heinrich Himmler, who in turn had been empowered by Hitler.

Wisliceny verbatim: 'Eichmann told me, he could also show me this order in writing, if this would ease my conscience. From his safe, he took a thin folder which he leafed through and then showed me a letter by Himmler to the Chief of the *Sicherheitspolizei* (security police) and the SD. This letter said in essence: The *Führer* had ordered the *Endlösung* of the Jewish question. The Chief of the security police and the SD, together with the Inspector of the concentration camps, were charged with the execution of the so-called *Endlösung*. All female and male Jews who were capable of working were to be temporarily exempted from the *Endlösung* and were to be put to work in the concentration camps. This letter was signed by Himmler personally.'

In this *Geheime Reichssache* (secret state matter) there was never a *Führer* Order in writing. Hitler stayed true to his principle of 1937: 'What one can convey verbally, one should not put down in writing, never!'

Eichmann also explained the meaning of the term *Endlösung* to his guest. It meant the 'planned biological extermination of the Jews in the Eastern Territories'. He, Eichmann was the person in the *Reichssicherheitshauptamt* who was charged with the execution of this order.

Next to the conduct of the war, the NS leadership considered the 'evacuation of the Jews' to be the matter of greatest importance. At a meeting in the *Reich* Propaganda Ministry, Eichmann was reminded of the *Führer* Order to deport the 60,000 Viennese Jews. There were only about 45,000 Jews to be found in the metropolis on the Danube. One should therefore make up the remaining 15,000 with Jews from Berlin. Thereupon the *Hauptsturmführer* was given the assignment to 'prepare a recommendation for the evacuation of Jews from Berlin' for *Gauleiter* Josef Goebbels.

In those days, the deportees were sent to the Warthegau (district in former Poland), to Litzmannstadt (Lodz). In 1941, one of Eichmann's colleagues, SS *Sturmbannführer* Höppner, reported from there: 'This winter, there is a danger that not all of the Jews can be fed any longer. It should seriously be considered whether it would not be the more humane solution to get rid of them by some quick-acting means. In any case, this would be far more agreeable than to simply let them starve.'

In the Warthegau, the first deported Jews and Gypsies were killed by poison gas from December 1941 onwards. The SS *Sonderkommando* Lange (Lange Special Unit) employed mobile gas chambers for the first time. A soldier reported: 'They drove into the prison yard and the Jews – men, women and children – had to climb into the gas wagon directly from their cells. I also saw the insides of the gas wagons. They were lined with tin sheeting and had a wooden grating on the floor. The exhaust fumes were fed into the interior of the wagon. I can still hear the banging and screaming of the Jews: "Dear Germans, let us out...".' As the 'Inspector for gas wagons' reported to his head office: 'Since December 1941, for example, with only three wagons 97,000 have been processed, without there being any deficiencies noted in the vehicles.'

In the occupied territories of the Soviet Union, *Einsatzgruppen* (task forces) of the Security Police and the SD rampaged among the civilian population. Hundreds of thousands were massacred, and not only Jews. Example Minsk: *Einsatzgruppe* B of the SS murdered all of the Jewish intellectuals. The rest were put into a ghetto. On 31 August 1941, a series of raids were conducted there and 916 people arrested. Next morning they were shot in a mass execution. During his interrogations in Jerusalem, Eichmann, pretending to be a sensitive person, described how he had taken part in such an action. He said that he had become ill. He had then climbed into his car and more or less fled the scene.

On 7 November 1941 alone, 12,000 inhabitants of the ghetto fell victim to the SS killers. The empty apartments were filled with new victims of the deportations. Mass murders in Kaunas (Kovno) and Riga followed. Between the end of November and the beginning of December 1941, more than 30,000 Jews from Germany and the Baltic States were murdered. Historian Raul Hilberg estimates that in the western part of the Soviet Union, during the second half of 1941, the four mobile *Einsatzgruppen* of the SS, numbering 3000 men, butchered approximately 500,000 human beings – most of them Jews.

And the infamous conference in the offices of the International Criminal Police Commission at No. 56/58 Am Großen Wannsee in Berlin had yet to take place on 20 January 1942. The invitation issued by the RSHA already stated that the matter for discussion was to be 'the preparation in terms of organisation, objective prerequisites and material requirements, of the comprehensive solution to the Jewish question in Europe'. Eight State Secretaries, one Ministry Director and six police and security experts, among them Adolf Eichmann, who had meanwhile been promoted to *Obersturmbannführer*, needed only ninety minutes to discuss and agree the technical details for the killing of eleven million Jews. With the extermination of about six million, they were to be successful in the end.

Now it was no longer a matter of deporting or resettling Jews, but of murdering them. Heydrich, according to minutes prepared by Eichmann himself: 'In place of emigration, there is now a further possible solution – based on the appropriate prior approval by the *Führer* – the evacuation of the Jews to the East. Such actions, however, are only to be seen as an evasive measure, albeit such practical experiences will already be gained thereby, as will be of great importance to the forthcoming *Endlösung*.'

Recorder Adolf Eichmann noted down the following decision by the conference in the words of his boss Heydrich: 'Under appropriate control and within the context of the *Endlösung*, the Jews are to be put to work in the East. Segregated according to sex, the Jews capable of working will be led into these territories as large labour columns building roads, whereby without doubt, a large proportion will drop out by means of natural depletion.' What was meant by this was death from starvation and exhaustion.

'The expected finally remaining stock will – because this will doubtlessly be made up of the most resistant part – require appropriate treatment, because it, representing the result of a natural selection, must be seen as being able to serve as the nucleus for a new Jewish resurrection, if it were to be set free.' Once again, what this meant was death, this time, however, not in the form of a 'natural depletion'. Later on in Jerusalem, Eichmann insisted that during the Wannsee Conference one had spoken very openly. For the minutes, he had been required to 'smooth over' and to 'tone down certain excesses', a certain 'jargon', to clothe it with 'official language'.

The highlight of the meeting was the discussion of the various means of killing. Adolf Eichmann should have been able to contribute quite a bit to this, because for some time now he was well informed. Since 3 September 1941 at the Auschwitz concentration camp, the victims of the NS regime were being murdered by means of a prussic acid compound called

Cyclon-B. In March 1942, the camp at Belzec was established, followed by Sobibor in May and Treblinka in July. There were concentration camps such as Theresienstadt, which had the character of retirement homes and could be put on display, and there were the extermination camps with their gas chambers. The worst of these were at Auschwitz-Birkenau and Lublin-Maidanek. It has been claimed that at Auschwitz alone a million human beings were put to death.

During the Nuremberg military trials, the former Camp Commander of Auschwitz, Rudolf Höss, implicated his accomplice Adolf Eichmann: 'Eichmann was at Auschwitz repeatedly and knew the procedures in exact detail.' In his notes, prepared during his captivity in Poland, Höss went much further: 'Eichmann introduced me to the method of killing inside lorries by means of exhaust fumes from the engine, as had been practised in the East up to then. This, however, could not be a consideration in view of the expected mass transports to Auschwitz. Killing by means of carbon monoxide gas through shower-heads in a bathroom, as was being done in some places in the *Reich* to exterminate the mentally ill, required too many buildings, and furthermore, obtaining the amounts of gas needed for such large masses was highly problematical. We did not come to a decision on this matter. Eichmann was going to enquire about a gas that would be easy to obtain and would not require any special installations, and then report back to me.'

Obersturmbannführer Eichmann, the unobtrusive recipient of orders, became the architect of the *Endlösung*. Whenever he recalled his actions later on during his interrogations by the Israelis, he played them down. He never deviated from the version that all he had actually ever done was to coordinate trains. Eichmann verbatim: 'But with the delivery of the transports to their designated terminals in accordance with the timetables set by the Scheduling Conference, my authority came to an end.'

In March 1943, Zvi Aharoni left the *kibbutz* with less than one pound in his pocket. 'Five years of hard work were as if blotted out. Within only a few hours, a whole chapter of my life came to an end. In Sarafand, where the local recruiting office was located, the formalities were quickly taken care of. Next day I already belonged to the forces of His Majesty. But not only I – my wife as well, who did not wish to stay behind alone in Alonim.'

The first three months were taken up by intensive exercises at the Sarafand training camp. In line with British tradition, great emphasis was put on correct drill. 'We were part of the "Palestine Regiment", which was composed of Jews as well as a few Arab volunteers. The chances of being shipped to Europe and serving at the front against the Germans seemed to be minimal, because all of the units of this Regiment were rumoured to remain in the Near East for the duration of the war.

'Therefore when I heard one day that they were looking for soldiers who spoke German, I reported immediately. After a brief language test, I was ordered to the headquarters of the Middle Eastern Forces in the Cairo suburb of Maadi. Overnight I advanced from simple soldier to sergeant. My unit was part of the Intelligence Service. Its job was to interrogate high-ranking German prisoners – and after the interrogation, to listen in secretly on their conversations with bugs. Six months later I was sent to the 8th Army in Italy as part of a mobile unit.'

In September 1943, Aharoni and his comrades received marching orders from Port Said to Naples. The convoy took six days to cross the Mediterranean. In the Straits of Messina one of the ships was attacked at night by German U-boats and destroyed by a torpedo. The days were taken up by alarm and defence exercises. No one knew whether this was for real or just training.

After a few months in Naples, attached to GHQ-CMF (Central Mediterranian Forces), Aharoni was detailed to join a small mobile unit attached to HQ-8th Army, somewhere near the frontline between Rome and Naples. This unit was quartered in tents, partially dug into the ground for greater safety.

Aharoni recalls: 'Many nights German planes came over dropping their bombs. We were not so much in fear of a direct bomb-hit on one of our tents. The chances for that were minimal. However, shells from our own AA defence were exploding overhead and small bits of shrapnel were frequently hitting a tent. We were therefore under order to leave our tents during an air-raid and to take shelter in the nearest stone building. As far as I know no one followed that order. I remember that whenever waking up during an air-raid I pulled my steel helmet over my face and tried to go on sleeping. If I was to be hit by a friendly shrapnel – at least not in the face.

'In May 1944, the Allied troops stood only a few miles south of Monte Cassino. The monastery was being defended by an élite unit of German paratroopers. It was the last desperate attempt to stop the Allied advance on Rome. In the early hours of 11 May, we watched more than a thousand four-engined Allied bombers unload their explosive freight on to the monastery and the surrounding hills. It lasted for over an hour. It sounded like a heavy thunderstorm. Later on, our attack began, led by units from New Zealand and the Polish troops of General Anders. The remaining Germans fought like tigers and therefore it took another three weeks, before our forces were able to take Rome on 4 June.

'In the autumn of 1944, things got quite hot once more when we saw ourselves faced by the last serious German counter-attack at Rimini. Some of our troops had to flee helter-skelter, leaving a large part of their equipment behind.

'The four years I spent in the British Army were an exciting and fruitful period of my life. I learned English and was soon able to enjoy the manner and mentality of the average Englishman. On top of that, we met many soldiers from distant lands like Australia, New Zealand, South Africa and the USA, and got to know each other.' The horizon of the little boy from the *kibbutz* was expanding ever more widely.

'I also managed to acquire quite a bit of Italian. We maintained good relationships with many common people. We liked them, and sometimes we even revered them. I will never forget a family of farmers in a little village called Chiaravalle not far from the Adriatic. We had dug in on a slope next to their vineyard. Within a few weeks we became friends and these people treated me almost as if I were their adopted son. When the front moved north and we had to fold up our tents, the mother wept openly.

'We witnessed how heavily the Italian civilian population had suffered during four years of war, under the German occupation and from the general shortages. I can still see those under-age prostitutes with their naked legs covered with chilblains. In the middle of winter they were inadequately, even scantily, dressed. They offered their services for a handful of cigarettes. I cannot forget the picture of a little boy, maybe nine or ten, who, fully dressed, jumped into the icy waters of the harbour in Naples from a small boat. He fished out a cigarette butt that a soldier had thrown overboard.

'During that winter of 1943-4 things were not very funny in Italy, nor was it a pleasure jaunt. We, the soldiers, also froze and we were constantly hungry. Even a sergeant did not warrant a bed, not even a mattress. We slept on the bare stone floor. We had to use a thin tarpaulin to lie down on. Each man only had a single woollen blanket. And in order to be able to catch some sleep in those unheated Italian houses during the harsh winter, we kept our combat fatigues and our great-coats on even at night. No, it was certainly not funny.'

In order to augment their sparse military rations, many of those from Aharoni's unit were constantly on the look-out for farmers who were willing to trade eggs or apples for cigarettes. Once a week, a mobile canteen came by. Then there were tea and biscuits. Once a week the mobile shower also appeared, and with it warm water and a clean towel. On particularly lucky days, fresh socks were handed out.

The terrible balance sheet of the Holocaust: by the end of 1944, the Nazis had murdered as many as three million Poles, more than 700,000 Russians, more than a quarter of a million each of Romanians and Czechs, over 180,000 Hungarians, up to 130,000 Lithuanians, over 120,000 German Jews, over 100,000 Dutch. The death statistics also include 75,000 French, 70,000 Latvians, 60,000 each of Yugoslavs and Greeks, and over 50,000 Austrians. Particularly in 1941 and 1942, the machinery operated by the 'Eichmen' ran in top gear. During this period, 3.9 million Jews were deported, beaten to death, shot and gassed.

One could recount millions of individual tragedies. A chronicler could portray the insanity of the Nazi death machine three-dimensionally in terms of names and lifelines. There are shattering stories about the fate of Jews from mixed marriages, about the destruction of the ancient Jewish community in Salonika, about the Warsaw ghetto and about Eichmann's final robber's raid against the Hungarian Jews. Many well-founded books written about the 'Eichmann men' describe the bloodthirsty gang of 'experts on the Jews' surrounding Eichmann. It is also important to realise that Eichmann's purge of Jews throughout the length and breadth of Europe would hardly have been possible without the support of local governments and Fascist organisations, such as the *Pfeilkreuzler* (the name is taken from their emblem, two crossed arrows) in Hungary.

One description of the horrors of the concentration camps must stand for all the rest – the account by eyewitness Kurt Gerstein. In 1942, Gerstein, whose secret sympathies lay with the *Widerstand* (resistance movement), was the senior epidemic-control officer with the Chief of Hygiene of the *Waffen-SS*. Gerstein was familiar with prussic acid and poison gas. The SS therefore sent him to the Belzec camp in south-east Poland. He was to develop new and more effective methods of mass gassing. The diesel engines used to produce carbon monoxide were highly prone to break-downs and had to be frequently repaired.

Gerstein came to Belzec and took a tour around the extermination facilities. The system was simplicity itself: Belzec was a small wayside station on the main line between Lublin and Lemberg. It consisted of two ramps and some barracks, one of which carried a sign saying *Kleiderkammer* (clothing store). When entering one saw, among other things, a counter marked 'valuables'. Whoever went through a door marked 'hairdresser' entered a room containing about one hundred chairs. The adjacent open passageway of approximately 150 metres in length was already enclosed in barbed wire. There was a sign pointing 'to the baths and inhalation rooms'. One was now in another building that resembled a bath-house. Gerstein recalls huge pots with geraniums and other plants. A Star of David made out of copper looked down from the roof. This building carried the name *Heckenholt-Stiftung* (Heckenholt Foundation).

Kurt Gerstein, who passed on his observations to the Allies already during the war, was present when a transport of 6000 Jews arrived and went through all the stages of extermination. 'When the train came in, 200 Ukrainians who had been specifically selected for this job pulled open the doors and drove the Jews out of the livestock cars with their leather whips. From a loudspeaker boomed instructions ordering them to take off all their clothing, any prostheses and eyeglasses. They had to tie their shoes together with a short piece of string that a little Jewish boy was passing out. Any valuables and money had to be handed in at the counter for valuables. The women and young girls then had their hair cut off in the hairdresser's barrack (an SS officer who was on duty told me: "They make something special for the U-boat crews out of it").'

The naked, despoiled mass of people moved slowly through the long corridor. Barbed wire to their left and right; behind it, heavily armed Ukrainians. The Gerstein report leaves no questions unanswered. 'They came nearer to the place where ... I was standing before the death chambers. Men, women, young girls, children, babies, cripples, all completely naked, moved past in a long line. At one corner stood a burly SS man with a loud, unctuous voice. "Nothing bad is going to happen to you," he told the poor creatures. "All you have to do is inhale deeply. That strengthens the lungs. Inhalations are a means of preventing infectious diseases. It is a good method of disinfection!"

'They asked what was going to happen to them. He answered: "The men will be employed in building houses and roads, but not the women. They will be given housework or required to help in the kitchen." ... They went up the few steps and into the death chamber, most of them mute, pushed forwards by those who were further back. An approximately forty-year-old Jewess with flaming eyes cursed her murderers. She was beaten on with a few whiplashes ... and disappeared into the gas chamber...

'Inside the facility, the people were crowded together by SS men. "Fill the place up nicely," Wirth (SS officer Christian Wirth) had ordered. "Seven to eight hundred into two hundred and seventy square metres each time." Then the doors were closed. During the ensuing interim, the rest of the people from the train stood around waiting. "Naked, in the middle of the winter," someone said to me, "but they will catch their death!' "That is what they are here for!" was the answer. At this moment I realised why the building was named Heckenholt Foundation. Heckenholt was the driver of the lorry with the diesel engine, whose exhaust fumes were being used to kill these unfortunates...

'The diesel engines were turned on ... twenty-five minutes passed. Many were already dead. One could see them through the small window when an electric light went on inside and briefly lit them up. After twenty-eight minutes there were only a few left alive. After thirty-two minutes, they were finally all dead.

'Some Jewish workers at the other side of the building opened the wooden doors. As compensation for this grisly work, they had been promised their lives and a small share in the valuables collected. The people in the room were still standing upright like basalt columns, because there was not one millimetre of space between them. They could neither fall down nor even lean sideways. Some families were still holding hands, even in death. It was hard work to pull them apart, when emptying the chamber to make room for the next lot.

'The corpses were thrown out, just as they were, discoloured blue, covered with sweat and urine, the legs soiled by excrement and menstrual blood. A few dozen workers searched the mouths of the dead, which they ripped open with hooks, for gold teeth. "Gold to the right, other things to the left!" Other workers searched rectums and genitals for hidden money, gold, diamonds and so forth. Dentists hammered out gold teeth, bridges and crowns... The corpses were then thrown into large pits, each measuring about one hundred by twenty by twelve metres, which had been dug next to the gas chambers.'

If one compares these recollections by Gerstein of the terminal point of Eichmann's chain of destruction with the testimony given by the architect of the *Endlösung* during his interrogations by the Israeli police, then a boundless cynicism comes to light. Adolf Eichmann told his investigating officer Avner Less that 'the evacuation could not just be carried out as simply as that... There could have been as strong a German force stationed there as you like, they still could not just have rounded people up, put them on cars and shunted them off, forward march and away! The whole story of the evacuation in the European countries was a chain of tough, endless negotiations. We had to order the trains from the *Reich* Traffic Ministry, from *Reichsbahnrat* Stange, and we had to contact the SS Central Administration and Economics Department. That is where the destinations were decided upon, because we, we did not know where to. It was not our responsibility to decide where the transports were to go.'

And with typical German attention to detail, the *Reichsbahn* (German state railway) offered rebates to its key client, the SS. It only charged the rate for holiday excursions by groups numbering more than 400 people. A nicety that is little known.

Eichmann increasingly worked himself up with attempts at justification, which were also to mark his trial in 1961 – the largest in the history of Israel: 'I had nothing at all to do with the killing of the Jews. I never killed a Jew, but I never killed a non-Jew either – I never killed any human being. I also never gave an order to kill a Jew, nor an order to kill a non-Jew, that I also never did.' Avner Less, the slightly built police captain who managed to remain fair during his more than 275 tortuous hours of questioning, then reproached him by saying, that he had 'delivered the people to their death'.

Eichmann, completely convinced of his innocence: 'Yes, well, that is correct in so far, Captain, that I had been given the order to evacuate. Not every person whom I evacuated was killed. I had no knowledge whatsoever about who was killed and who was not killed. Otherwise, when a count was made after the war, they could not have discovered 2.4 million Jews who were still alive.'

Whatever Adolf Eichmann may have done within the context of the Holocaust, afterwards he described himself as having been merely an exchangeable dummy. 'Had I not been there, then someone else would have had to take exactly the same decisions, based on the directives, orders and edicts of the chiefs of the department.' An outright lie, because Eichmann pursued the industrialised mass murder with great personal commitment. Despite the fact that his workload threatened to swamp him, he still always found the time to follow up the cases of individual Jews and to apply all the powers at his command to send the person concerned to his death.

Furthermore, when he realised that some Jews might escape him after all, Eichmann even ignored *Führer* Orders. According to a directive issued by Adolf Hitler at the height of the war, the *Reichsbahn* was to give top priority to the requirements of the *Wehrmacht*. This made no difference whatsoever to the organiser of the *Endlösung*. At any and all times, Eichmann was able to bully his way into obtaining rail transport capacity of huge dimensions, so that the death machine was not slowed down.

Dutch writer Harry Mulisch reported on the four-month-long Eichmann trial for the periodical *Elseviers Weekblad*. He recognised and unmasked the emotionless man in the glass cage in Jerusalem and described the machinery of the Holocaust once again from some correct observations.

'In the final analysis, it all boils down to the fact that Eichmann only believed in his own oath. This oath was his God and it lent godliness to the orders he received. It was stronger than the sufferings and the deaths of millions of innocents. The saying, "one man, one oath" held true for Eichmann. He had sworn his oath to Himmler personally in 1932, under totally different circumstances when there was no talk yet of exterminating the Jews, he at least was certainly not aware of such a possibility. And later on, there was no escape from the murder oath sworn long ago.'

Adolf Eichmann's work for *Reich* and *Führer* and *Reichsführer SS* came to an end for all practical purposes on Christmas Eve of 1944. That was when he left Budapest, shortly before the Red Army closed its ring of encirclement. In that year, he had sent half a million Hungarian Jews into the extermination machine. As late as November 1944, 'about 27,000 Jews of both sexes capable of marching and working' had been 'set in march for the territory of the *Reich*' on foot. These 'death marches' were Eichmann's final attempt to destroy the formerly flourishing Jewish community in the Hungarian capital.

In Budapest, the accountant of death was in his element. Asked about the exact number of Jews murdered, a moody Eichmann allegedly told a gathering in the officers' mess: 'One hundred dead are a catastrophe, one million dead are a statistic!'

In April 1945, *Obersturmbannführer* Adolf Eichmann set off on his last business trip to Prague. In Berlin, the final battle had by now been raging for quite some time. Then, like many other SS leaders, he fled into the Austrian mountains. He arrived at Ebensee near Bad Ischl on 1 May.

Aharoni recalls: 'In early 1945, after Italy had surrendered and the Germans had been chased out, our situation changed overnight. For four months, our unit was quartered in one of the finest villas in Florence, with a view over the river, not far from the Piazzale Michelangelo. Each day, I went to a large map of Central Europe and marked down the new front line. The distance separating the Allied armies in the West and the Russians in the East became shorter and shorter. In April 1945, they met at Torgau on the Elbe river and in May the Germans laid down their arms. The war in Europe was over.

'I will never forget that wonderful afternoon, when all the bells in Florence simultaneously began a deafening symphony. The calendar read the 8th of May.'

The mobile group was disbanded. Aharoni and his people went to Rome, where their parent unit had installed itself in *Cinecittà* (motion picture city). However, the volunteer from Palestine spent his final six months in the Army as an interpreter with the 'Field Security Service' of the British Army in Vienna. 'The Austrians told us horror stories about the cruelties and crimes of the Russian soldiers, who had reached Vienna before us. In the prevailing situation, everybody regarded us as liberators and protectors.

'The good life in charming Vienna compensated us for the hardships and deprivations during the war. No official reception or ball took place, without our being invited. We were given free tickets to all the premières at the opera and the theatres. I attended the world première of Werfel's *Jakobowski und der Oberst* in Vienna.

'In the autumn of 1946 I was honourably discharged from His Majesty's Forces. That took place where I had been recruited originally – in Palestine. I was given a set of civilian clothes and my outstanding pay of twenty-four pounds sterling. I was twenty-five years old and – after seven years with *Haganah*, the Palestine Police and the British Army – finally a civilian again.

'*Kibbutz* Alonim informed me and my wife that they would like very much to have us back. We gratefully declined. Life cannot be turned back. I was no longer the same person that had joined in 1938 and left in 1943.

'Even if it meant that we had to start from scratch, we opted for private business and decided to go and live in Haifa, the provincial metropolis in northern Palestine. I did not yet know what I wanted to do. However, I was young and filled with optimism. I believed that only the sky should be the limit.'

CHAPTER 3

Escape

*'You are being sought as a war criminal, but not we. If you were therefore ...
to disappear, you would be rendering a great service to your comrades.'*

Anton Burger, former Commandant of
Theresienstadt to Adolf Eichmann

After it was already far too late, the chief criminals of the Nazi régime showered each other with 'compliments'. 'This was during my very last days in Berlin, in the spring of 1945. It was then that *Gruppenführer* Müller said to me: "Yes, if we had had fifty 'Eichmen', then we must needs have won the war".' Even a dozen years later, statements such as this still filled Adolf Eichmann with pride. It never even entered his mind that this could also have been meant as a two-sided jest at his expense.

'On that day a high-ranking officer came who had brought hundreds of pages with all kinds of different printed letter-heads with him. All the gentlemen of Department IV could now be issued testimonials stating where they had worked during the past few years and what sort of duties they had been officially assigned to, and also any other kind of declaration and testimonial, which they could use as a disguise.'

The *Tausendjährige Reich* was crumbling into a thousand pieces and each and every one of those responsible was attempting to stage the best possible exit for himself. The culprits wanted to hide among the anonymous masses of their millions of victims, who were wandering about homeless in the shambles that had become Europe.

Once again, the humble *Obersturmbannführer* from Linz drew attention to himself as a fanatical civil servant who was convinced of the legality of his deeds: 'Among all of the officials in the *Gestapo* office in Berlin, I was the only one who did not care at all about such false testimonials.' He was soon to reconsider his over-hasty attitude.

Adolf Eichmann survived an Allied air attack on Brixlegg in Tyrol. He was on the way to carrying out his final assignment: 'Himmler told me that he intended to negotiate with Eisenhower and wished me to immediately take one hundred, two hundred – in any case all of the prominent Jews – from

Theresienstadt to safety in Tyrol, so that he could use them as hostages in his negotiations.' But it was already far too late for that. The *Gauleiter* of Tyrol, Hofer, was supposed to house the Jewish hostages. He refused even to listen to Eichmann.

Eichmann went to see his old friend and former boss, Ernst Kaltenbrunner, the last chief of the *Reichssicherheitshauptamt*, the Security Police and the SD. The latter had already come home to Austria, to the region around Bad Aussee. There, between the Toten Gebirge and the Dachstein, many prominent SS leaders went to ground. Here they were also close to the advancing Allies and could change sides in case of need. 'In Altaussee I reported to Kaltenbrunner, but the whole matter no longer interested him. I was given the order to form a line of resistance in the Toten Gebirge and to switch over to partisan activities. This was again a rewarding assignment and I went at it with ardent zeal.' And this despite 'feeling as if during the final days of Pompeii'.

'I was supposed to organise this resistance in the mountains with partially disabled and people who had not served at all. Anybody else would have rejected the assignment, but I was highly familiar with the mountains from my youth.' Horia Sima, the head of the Romanian government, together with several Ministers and Generals who had also fled, put themselves under the protection of Eichmann. 'I took the gentlemen living here in exile to the various Alpine huts and I myself, together with the rest of my men, then took shelter on the Rettenbachalm.'

These men were members of the *Waffen-SS* and, in the end, some pallid Hitler Youth – the scrapings from the barrel. Almost all were lacking in experience. On the other hand, the force disposed of large quantities of food, the newest weapons and lots of ammunition. They were supposed to defend what their prayer-leaders had so melodramatically called the *Alpenfestung* (Alpine Fortress).

Himmler's order no longer to fire on the British and Americans also fell in this period. When this order was received, Eichmann gave up: 'After this order was issued, I dropped all exercises with weapons completely and said to myself, "Now all I can do is send this whole lot home, if they want to go." From one day to the next, Eichmann's bureaucratic world dissolved. He 'now had to lead his own difficult life without leadership', could not 'obtain any directives from anywhere'. He knew, that from now on, 'no orders or directives would come from anywhere, there were no longer any applicable regulations to fall back on...'

During the early days in May, there was sheer despair: 'I can no longer describe the exact sequence of events during these final days, even with the best of intentions, because at the time I was living in a sort of state of shock. Then, when everything did finally collapse, I lost my zest for life. I was indifferent to virtually everything during these days, even had I been put up against the wall. Many others also experienced the same thing at the time; they had fought, worked, worried and feared for the *Reich* and now it was collapsing. The will to live was no longer there.'

While his former comrades, 'the gentlemen from Department IV', were escaping to Switzerland with 'gold and money and death and devil' (Eichmann in his recollections), the Eichmann personally paid off his team with 5000 *Reichsmarks* per man, and – it goes without saying – demanded receipts. Then he went to see the Romanian government-in-exile on the neighbouring Rettenbachalm. Together, everybody moved several hundred metres higher up the mountain.

Next morning, Anton Burger, former Commandant of Theresienstadt, came to see Eichmann: 'You are being sought as a war criminal, but not we. If you were therefore to ... disappear, you would be rendering a great service to your comrades.' After a short, embarrassing farewell ceremony, Adolf Eichmann and Jänisch, his assistant of many years, disappeared.

'In Altaussee I gave my wife a briefcase full of pearl barley and half a sack of flour as a final present. And poison capsules, one for each child and one for my wife, and I said to her: "If the Russians come, you must bite them; if the Americans or the British come, then you needn't." That may have been at the end of April or beginning of May 1945. Those were my only "provisions".' To anticipate the point: the Americans came and Vera Eichmann threw the capsules into the lake.

Several days after the leave-taking on the Alm, Eichmann and Jänisch ran into an American patrol near Ulm. They were arrested and taken to a small prisoner-of-war compound. During his initial interrogation, Eichmann claimed to be Adolf Barth, a *Luftwaffe* corporal. The name called to mind a grocer in Berlin-Britz, the Eichmanns' former place of residence.

The prisoner quickly learned that the American counter-espionage CIC (Counter Intelligence Corps), was giving officers preferential treatment. With the next change of camp, he therefore quickly advanced to become an *Oberscharführer* and finally changed himself into *Untersturmführer* Otto Eckmann, born on 9 March 1905 in Breslau.

Eichmann/Eckmann (in American-English these sound very similar) and his companion Jänisch were moved several times, including to the US camp in Weiden in the Upper Palatinate. 'After a time in Weiden, the Americans demanded that so-called labour companies be formed. I reported for this and since I was pretending to be a *Sturmführer*, I was assigned to the

Oberdachstetten camp in Frankonia as a platoon leader, whereas Jänisch and his unit were sent to the labour camp near Deggendorf on the Danube. This must have been in August 1945. I stayed there until early January 1946.'

In between, he spent several weeks in the Berndorf camp near Rosenheim, in Kematen, and in Cham, a town in the Bavarian woods. There he worked as a member of a construction unit.

Life in the camps became highly dangerous for him, because delegations of Jews, who were trying to identify their tormentors, kept appearing. 'On one occasion, we prisoners were supposed to watch a film about the extermination of the Jews, but we revolted and so we didn't have to watch it after all.' The interrogations also became increasingly annoying. Eichmann noted down later that in those days he had thought of suicide time and again. 'When I call to mind that the *Reich*, the dream and content of my life, lay there in ruin, then I choose death. When I consider that I do not know how long I can continue to conceal my true identity from the officers of the CIC, then I choose death – but I choose life when I think of my loved-ones, who have a right to their lives. And a right to my life... I choose life and throw the poison capsule down the drain.' The subordinate without a leader decided that 'things just have to go on...'.

With the Americans, it could not go on this way much longer, despite the fact that they had trouble administering their almost three million prisoners. Sooner or later they would surely have found him out. Besides that, several officers in the same camp either knew or guessed his true identity. In December 1945 Eichmann asked for an officers' meeting. Even in self-inflicted defeat, friends were noble, helpful and good: 'It was part of the unwritten code of honour, that an officer could only escape if all of his officer comrades or the responsible German camp commander had given their approval, because it was possible that the comrades left behind would be subjected to reprisals.'

Eichmann told the others that he intended to 'discharge himself'. He spoke vaguely of his plans to make his way to the Grand Mufti of the Palestinians in Egypt. The other officers agreed to his escape plan and some even helped him with it. 'Then one night, I carried out my planned escape. I left the camp with papers I had prepared under the name of Otto Heninger.'

Otto Heninger had been born in Breslau on 19 March 1906, was married, a Protestant and worked as a businessman in Prien on the Chiemsee. He carried a piece of paper with him on which his co-prisoner Hans Feiersleben had written down the address of his brother: District Forester Feiersleben, Forestry District Kohlenbach, Altensalzkoth near Eversen, County District Celle.

It was high time. The International Military Tribunal had long begun proceedings against 'Hermann Wilhelm Göring' and twenty-three other defendants. The greatest criminal trial in history was based on 5000 documents, many of which dealt with the millions of murders committed in places like Auschwitz, Maidanek and Bergen-Belsen. The whole régime was represented, by members of the Cabinet and the Party, the *Wehrmacht* and the *Gestapo*, the SS and the SD. Among the accused was Eichmann's last boss and old friend Ernst Kaltenbrunner. The trial in Nuremberg lasted for 218 days and the transcripts filled 16,000 pages. The court heard 240 witnesses and admitted about 300,000 sworn affidavits. Time and again a hitherto largely unknown name was mentioned: Adolf Eichmann.

'It must have been in the summer of 1946 or the summer of 1947, when on the border of the Lüneburger Heide, I came into possession of a whole pile of old newspapers, whose articles, among other things, were about me under such headlines as: "Mass Murderer Eichmann"; "Where is the Mass Murderer Hiding?" I became alarmed when I read that the "infamous mass murderer Eichmann was last held in the camp at Oberdachstetten under the name of *Leutnant* Eckmann". In addition, the date of my escape from the camp was also correctly given and the article went on to say that "he was attempting to reach the Grand Mufti by secret paths he alone knew of". I then said to myself that I had probably got out just in time.'

For a time, Otto Heninger lived in Prien on the Chiemsee. Kurt Bauer, *Scharführer* of the *Waffen-SS*, who had escaped from the US camp with him, had introduced Heninger to his widowed sister, Nelly Krawietz, in Prien. She immediately took a liking to SS man Heninger and arranged for him to find a place to stay on a farm.

In Prien, however, Heninger was not really able to relax, because the place was swarming with US military police. He confided in Nelly, told her that his real name was Eichmann and that he had been involved in the persecution of the Jews. He would prefer to go to North Germany where he also had a contact address. Nelly had never heard of Eichmann. Together they took a train to Hamburg. There they parted.

Eichmann/Heninger went to Eversen in the Lüneburger Heide, not far from Celle. For several years he chopped down trees and raised chickens. In his new surroundings, everything was very peaceful. Nobody asked awkward questions. Life followed a different rhythm than in the big cities, where reconstruction had already begun.

Otto Heninger did not make much money. It was barely sufficient for survival. And yet, a bit was always left over for the travel account. Heninger wanted to leave this country which was no longer his own. The danger that

he too could be brought before a tribunal and – with a high degree of proba-
bility – be sentenced to death, appeared to him all too likely.

More than ten years later, Adolf Eichmann was still able to recall 'that
during the initial years following 1945, I was being sought by the police, first
by the Allies and later also by the new German police. If it is true what the
papers wrote, then Wisliceny was promised his life under the condition that
he would produce me dead or alive.'

Dieter Wisliceny, his former boss and subsequent subordinate and friend,
had actually tried to save his own skin at Eichmann's expense. First of all, he
testified as a witness at the Nuremberg war crimes trials. The corpulent
Sturmbannführer felt he had been abandoned by his own former side and so
he talked incessantly about the Nazi system and the horrors committed
against the Jews. But that did not save him. The former *Judenreferent*
(officer for Jewish affairs) of Slovakia was later brought to trial in Pressburg,
sentenced to death and executed.

In his cell in November 1946, Dieter Wisliceny wrote a twenty-two-
page summary on the subject of the *Endlösung*. Close friend of the family
and godfather to Eichmann's son Dieter Helmut, born in Prague in 1942,
Wisliceny also gave the investigators a 'personal description' of Adolf Eichmann.

'He is about 1.76m tall. He walks slightly bent forward and has a poor
stance. He is quite bow-legged, which is particularly noticeable when he
wears boots. His body is extremely thin. He has thin, dark blond hair and a
very high forehead. The shape of his skull is narrow and long, particularly
noticeable are his hollow temples... In his upper jaw he has two gold bridges
and also many other fillings in his teeth. I would recognise the gold bridges
even in his corpse, because we went to the same dentist.'

Wisliceny's proposal: 'I am able and prepared at any time to help in the
search for Eichmann and in his identification. I would recognise him under
any disguise or despite other changes... I am convinced that I would only
need a few weeks to pick up Eichmann's trail... I therefore suggest having me
attached to an American task force that is to be given the special assignment
of searching for Eichmann.'

This wish was to be denied him. For a long time now, other men with
much patience, energy and world-wide connections were already on the trail
of the former *Judenreferent*. One of them lived in Linz, by coincidence only
a few blocks away from Eichmann's parents. His name: Simon Wiesenthal.
He was himself a survivor of the Mauthausen concentration camp and was

to make the search for Nazi criminals his life-long work. No one else deserves the term 'Nazi-hunter' more than he.

Wiesenthal, who is eighty-seven today, worked closely with the American secret services and with representatives of the Jews in Palestine. The major concern of his co-religionists was the *aliyah*, the transfer of the European Jews to the Promised Land. On the organisational side, this was the assignment given to Arthur Pier from Vienna, who had fled from the Nazis at the age of seventeen. He came back from Palestine under his new name of Ascher Ben Nathan and, for a time, became Simon Wiesenthal's partner. Many years later Israel appointed him to the position of Director-General of the Ministry of Defence and, later, as its first ambassador to the Federal Republic of Germany.

In Vienna, during the early months following the war, Arthur Pier represented – among others – the Jewish Agency and the Jewish self-defence army *Haganah*, nucleus of the Israeli armed forces. He founded the first Jewish Document Centre and brought to it his own, still modest archives on the most important Nazi criminals. The list was headed by a name Pier had heard from many European refugees: Adolf Eichmann.

Simon Wiesenthal initiated the first search of the premises of the Eichmann parents in Linz. The father stated that the son had not returned from the war. This was during the days in which the latter – coming down from the *Alpenfestung* – spent time with his wife and three sons in Altaussee on several occasions. Austrian police then checked on the premises at No. 38 Fischerndorf in Altaussee. Here, with beginners' luck, they stumbled upon SS *Hauptsturmführer* Anton Burger, the former colleague of Adolf Eichmann. A few days later, agents of the American CIC knocked on the door of No. 8 Fischerndorf, home of Vera Liebl and her children.

The plump Czech woman admitted that her divorced husband had been the much sought-after Adolf Eichmann. She had divorced him in Prague in March 1945 and had resumed her maiden name. In April she had come to Upper Austria and now had to support a family of four all by herself. Wiesenthal also visited this resolute woman, but made no progress either.

He was obsessed with the idea of catching Eichmann and bringing him to trial. The first thing he needed was a photograph of the fugitive. This turned out to be far from easy, because Eichmann had always avoided photographers during his career at the centre of power. Therefore he decided to enlist the help of Manus Diamant, a handsome Pole who had survived the Holocaust in Kattowitz and already worked against the Nazis in Hungary. Wiesenthal and Pier used all their powers of persuasion to induce Diamant to become a 'Romeo agent'. At first he refused to have anything to do with the wife of the persecutor of the Jews. 'I'm supposed to kiss the same lips that Eichmann kissed?'

Finally, however, he agreed to become the Dutch collaborator Henryk van Diamant and began to woo several SS 'widows'. Although marginally successful, he made no progress at all with Vera Liebl. Only her sons developed something of a liking for the friendly visitor. But one day, when Diamant announced he was planning to take them out in a boat, Wiesenthal smelled a rat. He rushed down to the Altaussee lake and confronted the Pole. Diamant did not deny that he had intended to drown Eichmann's children. After all, he had lost his whole family, including his own three children, in the concentration camps.

Wiesenthal was able to dissuade Diamant from this fatal plan and encouraged him to continue his special mission with lonely women. This time, however, he concentrated his interest on Eichmann's former mistresses. Simon Wiesenthal: 'During my investigations after the war, I was able to discover nine such ladies who had maintained intimate relations with him for shorter or longer periods.'

One of these was Margit Kutschera from Munich, who had helped to liven up his nights in Budapest. Her photographs with the likeness of the *Obersturmbannführer*, however, had all been lost when the Russians marched in.

Manus then discovered Maria Mösenbacher, aged about forty, from near Linz. He became friendly with her and spent much time in her apartment. There he discovered an album with photographs and a picture of Eichmann. The phantom had finally been given a face, albeit dating from the year 1935.

Towards the end of 1947, Simon Wiesenthal learned that Vera Liebl had presented a declaration by a certain Karl Lukas of Prague to the district court in Bad Ischl. In it, the man stated that he had seen Adolf Eichmann killed on 30 April 1945 during the fighting in the Czech capital. She now wanted her former husband declared dead. This sort of procedure was common in those days, because such a document could secure rights to a pension or make weddings possible.

Wiesenthal believed the declaration to be a fraud. First, he provided the court with affidavits sworn by witnesses who had seen Eichmann alive in Bad Aussee in May 1945 and in Cham in June 1945. The Nazi-hunter also had enquiries made in Prague and received the sensational information that Karl Lukas was Vera Liebl's brother-in-law, the husband of her sister Maria. The whole edifice of lies collapsed and the alleged widow was left without a death certificate.

Simon Wiesenthal today: 'In retrospect, this action was the most important thing I did in the whole Eichmann affair. Had he been declared dead, his name would have been crossed off all the wanted lists and his case would have been closed. Later on, it would have been impossible to renew the search for him. A man who is presumed to be dead is not searched after anywhere. Many NS criminals had themselves declared dead and thereby managed to escape their just deserts. Later on, they lived under a new name and sometimes even with their former wife.'

The highly regarded NS documentator wrote many books in the course of his life, including his memoirs *Justice Not Revenge*. In them he records that the Nazis murdered almost six million Jews: 'Sometimes I asked myself whether Eichmann ever talked about such numbers with his wife or with his children, and how they might have reacted. How did *Frau* Veronika Eichmann-Liebl manage to live with a man who was responsible for the deaths of almost as many human beings as the total number of people living in Austria? Did she believe the accusations raised against him were only malicious slander or did she, on the other hand, hold the murder of the Jews to be a meritorious achievement? Probably it was neither the one nor the other, but more likely a conviction that her husband had only "done his duty". What sort of a duty that was must have been of complete indifference to *Frau* Eichmann. I have no other explanation for how she could otherwise have done what she did: she fought to have Eichmann's escape remain a success and also, to be able to live with him again, by pretending that he had died.'

On 20 March 1946, Otto Heninger from Breslau registered as a new citizen with *Bürgermeister* Rickmann at the town hall in Eversen in Lower Saxony. He was assigned living quarters in a barrack on the grounds of the District Forestry of Kohlenbach. Together with him, there were also twenty discharged soldiers from the Soviet-occupied East, who had now become homeless. In Kohlenbach the barrack was simply referred to as 'the island'.

All of the 'islanders' were employed by the local company Burmann & Co. and worked as lumbermen. Sister Ruth of the Red Cross cooked and cleaned for them. When a reporter from *Stern* magazine visited him in 1960, Eduard Tramer, who had been one of them, recalled: 'I lived and slept in the same room with Otto Heninger. He was what you would call a "real mate". What we liked best about him was his outspoken sense of justice. He always paid attention that the food portions were justly distributed. He never joined us in playing *Skat* (the Germans' favourite card game) or blackjack, which we played a lot in our free time. He gave the impression of being more intelligent than most of the mates on "the island'. I can still recall that he spoke with a slight Austrian accent.'

Otto Heninger was a loner who never talked about himself. He usually wore an old *Wehrmacht* uniform that had been altered in the Bavarian style and a shabby green hunter's hat. When his employer went bankrupt in 1948 because of the currency reform and the successor company, Brauns, also failed to survive for long, he took a lease on a meadow in Altensalzkoth near Celle owned by Anna Lindhorst, a war widow, and began to raise chickens. 'The work was hard, but the personal relationships were very comradely. By saving diligently I was able, over the years, to accumulate enough money for a voyage overseas.'

Until then, Eichmann still kept in touch with the vivacious widow whom he had met on the first stage of his escape in Prien on the Chiemsee. Nelly Krawietz, who by now was on friendly terms with the indulgent occupation forces from across the ocean, travelled to the Lüneburger Heide from time to time with thick packets of food ('I was alone, he was alone...'). In 1950 he wrote her a letter saying goodbye. He intended to go to the Soviet Zone and give himself up to the Russians. They would either accept him or they would execute him. In any case, he would be dead as far as the rest of the world was concerned. 'If you have not received any sign of life from me within four weeks, you can make the sign of the cross above my name.' Besides, he wanted to thank her for all that she had done for him.

Nelly Krawietz from Prien was destined never to hear from Otto Heninger again. In 1953 she moved to Baltimore and married George Kuehn, owner of a delicatessen store. It was only in 1960, when again a widow, that she was to learn all about Adolf Eichmann.

While Eichmann/Heninger was living unobtrusively and unpolitically in the Lüneburger Heide, Simon Wiesenthal suspected him of still being in or around Altaussee. A high-ranking police official informed Wiesenthal on 20 December 1949 'that Eichmann intends' spending New Year's Eve with his family in Altaussee'. Together with members of the local police, Simon Wiesenthal and his people prepared an ambush – but to no avail. Rumours flew. Eichmann was allegedly seen in Cairo and Damascus, and was reported to have been 'exposed' as being employed as a training officer for a new Arab army. The fugitive, however, was closer than anybody realised.

In the spring of 1950 he gave up his modest quarters in the Lüneburger Heide. He told his landlady Anna Lindhorst that he was going to Scandinavia, where he intended to work as an electro-mechanic. District Forester

Feiersleben would come to collect his chickens. And that is what happened. Eichmann disappeared from Altensalzkoth, where no one had looked for him for many years. Together with three other men, he crossed two European borders on his way to Rome. The first time there were no controls at all. In the Austrian-Italian mountains, however, the group literally stumbled into the arms of a border patrol. Two of the illegal immigrants escaped on foot, one of them Adolf Eichmann. He was never again to return to Germany.

Those involved or in the know took great pains to cover up any tracks made during these weeks. After all, this touched on the pro-Nazi activities of the Catholic Church and the Red Cross. Eichmann's decision to leave Europe was allegedly influenced by *Odessa* (*Organisation der ehemaligen SS-Angehörigen*), the 'Organisation of former SS members', which was as prominent as it was mysterious. To the present day, no one has been able to explain convincingly who was behind *Odessa*, how the organisation to help fugitives was structured and who was funding it. It has frequently been suggested that the whole thing was merely an invention that was easy to 'sell' and could readily be combined with all sorts of conspiracy stories.

Holger M. Meding, a highly reputable expert on Latin America at Cologne University, came to the following conclusion in his study *Escape from Nuremberg?* 'This organisation of former SS members appears in the 1946/47 files of the American secret service CIC (Counter Intelligence Corps), without the investigators, however, being able to obtain concrete information on its formation, structure and activities – despite intensive investigation – so that the agents finally assumed that a few small unimportant groups and circles of former SS men had adorned themselves with this secretive name in order to surround themselves with a whiff of mystery. There are no further known facts, only assumptions.'

Simon Wiesenthal's information on *Odessa* began in the region of Altaussee. Decades previously, the dedicated Nazi-hunter claimed to have identified the centre of the Nazi underground movement *Spinne* (spider) as being located not far away in Gmunden. Wiesenthal in his memoirs: 'A second organisation operating in the Steiermark (a province in Austria) was the so-called *Sechsgestirn* (six-point star), to which Anton Burger – whom the police had discovered when they were looking for Eichmann and had entered the wrong house – maintained close contacts.'

Both Nazi organisations, the *Spinne* and the *Sechsgestirn*, were rooted within the larger organisation of industrialist and Nazi sponsor Theodor Soucek, which had its headquarters in nearby Graz. Being somehow interlinked, in the final analysis all of these organisations formed the network upon which *Odessa*, which by that time had already developed its full capabilities, could rely. 'This network obviously gave Eichmann a sense of security that was greater than the fear our network was able to induce. Thank God that he underestimated us to some degree.' Given that measure of mystery, legends and myths about hidden Nazi treasure, chests or even U-boats full of gold bars and bundles of dollars, were not far off. This attracted thriller-writers who, when all was said and done, made it quite impossible any longer to separate fact from fiction.

Adolf Eichmann – and this is a verified fact – made his way to Italy via the 'convent route'. As the name implies, Nazi officials on the run sought the protection of monks. They went underground into convents and told everybody that they 'wished to find their way back to the Cross of Christ'. Because activities of this sort required higher approval, there was also a 'godfather', the dean of the national German church of Santa Maria dell'Anima (Holy Mary of the Spirit) in Rome, bishop Dr Alois Hudal, himself an Austrian.

Already during the early days of the *Tausendjährige Reich*, church-leader Hudal had established friendly relations with the Fascists. In 1936 he published his book *The Foundations of National Socialism*. He sent Adolf Hitler a copy with the fervent dedication: 'To the Siegfried of German greatness'. Hudal was always in close contact with the German occupation forces and, after the war, became one of those who helped fugitives.

In his memoirs, published under the title *Roman Diary*, Hudal openly addressed himself to this taboo subject and admitted that after 1945 he had devoted his 'total charitable efforts primarily to the former members of the NS régime and Fascism, particularly to the so-called war criminals'. According to Hudal his protégées were 'being persecuted by Communists and "Christian" Democrats, often by means whose methods were hardly different from some of those of their former adversaries, despite the fact that these accused were often personally completely blameless, only the executive organs for orders from their superior authorities and therefore only the sacrificial offerings for the expiation of greatly mistaken developments of the system itself'. Hudal's closing remark is characteristic of the stance taken by a very active segment of the Catholic Church at the time: 'I thank ... the Lord that He opened my eyes and also granted me the undeserved gift of having been able to visit and console many victims of the post-war era in their dungeons and concentration camps and – by means of false identification papers – of having torn quite a few of them from the grasp of their tormentors for escape into happier lands.'

Hudal was not the only one. Already during the war, *SS Gruppenführer* and *General der Waffen-SS* Karl Wolff had met with Pope Pius XII in private audience. The Vatican was also present at the negotiation table when the

Armistice was being discussed. The Church expected a power vacuum in post-war Italy and intended to occupy a decisive position.

This was something that Germany's most highly decorated fighter pilot, *Oberst* Hans-Ulrich Rudel, was quick to appreciate. He, too, managed to find his way into exile in South America with the help of the Church: 'In other respects, one may regard Catholicism however one may wish. But for the sake of decency it should not be forgotten, how much valuable substance of our nation was saved, often saved from sure death, during these years by the Church, particularly by humanly outstanding individual personalities within the Church.' Historians agree that about 300 Nazis were spirited away. Eichmann also passed through the benign apparatus of the Catholic tacticians. He was sheltered by the Franciscans until all necessary papers had been obtained. Anton Weber, a Bavarian Father of the Saint-Raphael Community, took care of the architect of the Holocaust and maintained afterwards that he had never been aware of his true background.

That was the first step. The persons being sought disappeared into the safe houses of the clergy. The Italian Red Cross provided identification papers and the Argentinian Immigration Commission in Genoa stamped them. If the fugitive was able to pay for the passage, there were no further obstacles to his sea voyage to the southern hemisphere. In extreme cases, the Church was again helpful and donated the ticket out of Hudal's secret funds. These in turn were partially made up of donations, many from members of the Church in America.

Eichmann was able to purchase a second-class ticket from his own pocket. He had slaved away in the Lüneburger Heide for many years in order to be able to do so. On 14 June 1950, the Argentinian Consulate General in Genoa granted him an entry visa and the 'retired' *Obersturmbannführer* boarded the *Giovanna C*. A photograph shows him on deck with two companions. Eichmann, wearing a hat, a black overcoat and a bow tie, appears well off and content. He arrived in Buenos Aires on 14 July 1950. Again, a completely new life was to begin, but for the last time.

Twenty-five-year-old Zvi Aharoni and his wife Ge'ulah now lived in Haifa, where the stringent life-style of pioneers intermingled with the easy ways of the Mediterranean. The issue now was to build up a new existence. Some days were rosy and full of plans, others were unhappy and offered no perspectives: alternating hot and cold showers of emotions. The Aronheim/Aharonis moved closer together. Mother Eugenie lent her son some money so that he could afford the key-money on a small apartment on

Mount Carmel. Zvi took a number of different jobs, but was not really happy at any of them. For a few months he even tried his hand as an assistant in the accounts department of Palestine Railways.

Again, brother Yochanan helped out. He was able to talk the Jewish Agency into a small scholarship for an ex-soldier and Zvi enrolled as a student at the Technical University in Haifa. His ambition was to become an architect.

Because there was never enough money, Zvi and his wife Ge'ulah were constantly on the lookout for part-time work. She took on a job as a cleaner, while Zvi worked two nights a week unloading heavy crates of oranges from railway freight cars and loading them onto freighters in Haifa harbour. This was back-breaking work for the physically weak student. Often he did not return from the harbour until five o'clock in the morning, only to be sitting in the classroom three and a half hours later.

Then something occurred that was to overturn all civilian plans for the near future. It was 29 November 1947, a momentous date in the history of the Near East. The General Assembly of the United Nations voted in favour of the foundation of the State of Israel. Before that, the British had decided to withdraw from former Palestine and had announced their decision. On 15 May 1948, the last soldier of the Crown would embark from Haifa. The Mandate for Palestine would go back to the United Nations. The British Empire was unable to solve the conflict between the Jews and the Arabs. Now let the UN have a try.

Aharoni recalls: 'I cannot forget that night. It was late afternoon on the east coast in America and almost midnight in the eastern Mediterranean. We clung to the wireless receivers. Up to the final moment it was not clear whether we would achieve the required two-thirds majority. The Arabs fought to prevent the partitioning of Palestine with all their petro dollars and with all the political influence which they already had at the time. For them, this little strip of land was an inalienable part of the great Arab empire. It was not for sale. If the colonial powers were ever to leave, then no one but they should control it. The Arab continent would not carry a foreign bridgehead.

'We Jews, on the other hand, lived with the daily longing for our own piece of land. Size did not matter. Hundreds of thousands of the survivors of the Holocaust were stuck in camps in Europe and Cyprus, victims of the restrictive immigration policy of the British Mandate government. When it became clear that we had achieved the required majority, Jews all over the world – figuratively speaking – danced in the streets.

'Unfortunately, joy was only to last for a brief time. The war in Palestine began the very next day. The British were still present in their Mandate and had to maintain law and order, at least theoretically. This prevented open war between the local adversaries and the invasion by Arab armies, at least until the start of the Israeli war of independence on 15 May 1948.

'The day after the vote in New York, Arab guerrilla forces came over the border – primarily from Syria – to reinforce the local insurgents. When shooting broke out between the Jewish settlers and the Arab *fedayeen*, British soldiers mostly looked the other way. The representatives of the shrinking world empire had written off Palestine. The Jews had to build their own defences in great haste. The still illegal *Haganah* began a country-wide campaign to recruit volunteers. These were no longer local disagreements and skirmishes, this was war. It would answer the question of the life or death of the nation. The *Haganah* took over security duties and no one was prepared to question its authority. *Haganah* was now in command.

'Only days later, my life as a student came to an end. My whole class was converted into a company of the *Haganah*. Before I had really realised what was happening, we were already in Upper Galilee, reinforcing the defences of the beleaguered Jewish quarter in Safed. Since I had attended a course for non-commissioned officers at Alonim during my time with *Haganah*, I was immediately given command of a sector.

'One month later, our unit was incorporated into the Carmeli-Brigade which was soon to become famous. I was now in command of a platoon. As a consequence, I had to take part in almost every battle along the northern front during the first Arab-Israeli war. I had again become a soldier. But this time it was real. It was a matter of life and death. Either they or we...'

Haganah did not come on the scene as a neatly dressed army. Hardly anybody wore a real uniform. The weapons came from the four corners of the earth and belonged to completely different systems. The officers had no insignia of rank. There were no training camps, no military vehicles, let alone troop transports, no military police and no prisons. But morale was high and discipline exemplary.

In 1948, Zvi Aharoni took part in many battles. He often risked his life, particularly drastically during the defence of Ramat Yochanan *kibbutz* in Lower Galilee. In April, Arab irregulars who had come over the Syrian border succeeded in occupying two villages overlooking Ramat Yochanan. Thereupon the inhabitants of the agricultural community became constant targets for Arab snipers. By day, no one could leave the stone houses. The livestock was shot in the stables. The order to clear the two Arab villages on the heights was given to the 21st Batallion and to B Company, 22nd Batallion – Zvi Aharoni's company.

The 21st Batallion was to take the village of Khirbet El Kasatr, which lay closer to the *kibbutz*, whereas B Company was to deal with Khirbet Hoshe, a more distant settlement. For this, B Company was split. The majority of the soldiers were ordered to attack the village frontally, while a platoon of twenty-five men, including Aharoni, was to bypass the village from the south and occupy a chain of hills that dominated the whole terrain. This was intended to prevent the reinforcement of the Arabs after the village had been taken, or at least to make it more difficult.

At first light, the Israeli units stormed both villages and the neighbouring heights without meeting any opposition. As it turned out later, the Arabs – mostly first-class Druze warriors from southern Syria – had always left the villages at night in order to rest and eat in the neighbouring town of Shefar Am. Each morning they came back refreshed. It happened this time, too, just as the *Haganah* was in the process of occupying the villages.

The platoon to which Zvi Aharoni belonged had been spread out over three hills, without any one group being in contact with either of the two others. When the advance guard was overrun by the returning Arabs, the survivors fled in the direction of the *kibbutz*, without their comrades being aware of what was happening.

Suddenly and unexpectedly, Aharoni's group was attacked by four Arabs and engaged in a fire-fight. Before he realised it, Zvi Aharoni was all alone. The others had sought safety with the speed of lightning. He wanted to return the fire, but his sub-machine gun jammed. His single hand grenade rolled away when he threw himself down to take cover behind a boulder. Completely unarmed and almost helpless, he came under machine-gun fire from close by. Only when the Arabs briefly stopped shooting, apparently in order to reload, did he succeed in escaping. He ran down the hill in zigzags.

By a miracle, Aharoni escaped the Arab sharp-shooters. The remainder of his platoon collected in the valley between the two villages. Now there was fire from all the hills around. Arabs appeared everywhere and attacked the Jewish defenders. The battle for Ramat Yochanan was developing far more dramatically than the *Haganah* fighters had ever expected.

Aharoni recalls: 'In my company alone, we had lost twenty-one men. We succeeded in inflicting about three times as many casualties on the Arabs and in holding the two villages. Under cover of darkness we retired in order to bring the wounded to safety and obtain supplies. The following morning when we again tried to occupy the two villages, we found that the Druze had pulled back into the surrounding mountains and given up the siege of the *kibbutz*. We had won the battle.

'At Ramat Yochanan I crossed my personal border. Before then, I had been a soldier. On that day, I became a fighter. I had seen blood for the first time. I had seen others being killed: on both sides. I now knew what the fear of death meant.'

About three weeks later, the last British soldier left the Palestine Mandate and on 31 May 1948, *Haganah* became *Zahal*, Hebrew for 'Israeli Defence Forces'. Only hours after David Ben Gurion, founder of the State of Israel and its first Prime Minister, had announced the birth of the Jewish state at a ceremony in the Tel Aviv Museum, the regular armies of five Arab states crossed the borders into Palestine. But as usual, whenever the Israelis were attacked, they quickly seized the initiative. Theirs was the higher motivation and they were the better soldiers, despite the primitive conditions.

Bitter fighting followed, in the south against the Egyptians, in the centre against the Jordanian Legion and the Iraqis, and in the north against the Syrians. The Arab forces, however, did not coordinate their plans of attack and were hardly able to achieve any gains on the ground. The UN Security Council enforced the first cease-fire on 1 June 1948. The Israelis took advantage of this phase to re-organise their forces and to import heavy weapons.

A new partition plan was again rejected by the Arabs. Therefore war broke out anew on 9 July. The Israelis captured strategically important ground. There were to be still several more cease-fires and clashes of arms. The Egyptians surrendered in the so-called Faluja pocket and agreed to an end to the fighting on 24 February 1949. Within five months the Lebanese followed, then the Jordanians and the Syrians. The 'green line' had been established as the borders to the West Bank and the Gaza Strip.

After the second cease-fire, Zvi Aharoni attended a training course for officers. During this time his company was involved in a military operation similar to the earlier one at *kibbutz* Ramat Yochanan. This time the assignment was to relieve *kibbutz* Manara in the north. However, success was only achieved at high cost. When the newly promoted officer Aharoni returned, many of his comrades were no longer there. Not a single officer in his company had survived the battle: they were all either dead or wounded. The very same day he was given command of B Company. The war went on. When the final armistice was concluded, Aharoni was unhurt and a captain.

Only after the fighting was over did a high fever put him into the hands of the doctors in the Haifa military hospital for two months. The diagnosis read typhoid, although this was never confirmed. Meanwhile, the Aharonis' first child was born, a boy. Zvi was only to see him eight weeks later. Until then, he lay in an isolation ward completely cut off from the rest of the world.

'When I was permitted to leave the hospital, I must have looked like a walking skeleton. I had lost fifteen kilos and I even lacked the strength to climb up one flight of stairs. After two weeks in a convalescent camp I was sent to the central military transit camp near Tel Aviv. There I was to be given a new assignment in accordance with my rank. All of the interviews with possible future superiors ended in a rejection. The way I looked, that did not surprise me. Then one evening, when I was looking for a ride to Tel Aviv, it happened. An unexpected encounter was to change my life and to promote me to a leading position with one of the best secret services in the world within a few months...'

The pick-up truck stopped at the gate of the camp and Zvi Aharoni recognised an old friend from former army days in Italy. He was Bobby Rodan, whom he had not seen for four years. During the drive to Tel Aviv the two of them talked. It was Bobby who made the suggestion to leave the fighting forces in order to look for success on the secret, invisible front.

The term 'General Secret Service' – *Shin Bet* or *Shabak* – meant absolutely nothing to Aharoni and he asked many questions. Bobby referred him to a mutual acquaintance who had served with the same British unit in Italy. His name was Isi Dorot, cover name 'Dafni', and he had already advanced to become Deputy Director of this new, unknown service *Shin Bet*, the internal Security Service. Slightly built Dorot came from Poland, had arrived in Palestine in 1936 as Isidor Roth and had learned the art of interrogation from the British. Even before the founding of the state, he had joined the secret service of the *Haganah*. Bobby gave Aharoni the home telephone number of Dorot and that same evening the two men met and talked about the past and the future. When Isi heard that Aharoni was in the transit camp, he offered him a job in the interrogation section of *Shin Bet*, which consisted of only two members at the time. The rest was a sort of ritual. Zvi Aharoni had to present himself to the chief of the new secret service, Isser Halperin, who would later call himself Harel and become world-famous.

'We agreed to meet in Kapulski's Café in Jaffa, not far from *Shin Bet* headquarters. The interview was short and consisted of only ten to twelve questions. Apparently I left a good impression, because the decision to employ me reached me within days. In those days, *Shin Bet* was still a department of the Israeli armed forces. We were organised along military lines and wore uniforms. We had to carry out interrogations of suspected spies or terrorists.'

In this context, there is a little episode that Ian Black and Benny Morris relate in their history of the the Israeli secret service. After a few general questions, Isser Harel had wanted to know from Zvi Aharoni: 'What do you think about dissidents?' What he meant were the right-wing and extremely violent groups of the *Irgun* and the *Stern*. In Hebrew the word *porshim* stands for dissident. At the time, Zvi Aharoni was still discovering the refinements of the Hebrew language. He was not familiar with the term *porshim*, but was embarrassed to ask what it meant. The subject appeared to be very important to Harel. Since the word sounded very much like *posh'im* – criminals – he took a quick decision and answered clearly and unequivocally: 'I am absolutely against them.' Isser was very pleased, and the short, slightly built refugee boy from Frankfurt on the Oder had a foot on the lower rungs of the career ladder.

He was now part of the Israeli State Security Service, in Hebrew *Sherut ha-Bitachon ha-Klali*, that David Ben Gurion had just created by cell division of the Intelligence Service. Since the foundation of the state, there had only been the SHAI, also known as *Sherut Jediot* or simply Secret Service. Now there were special services, one each for internal and for external affairs, one for the military and one to organise Jewish immigration.

In 1951, the next restructuring took place: on 1 April the feared and famous *Mossad* – in Hebrew *ha Mossad le-Modi'in ule Tafkidim Meyuhadim* (Institute for Reconnaissance and Special Assignments) was founded. The *Shin Bet* also finally became a civilian authority, responsible solely to the office of the Prime Minister.

The ambitious ascetic Isser Harel was thirty-nine years old at the time. Born in 1912 in Witebsk, in Russia, he came to Palestine with his family at an early age. A *kibbutz* near Herzliya then became his new home. Harel, alias Halperin, worked at harvesting fruit and soon joined the *Haganah*. However, he was only to find his true calling with the secret wing SHAI and in operations against the Arab enemies.

This reticent, extremely cautious and boundlessly suspicious Russian exile was quickly numbered among the élite. In 1948 he succeeded in obtaining the Jordanian plan of attack. That opened all doors for him. Isser Harel was to found *Mossad*'s world fame. In his private life, however, he remained a lonely man. Israel's politicians feared his power, his colleagues his puritanical and pitiless manner. Prime Minister Moshe Sharett called the diminutive agency chief (only 1.55m tall) 'a devil in the body of a dwarf'. No chief of an Israeli secret service ever had so much influence, none was so heartily disliked and controversial as Harel.

The chronology of his career: Isser Harel remained as Director of *Shin Bet* until September 1952. That same year, mainly by means of intrigues, he succeeded in having Reuven Shiloah, Director of the *Mossad*, removed from office. Since Harel stood very high in Ben Gurion's favour, he was appointed to succeed Shiloah. His former deputy at *Shin Bet*, Isi Roth, succeeded him as the new Director of the internal service. Isi Roth was not a leader and therefore the ambitious Harel was able to pursuade Ben Gurion to let him keep control of *Shin Bet* as well.

When Roth was transferred to *Mossad* a few months later and was succeeded by Amos Manor, nothing changed. During the whole of his time in office, Harel controlled both services. Simultaneously, he was the permanent Chairman of the 'Committee for Security and Intelligence', to which, in addition to *Mossad* and *Shin Bet*, belonged the police, the military intelligence service *Aman* and even the intelligence section of the Foreign Ministry, *Machleket Hacheker*.

He was only to lose his power after Adolf Eichmann was long dead. The most wanted of all the Nazis, however, never had any chance, while still at large, to understand the system of his adversaries and therefore could not take any serious counter-measures. It was only a matter of time, before Isser Harel and his team – including resourceful Zvi Aharoni – would begin the operation that would lead to the arrest of the man who had committed the incomprehensible against their people.

Chapter 4

Argentina

'I was but a faithful, orderly and diligent member of the SS and the Reichssicherheitshauptamt, filled with idealistic feelings towards my fatherland, to which I had the honour to belong.'

Adolf Eichmann

The eighth largest country on earth – a virtually uninhabited pampas state extending 3800 kilometres from north to south – was ruled by a general, who had already made himself a legend: Juan Domingo Perón. He was both a Fascist and a social revolutionary, an admirer of Benito Mussolini, and a staunch believer in Hitler's ultimate victory. He gained the love of his people because he imposed the most radical social legislation anywhere in the Americas. Half a century ago, Argentina already had employment protection and pension rights, social housing and the forty-hour working week. For this, the *descamisados* – 'those without shirts' – followed Perón and his legendary wife Eva Maria, called 'Evita', with boundless affection. When she, 'the angel of the poor', died of leukaemia in 1952, the 'nation of the tango dancers' fell into a deep depression.

Peron came to power during the war and had supplied the anti-Hitler coalition with raw materials and food. This made his country rich and provided the people with many new jobs. Subsequently, Argentina accepted almost any immigrant who applied for a visa and a job. Few were asked any questions. Before the war, the German Jews had thronged in, afterwards it was the Nazis. To prevent anything going wrong in individual cases, substantial bribes were allegedly paid. Despite the fact that Germans were not allowed to leave their destroyed *Reich* without the permission of the occupation forces, Argentina immediately opened up her gates and did not ask about *Entnazifizierung* (denazification) or for police documents certifying good conduct.

A grateful *Jagdflieger-General* (General of Fighter Pilots) Adolf Galland: 'All over the world the barriers of hate against all things German were still up. Here, among the Argentinian armed forces, we did not encounter any prejudices. In their eyes we might well have lost the war, but not our honour.'

Scientists and technicians were preferred, because Perón wanted to lead his country rapidly from the Third World into the First World. He even paid their air fares. In this way, several thousand highly qualified immigrants came in, many of them from the armaments industry. During the Perón era, about 40,000 people of German stock are alleged to have arrived.

Because the visionary Perón had little understanding of economics, he continued to rule his land until it teetered on the edge of bankruptcy in 1955. Then the Americans, whose traditional influence had been challenged by the social reformers, stepped in behind the scenes and forced the idol of the masses into Spanish exile by means of an economic boycott and a military *putsch*. Argentina continued to exist and, within its borders, many men such as Adolf Eichmann. The General conceded them 'humanitarian reasons', because he considered them as being endangered by the victors' tribunal in Nuremberg.

Besides Eichmann, many other wanted Nazi criminals found safety in Argentina, such as Eduard Roschmann, former Deputy Leader of the Riga ghetto, Josef Schwammberger, Commander of the ghetto in Przemysl, and Josef Mengele, the former camp doctor and *Todesengel* (Angel of Death) of Auschwitz.

The list could be extended by the names of many other known bigwigs of the *Wehrmacht* and the Party. Historian Holger M. Meding claims that about 500 escaped Nazis came to Argentina. In his study he writes: 'The hard core of those who would not have escaped severe sentences even under the most auspicious circumstances, probably numbers between three to five dozen persons. Often under false names, they took up residence in the centres of German settlement, in the capital and in the provinces of Buenos Aires, Cordoba, Misiones and in the area around Bariloche.'

By far the majority have died in the meantime. Only a few are still subjects of interest for Simon Wiesenthal, for European state prosecutors or courts. The most recent case is that of SS *Hauptsturmführer* Erich Priebke, who was involved during the war in the collective shooting of 335 Italians in the Ardeatine Caves near Rome and who later fled to Argentina. He opened up a hotel in the remote Andean city of Bariloche. After a lengthy legal tug-of-war, it was decided in 1995 to extradite the eighty-three-year-old to Italy.

Adolf Eichmann stepped on to Argentinian soil on 14 July 1950. He was relieved and felt safe again for the first time in a long while. The architect of the *Endlösung* was received by a net that had been specifically created for Nazi criminals. On Perón's order, an organisation along secret service lines had been established – the *Secretario de Informaciones* – which was there to help political refugees. Special cases like Adolf Eichmann, Josef Mengele or Josef Schwammberger were cared for by the 'Special Commission Peralta' (Santiago Peralta was one of the directors of the Immigration Office), under the overall responsibility of Rudi Freude, Peron's private secretary.

Historian Meding: 'Argentina wanted to make sure who it was letting into the country by bypassing the existing regulations, on the one hand because of a certain scepticism towards these internationally wanted, but possibly also, in order to be able to make use of these people should the need arise, something that was actually attempted later on.' After an initial investigation and the obligatory medical examination, the refugees were issued an identity card, called *cedula*. In a conspiratorial manner, they were then supported during the initial months and were helped to find suitable employment.

Eichmann, who now called himself Ricardo Klement, was registered in the Argentinian records as 'stateless'. He declared that he was a bachelor with a secondary level education and knowledge of both German and English. He was the natural (illegitimate) son of Anna Klement from Bolzano and had been born there on 13 May 1913. By trade he was a mechanic. Klement deposited his ten fingerprints when he applied for an identity card on 3 August 1950. On 2 October 1950 he received his *cedula* with the number 1378538. Now he felt he was truly free.

At first he lived at No. 1429 Monasterio Street, in the Florida district of Buenos Aires. He did not want to make any mistakes and endanger his silent integration into Argentinian society. He therefore entrusted himself to Horst Carlos Fuldner, a friend of Perón and a banker with the Fuldner-Bank at No. 374 Avenida Cordoba. For four months, Fuldner found Klement/Eichmann a place to stay with Fernando Eifler, a man of German descent. During this time, he supported himself with odd jobs. In 1960, *Stern* magazine reported that Eichmann had been employed as a mechanic in a small metal-working company. He had been very diligent and had been promoted to shift leader after only a short time.

This was followed by the CAPRI period. CAPRI was a company belonging to Fuldner, the initials standing for *Compania Argentina para Proyectos y Realisaciones Industriales Fuldner y Cia* (Argentinian Company for Industrial Planning and Realisation Fuldner & Co.). This embraced, among other things, a recruiting organisation for the production plants of the Argentinian Air Force. It also maintained close cooperation with the state-owned water and power concern, *Agua y Energia Electrica*.

Fuldner brought high-ranking military people such as Galland and Rudel into the country – but also the former Chief Design Engineer of the *Focke-Wulf-Flugzeugbau GmbH* in Bremen, Professor Kurt Tank. The Perón government placed a large facility in Cordoba – the *Instituto Aerotecnico* (Aerotechnical Institute) – at the disposal of Tank and his team, which was soon to grow to fifty engineers and technicians, and gave him almost unlimited funds. His assignment was to develop a jet-propelled fighter aircraft.

The German and Argentinian Fascists got on well with each other. They both practised a Catholic-influenced anti-Semitism. In the Argentinian armed forces, which are steeped in tradition, not a single Jew has been admitted to an officer's career to the present date. The only exceptions are doctors and dentists.

German-Argentinian Fuldner was allegedly born in Buenos Aires but educated in Germany. Police file No. CF A.3380 of 24 March 1962 contains the following verbatim entry: 'During the last World War he was an officer in the SS with the rank of captain. At the end of the war he fled to Spain, from where he returned to our country, being an Argentinian citizen. It is assumed that he is on one of the lists of those being sought by the court in Nuremberg. He eventually accepted a position with the Immigration Office. Some time later he returned to Europe, in order to help Professor Tank's collaborators with their emigration to Argentina. On this occasion he spent approximately one year there. During this time he was supplied with money by the Air Office and the Information Office of the President. One presumes that he successfully carried out his self-assigned task of also bringing people into the country, who were not employees of the already mentioned Professor.'

The mysterious Horst Carlos Fuldner, who in 1953 even appeared as an official of the Office of the President, had a partner named August Siebrecht. This former AEG representative, who had been deported from Chile after diplomatic relations with Hitler's Germany had been severed, had come to the country of his friend Perón and after the war had advanced to become 'coordinator for undercover immigration' (to quote Holger M. Meding). At the height of his activities, he took care of 700 scientists and engineers – many of them Nazi criminals.

One of his clients, Adolf Eichmann alias Ricardo Klement, was placed with CAPRI. The company was investigating the waters in Tucuman and Santiago del Estero provinces under government contract. It was to develop a concept for the construction of dams and hydroelectric power plants. At certain times, no fewer than 300 men worked on this project, many of them and certainly the most important, of German origin. One of the most prominent was a Dr Dardieux, who under his real name of Siegfried Uiberreither, had been the *Gauleiter* of Steiermark province in Austria from 1938 to 1945.

The technical branch office of CAPRI was located in the abandoned village of Cadillal, thirty-two kilometres from the provincial capital Tucuman and 1100 kilometres north-west of Buenos Aires. Whoever worked there could only be reached by letter via a post office box in Tucuman. Ricardo Klement and many of his colleagues shared this address and their *cedulas* were issued under *casilla de correo* 17 (PO Box No. 17).

Klement's new identification card was issued on 8 February 1952. The provincial administration in Tucuman opened file 389,071 on him. During a personal interview, Klement said his profession was a hydrologist. The other data was identical with the 1950 version.

Klement/Eichmann lived in La Cocha, a little village in the mountains. His landlord, Miguel Martinez, recalls a silent oddball. He spoke little Spanish, got up in the morning before all the others and avoided people. He received mail from abroad under the name of Ricardo Klement. After about a year, he moved to nearby Graneros, into a modest house. In September 1952, the whole camp was moved to Rio Portrero, to the village of Las Estancias.

Despite the fact that CAPRI was originally a camouflage organisation, the company did meet its obligations. For several years, it investigated water levels and rainfall and made recommendations on the construction of dams, artificial lakes and irrigation installations.

At Christmas in 1950, a letter for daughter-in-law Vera arrived at the home of Adolf Eichmann's parents at No. 3 Bischofstrasse in Linz. When she saw it, her heart began to pound. The handwriting was very familiar. The sender's name was Ricardo Klement and as a contact address he gave Rio Portrero, Tucuman Province, Argentina. It was the first sign of life in five years from her missing husband.

The mother bringing up three children by herself had almost given up hope of ever hearing from him again. However, in the end, family ties had overcome his fear of being discovered. The letter said that 'the uncle of your children, whom everybody presumed dead, is alive and well'.

From then on she began speaking to her three sons, who were now eight, ten and fourteen, more and more frequently about an uncle Ricardo who was surveying the mountains and jungles in South America and riding through the gorges on his white horse 'El Bravo'. It was very nice there, and therefore they would probably go to visit uncle Ricardo one day. She gave herself ample time to prepare the journey: no one was to discover her real intent. One of her stratagems was to wait a whole year before applying for a German passport under the name of Veronika Liebl. The reason given: she was of Sudeten-German descent and had been married to an Austrian called Eichmann, who was now deceased. The trick worked.

Vera Liebl/Eichmann left Austria with her sons around Easter in 1952. They went to Genoa carrying tickets for the passenger liner *Salta*. Nobody pursued them. No one took an interest in the family of the missing man, who had been involved in murder by the millions.

Klaus Eichmann, who was sixteen years old at the time of their emigration, gave an extraordinary interview to the illustrated magazine *Quick* in 1966: 'During the passage, mother lay in her cabin with a biliary colic, my brothers and I were only seasick once. We arrived in Buenos Aires on 28 July 1952, two days after Evita Perón had died... There were several gentlemen waiting at the dock. They were very kind to us. I did not know any of them. Later on in the hotel, another man joined us. Mother said: "Children, this is uncle Ricardo." He gave us one hundred pesos, a lot of money in those days. We bought ice cream, sweets and I bought my first cigarettes. Then we went out to eat with uncle Ricardo.'

The following day, the reunited Eichmann family took the train to Tucuman and then a lorry to Rio Portrero, the place were 'uncle Ricardo' worked. A few weeks later he disclosed his identity to his sons. They enjoyed to the full the contrast with dreary post-war Austria. 'That was a marvellous life out there in the wilds. We had no electric light, but we had horses instead. When we came out in the morning, the first thing we did was to catch the horses with lassos. But life also had a more serious side for us. We learned Spanish at high speed. Father ordered me to learn one hundred words a day, neither more, nor less. It had to be exactly one hundred words. Our father was very correct, everything had to be just so, everything had to be in exact order.'

The cardinal rule in the family was: keep your mouth shut. The Eichmanns lived in self-imposed isolation and did not react to invitations by other CAPRI employees. Only Horst Adolf, thirteen at the time and nicknamed 'Waston', did not obey the rules. He chattered on incessantly and about everything. He told Argentinian acquaintances that Klement was his stepfather. His real father had died in the war. In Germany they had formerly lived a life of luxury, in a villa with a big garden, and had owned several cars. Furthermore, the soldiers had treated his father with great respect.

Nazi-hunter Simon Wiesenthal soon learned that the family of the exterminator of the Jews had disappeared. The tip came from Altaussee: 'She (Vera Eichmann) had taken the children out of school in the middle of the school year, despite the fact that they would not be accepted at any other Austrian or German school without a school-leaving certificate. While the rent on the house was still being paid and none of the furniture had been carted away, as would have been the case with a move of house, the neighbourhood suspected the truth immediately. Frau Eichmann was obviously in the process of getting away. Presumably to South America, to Brazil, according to rumours.'

The most important piece of information came from an unexpected source. Simon Wiesenthal visited an elderly Austrian baron to look at his stamp collection. The two of them began talking and naturally came to Wiesenthal's main topic, the Nazi war criminals. At this point the host pulled out a letter from an old friend who had emigrated to Buenos Aires. The last paragraph said: 'I saw that dirty pig Eichmann who had pushed around the Jews. He lives near Buenos Aires and works for a water company.'

The machinery of the victims' organisation went back into gear. On 24 March 1953, Simon Wiesenthal passed this new information on to the Israeli Consul in Vienna, Arie Eschel.

When the Argentinian economy went rapidly downhill, CAPRI owners Fuldner and Siebrecht also felt the effects. They had to lay off people and finally to apply for bankruptcy. By then, only the dam and the artificial lake on the Rio Hondo in Santiago del Estero – the largest facility of its kind in Argentina – had been completed.

The Eichmanns continued to live in El Cadillal until July 1953. The three boys did not like having their pictures taken and Klaus, the eldest, got engaged to a girl from Concepción, whose family was spending its holidays in the Tucuman area. The Eichmanns corresponded with relatives and former friends. There were no exciting events.

Eichmann is alleged to have written articles for Nazi-orientated newspapers on occasion. Simon Wiesenthal claims to have found out that in 1951 the subject of his investigations was in contact with the *Deutsche Reichspartei* (German Reich Party) which was later dissolved, and had written an article on the Jewish question for its organ, the *Reichszeitung*. The piece was signed by Alfred Eichenwald, probably a fictitious name.

In July 1953, Veronika and Adolf Eichmann returned to Buenos Aires with their three sons. The 'retired' *Obersturmbannführer* was now unemployed. He had to try to survive on the open job market. During the next seven years, he proved time and again how little he was able to adjust to the working world. Adolf Eichmann was orderly, diligent, accurate, polite, modest and obedient. But he was incapable of working on his own initiative; he depended on precise instructions.

The family moved to Olivos, No. 4261 Chacabuco Street, on the northern fringe of the capital. Together with two Nazi comrades from CAPRI days, Eichmann opened a laundry. A few months later the company went bankrupt. Eichmann also failed with a textile store and as the transport department manager of a company making sanitary appliances. He took a job as manager of the 'Seven Palms' rabbit farm in the little village of Joaquin Gorina, seventy kilometres from Buenos Aires. The farm belonged to distant relatives who had returned to Europe.

Eichmann had charge of 1000 rabbits and 5000 chickens – an unprecedented decline in status. He had his hands full scratching out a modest living for his family.

Question to Klaus Eichmann by *Quick* : 'You had found out by now that your father had been an SS leader and had been specifically involved in the "Jewish question". Did you ever try to talk with him about these things?'

Answer by Klaus Eichmann: 'Rarely. He always said: "Children, there was a war on and we want to forget all that. War is war," father said. "I do not want you to ever join the military or to go into politics..." father ordered. You will not believe how strict he was. Our old man was very strict.'

The Eichmanns' family life was anything but harmonious. The sons, who had been fatherless for so long, either were not able or did not want to submit themselves unconditionally, whereas the head of the family was used to a clearly structured hierarchy. After Adolf Eichmann had read a book on atomic physics, he wrote a short note on the cover, in which he expressed his doubts that his children were intelligent enough to understand it: 'Unfortunately I must fear that, given the degree of ignorance of my three sons, all of this will mean no more than empty straw to them. And this I regret!' Eichmann, during his interrogation in Israel: 'Because in the intellectual development of their, let us say, abilities, my sons showed themselves to be so completely disinterested, that I wrote that as a warning.'

In the autumn of 1953, a fourth son was born to the Eichmanns: Ricardo Francisco. Ricardo, after the cover name of his father and Francisco, the name of the Father who had helped Adolf Eichmann to escape to Argentina. One thought became almost an obsession. This child, the father determined, should never hear any prejudices and lies about him and his deeds. It must know from the very beginning that all he had ever done was to fulfil his duty and to obey the commands of his fatherland.

Besides Wiesenthal, not a single official institution of the Jewish state or any of the international Jewish organisations was yet actively looking for the architect of the *Endlösung*. The next initiative was therefore again taken by the Nazi-hunter's documentation centre in Linz. Wiesenthal approached Nahum Goldmann, President of the Jewish World Congress in New York, an umbrella organisation for Jewish communities in more than seventy countries. In his letter Wiesenthal informed Goldmann that he had good reasons to believe that Eichmann was living in South America, probably in Argentina, and that his wife and children had recently left Germany in order to join him. Wiesenthal requested assistance from the Jewish World Congress in order to follow up this lead.

Two months later an answer came, not from Goldmann himself, but from the New York rabbi Abraham Kalmanowitz, who had been authorised to reply: 'It would be important to learn Frau Eichmann's precise address and the name she is now living under, because your letter does not give Adolf Eichmann's exact place of residence'. Furthermore, the reply added that the JWC assumed that the war criminal was in Syria and not in South America.

Wiesenthal suggested to Kalmanowitz that he would send an investigator in order to discover Eichmann's address in Argentina. For this, however, he would need a budget for travel expenses not in excess of 500 US dollars. The functionaries in New York did not even reply to this request. There were no 500 dollars available to look for Eichmann. Wiesenthal was beside himself. The hunt for Eichmann was put off for five whole years. Furthermore, Wiesenthal was no longer able to finance the running of his office on the present scale. In 1954, he packed up 532 kilos of Nazi documents and sent them to the *Yad-Vashem* archive in Jerusalem. The only item he kept back was the file on Eichmann.

A frustrated Wiesenthal in his memoirs: 'At this time, the American Jews obviously had other problems. The Israelis were no longer interested in Eichmann, they had to fight for survival against Nasser. The Americans were no longer interested in Eichmann, they had to defend themselves against the Soviet Union in the Cold War. Except for a few like-minded fools, I had the feeling I was completely alone.'

In Argentina, the wanted man was now concentrating mainly on his family. He stayed away from the German community, but still maintained close contact with old comrades from the SS. National Socialism had a long tradition on the Rio de la Plata. The first local group of the NSDAP had been formed in Buenos Aires as far back as April 1931. This was to have been the base for the Fascist mission to recruit all people of German stock in the whole of South America.

The *Landesgruppenleiter* (country party leader) sent to Argentina was Willi Köhn. By 1935 he had recruited 2000 members and had developed a right-wing infrastructure. On 1 May 1936, 16,000 Hitler supporters had marched through the streets of the southern metropolis. The 50,000 Jews who had fled from the Nazis to Argentina reacted in fear.

Two worlds collided head on and, far from their actual homeland, the mutual hatred of two opposing German factions flared up. Balder Olden, an emigrant persecuted by the Nazis, came to the conclusion that Buenos Aires resembled a village split in two by an hereditary feud. 'We have a theatre, and so does the other side, we each have a newspaper, a school, associations, presentations – within the same environment a German world and a German non-world'.

Werner M. Finkelstein, a publisher who had fled from Berlin to Buenos Aires in 1939, saw things in the following light: 'From 1937 onwards, tens of thousands of Jews streamed into Argentina, because thanks to the flourishing corruption, this was one of the few countries for which one could obtain a visa, in other words buy one. In addition to that, in Argentina there was also the possibility of entering the country without a visa, if one came as a first-class passenger. First class was synonymous with capitalist. Whoever travelled first class could leave the boat without being bothered by the immigration officials.

'The Jewish and non-Jewish immigrants always kept their distance from each other. Everybody knew about everybody else, whether he was a Jew or a Nazi. The German clubs did not accept Jews. One could put up with that. It was only after the war at receptions in the embassy or the *Goethe-Institut* that we saw the Nazis close up. It was always an ugly feeling to meet people who were older than thirty-five. That led to bad blood, assumptions, suspicions, unbridgeable ditches.'

After the war, right-wing Germany kept fit in the *Teutonia* rowing club and the *Austria* sports club. The Navy socialised in the *Kameradenkreis* and the *Waffen-SS* had its own circle. National Socialist ideology was upheld in the evil immigrant magazine *Der Weg*. One of its editors was the Belgian Nazi Willem Sassen, who was wanted by the police in Holland. His motto: 'Our front is thinly held, but deeply echeloned.'

Opposing this stood South America's oldest German-language newspaper, the *Argentinische Tageblatt*, founded in 1889, and the *Freie Deutsche Bühne* (Free German Stage), a theatre in exile. Its counterpart was the *Deutsche Theater*. This is where Willem Stassen appeared on-stage. He also dominated the *Dürerkreis*, a cultural association in the *völkische* (nationalist-racist) style. *Der Weg* was published by the *Dürer-Verlag* with offices in the *Dürerhaus*.

The *Tageblatt* helped Jews and other opponents of the Nazis to emigrate to Argentina, provided medical aid and financial support, and furthered integration into the employment market.

Collaborator Willem Sassen and the prominent refugee Adolf Eichmann went hand in hand for a time. Sassen had quickly learned of the presence of the exterminator of the Jews. The two like-minded men allegedly first met through Otto Skorzeny, who had freed Mussolini, and then saw each other frequently. Finally, Eichmann gave in to Sassen's insistent requests for a major interview: he dictated his memoirs into the microphone of an old recording machine.

After Eichmann had been abducted, Sassen sold the recorded material to the world press for a handsome sum. Eichmann's statements appeared in the *Stern* and in *Life* Magazine, among others. Holger M. Meding claims: 'After Eichmann's execution, Sassen gave a part of the fee to his widow.'

During the time he was meeting Sassen, Eichmann lived very unostentatiously. His only hobbies were 'educative literature and playing the violin' (*Stern*). Avner Less, the Israeli interrogation officer, questioned him about several books he had read and commented on in those days.

One example was *Die letzten Tage der Reichskanzlei* (*The Final Days of the Reich Chancellery*) by Gerhard Boldt. While studying the book, the 'retired' *Obersturmbannführer* discovered that the author had apparently begun to develop doubts about the justice of the Nazi cause during the final days of the war. As a consequence, Eichmann crossed out 'Boldt' wherever the name appeared in the text and replaced it with terms such as 'scoundrel', 'traitor' or 'swine'. Boldt informed his readers that the once-arrogant NS bigwigs had begun to fear for their power and lives during the final days of the *Reich*. Eichmann's hand-written comment: 'The author of this book is a stupid asshole! The swine is called Boldt!!!' And elsewhere the enraged organiser of the *Endlösung* noted: 'One should peel the skin off the author's living body, he is so despicable. With swine like these, the war had to be lost!'

At the end of the book, Eichmann summed up:

'1. Anybody can live as he likes.

2. But then, one is not permitted to set oneself up as an officer; because

3. Officer = doing one's duty according to one's oath to the flag!'

Eichmann read the accusations made against him by his former friend Dieter Wisliceny, who had been executed in Pressburg in 1947, and showered him as well with obscene comments, calling him a 'bottomless swine' and an 'asshole with ears' in his marginal notes. Eichmann to Less: 'While reading, I was always seized by a holy rage and in this mood, I reached for a pencil and wrote down whatever seemed necessary for me to say at the moment.'

Eichmann condemned as the 'blatherings of a journalist' the following conclusion drawn from its investigations by *Stern* magazine, which helps to explain the violence of his reactions: 'Acquaintances and friends who spoke with him in those days in Argentina, describe him as a man who had been inwardly destroyed, who, while recognising his unspeakable guilt, did not dare to admit it even to himself, but rather continued to search in grim anger for formal excuses, so as not to have to condemn himself.'

At the end of his ninety interrogations, Avner Less presented a series of self-revelations by Eichmann, which he had formulated in broken Spanish while still at liberty in Argentina. They furnished a further, important key to understanding the Nazi criminal:

'I am slowly becoming tired of living as an anonymous wanderer between the worlds. The voice of my heart, which no man can escape, has always murmured to me that I should try to find peace. I would also like to make peace with my former adversaries. Maybe this is a trait of the German character. And I would be the last person in the world who would not be willing to give himself up to the German authorities, were it not that I have to consider that the interest in the political aspects of the matter could still be too great, to permit a clear, factual ending of the affair.

'Far be it from me to wish to doubt the justice of a verdict by a German court to even the slightest degree, but I am still in no way sure about the legal status within the due process of law, that a former recipient of orders has today, who had to act faithfully in accordance with his previously sworn oath of office and to carry out the orders and directives received.

'I was but a faithful, orderly and diligent member of the SS and the *Reichssicherheitshauptamt*, filled with idealistic feelings towards my fatherland, to which I had the honour to belong. I never was a mental swine or a traitor.

'Despite conscientious self-examination, I must conclude for myself that I was neither a murderer nor a mass murderer. Nor in any way were my subordinates. But to adhere strictly to the truth, I would like to accuse myself of having aided and abetted killing, because I passed on the deportation orders I received and because at least a part of these deportees were killed, albeit by a completely different unit. I said, I would have to accuse myself of having aided and abetted killing, if I were stringently and ruthlessly to judge myself.

'What I still do not see clearly is whether I have the right to do so with regard to my immediate subordinates. On this point, I am still caught in an inner conflict. My subjective view of the things that took place was my belief in the necessity of a total war, because I had always to believe increasingly in the constant declarations by the leadership of the former German *Reich*, "Victory in this total war, or downfall of the German nation". Based on this attitude, I did my duty as ordered with a clear conscience and a believing heart.'

Robert Pendorf commented on this in 1960 in *Stern* magazine: 'A truly terrible document, this attempt to entrench himself behind the oath to the flag, duty and obedience, far worse than the confessions by the brutalised murderers in the concentration camps, who, being hardened and incapable of realising what they were doing, counted a human life as nothing.

'Because this Eichmann was neither brutalised nor hardened, but according to his own believable assertions, was rather sensitive. And yet, this man signed – seeing and knowing – the deportation orders, which meant death for many hundreds of thousands. A macabre example of the total misapprehension, the total perversion of the original Prussian definition of duty, which had put the sense of responsibility of the recipient of orders next to and above mere obedience and of which, under the Swastika, only one half was left: *Kadavergehorsam* (blind obedience).

'It is this deadly, murderous perversion to which Eichmann refers when he tries to justify himself with his "oath to the flag" and his "obedience to duty". It is a hopeless attempt. Because Eichmann was neither too stupid nor too primitive, not to be able to recognise what it was he was doing, with or without orders. He was a bureaucrat in charge of murder, and he knew that he was, during all the time that he was. He had no compunctions, nor the desire to appeal against his orders. And for this he will have to bear the responsibility.'

CHAPTER 5

Israel

'This is simply unbelievable! Here we have the name Klement. Two completely independent sources, who are strangers to each other, mention this name. Any second-class policeman would be able to follow such a lead.'

Fritz Bauer

The *Shin Bet* of the 1950s was a colossal beginners' event. Zvi Aharoni described the situation of the secret service organisation in the manuscript of a book that was never published:

'We tried to learn, we tried to improve ourselves, tried to make professional competence our hallmark and to surpass all the others. It was a great challenge, but on the other hand, we had the advantage that we were starting from scratch. We were not blocked by any hallowed traditions or outdated habits. While we had a lot to learn and to create our own traditions, we had our heads clear and no one had imposed any limitations on us.'

The most important duties of the internal service included protecting state secrets and governmental and military institutions. *Shin Bet* was also responsible for counter-espionage and for the surveillance of Israeli and Arab extremists. Particularly during the initial phase of the Cold War – while its 'hot' offshoot, the Korean war, was raging – diplomats from the Eastern Bloc practised large-scale 'reconnaissance'. Isser Harel was virtually obsessed by the hunt for Red agents. In the mid-Fifties, the Soviet Mission in Tel Aviv employed about sixty people. The Russian-born Harel was convinced that many of these former compatriots belonged to the KGB.

Over the years, politicians from all parties were to discover that the internal service was also keeping watch on political parties. Harel reported details of the activities of the opposition parties *Mapam* and *Maki* to the ruling *Mapai*, which in principle he could only have learned about through bugging. Despite this, the first Inspector General of Police, Yehezkel Sahar, claimed as late as 8 May 1957, that Israel 'has neither a secret service nor a political police'. One month later, David Ben Gurion came out with the truth in a sensational statement made in the *Knesset* :

'The Israeli secret service is serving three purposes. Ninety-five per cent of the budget and the staff are being used for counter-espionage. *Shin Bet* is working very successfully in this area. Secret court proceedings have already taken place.' The Prime Minister then described the other two priorities with carefully chosen words: 'Splinter groups of terrorist organisations' and an ominous 'fifth column' – in plain language, the Arabs in Israel.

Zvi Aharoni was promoted to the head of the interrogation section after only one year. In 1954, he moved up to become a department head and now belonged to Harel's leadership team.

'We developed new methods of interrogation that had nothing to do with the traditional practices in this part of the world. When dealing with Arab prisoners, the interrogation officers of the police often only relied on beatings and worse. During my days, the cardinal rule was: no internee of *Shin Bet* was ever to be exposed to physical violence, no torture, not even a slap in the face. We quite deliberately wanted to differentiate ourselves from our Arab neighbours and from our British teachers.'

Having been influenced by the Prussian virtues, Aharoni's guidelines were adherence to the law, morality and efficiency. Israeli law, stemming from England, clearly stated that confessions obtained by force were inadmissible in court. As for morality: 'One cannot make up for one wrong by another wrong,' said Aharoni. To beat a prisoner meant becoming a criminal oneself.

'I personally questioned hundreds of prisoners and suspects. There is not one among them that I could not face at any time without a clear conscience. These people broke the law, I did not. Every one of these criminals recognised my stance and respected me. This is a part of the balance-sheet of my life.'

Part three, 'efficiency': 'We were never out merely to obtain so-called confessions. Clear results and information were important to us. The truth. It is not a great art to put so much pressure on someone that he will confess to anything you want to hear. There are examples enough of people who confessed to imaginary crimes, just to escape the pressure of their interrogators. My men knew that they could use any psychological trick and also apply a certain pressure. But blows, threats and false promises were forbidden. As long as I was in charge, this was strictly adhered to.'

Aharoni was deeply shattered when he realised, long after his retirement, that the rules had changed and that the ideals of his past no longer applied, that with the occupation of the West Bank and the Gaza Strip, Israel had become a different country.

In September 1957, the starting signal was given for the most successful of all known Israeli secret operations, 'Operation Eichmann'. The signal came from a totally unexpected direction. Fritz Bauer, who at the time was the *Generalstaatsanwalt* (State Attorney General) for Hesse, had a strong personal interest in the prosecution of Nazi criminals. The liberal Jewish lawyer, born in Stuttgart in 1903, had formerly been the youngest judge appointed during the Weimar Republic. Together with his friend Kurt Schumacher, he had resisted the National Socialist tide. For having done so, he lost his position in 1933 and was dragged off to a concentration camp.

Fritz Bauer was released in 1936 and emigrated to Denmark. When the *Wehrmacht* marched in, he was imprisoned for the second time. Bauer succeeded in escaping to Sweden. Until the end of the war, he worked there as a lecturer on business and economics at the University of Stockholm. After that, he again worked for the Danish government. It was only in 1949 that he returned to a new Germany, became President of a federal court, then State Attorney General in Brunswick in 1950 and subsequently in Frankfurt in 1956.

This influential jurist committed himself to a reform of the penal code and the corrective system, to re-socialisation and to the social responsibility of the judicial system. He personally visited prisons and sought communication on a person-to-person basis with the inmates. In the NS field, he demanded 'justice, not revenge', just as did Simon Wiesenthal. During the late 1950s, this kind of demand was called *Nestbeschmutzung* ('fouling one's own nest'). For Fritz Bauer, it was *Nestsäuberung* ('cleaning one's own nest'). His wish was 'to hold court on the most dangerous factors of our history'.

Increasingly, he came to discover the resistance that prevailed within a judicial system that was still employing many jurists from the days of the National Socialist wartime courts. Furthermore, the political climate during the Adenauer era did not appear to him to be suitable for reviewing capital cases such as that of Adolf Eichmann. After four years of strenuous effort, he succeeded in setting the famous Auschwitz trial in motion in 1963. After seventeen defendants had been sentenced for murder in 1965, the German nation was better informed about the atrocities of the Third Reich than ever before.

The much vilified Fritz Bauer informed the Israelis in September 1957 that he had received some information according to which Adolf Eichmann was living in Olivos, a quiet northern suburb of Buenos Aires. The exact address: No. 4261 Chacabuco Street. An area with small single-family homes and two- to three-storey apartments – modest middle-class. Isser Harel: 'All this took place in secret and with the utmost caution in order to prevent the public from learning of our interest in the criminal.'

Bauer had every reason not to talk to his own countrymen but rather with the victims and the descendants of the people who died in the Holocaust. In previous cases, Nazis on the run had been warned of impending actions and immediately gone underground again. The most prominent case occurred in 1959. The infamous *Todesengel* of Auschwitz, Josef Mengele, lived in Buenos Aires under his real name until the summer of 1959, despite the fact that he had immigrated ten years previously under the name Helmut Gregor. His Argentinian identity card carried the number 3940484.

The key figure in the Nazi scene, Willem Sassen, had already brought Eichmann and Mengele together in 1952. They met from time to time in the centrally located ABC-Café. However, they did not have much to say to each other, because the well-off doctor classed his former SS comrade, who was struggling to survive, as a down-and-out, leading a 'broken, tragic existence' (Sassen), and therefore despised him.

In 1959 the German legal authorities requested the extradition of Mengele from the government of Argentina. They observed officially correct procedures and sent the request via the German embassy in Buenos Aires. Only days later, Mengele packed his bags, disappeared and then turned up in Paraguay. He had obviously been warned by a sympathiser in the embassy.

In those days, *Mossad* and *Shin Bet* were both under the joint leadership of Isser Harel. Compared to today, the foreign secret service was more of a family affair, where everybody knew everybody else. Internal photographs show middle-aged gentlemen in black trousers and white shirts engaged in strenuous conferences. The team was relatively small and therefore it was to take several more years before the service was even given its own office building. Initially, Harel's *Mossad* was housed – and fairly primitively at that – in some buildings of the former German Templar colony Sarona, on grounds belonging to the Ministry of Defence – *Hakirya*.

Astonishingly enough, in the Fifties there was no special department that was seriously concerned with the fate of wanted Nazi criminals. The files on men such as Adolf Eichmann, Hitler's secretary Martin Bormann or Heinrich (*Gestapo*) Müller, were kept openly in one of the offices. This section, however, had no operative agents of its own. Therefore, if new information had to be checked on, a telex went out to 'our man in Buenos Aires' or 'our man in Panama', wherever the case arose.

The *Mossad* residents in those countries were generally overworked, because they had huge areas to cover and were constantly being flooded with various requests. It thus sometimes took weeks or even months before the representative concerned got around to dealing with the case. As a result, hardly anyone at headquarters expected a quick and efficient treatment of the assignments. In important cases, therefore, an agent was sent out. He had to handle the problem together with the local resident and if possible solve it.

In view of the clear information on Adolf Eichmann and his presumed place of residence, Harel decided to send an agent to Buenos Aires. The importance of the source – Fritz Bauer – and the target – Adolf Eichmann – left no other choice. Despite this, Harel was in no hurry. It took all of four months before the agent was sent off.

The man chosen by Isser Harel had many years of operational experience. One of his advantages was that he spoke fluent Spanish. He left Tel Aviv in January 1958 destined for Argentina. His only assignment was to check the Chacabuco Street address in Olivos. After two weeks he returned to *Hakirya* and assured his chief that Bauer's information was definitely without foundation. In his view, it was absolutely unthinkable for a man of Eichmann's standing to be living in such a poor neighbourhood. The *Memu-neh* – Harel's self-adopted title as director of both secret services – accepted this conclusion without even a moment's reflection. For him, the Chacabuco Street affair was closed.

Fortunately for the case and unfortunately for Eichmann, when Fritz Bauer learned of the negative result of the preliminary enquiry, he refused to give up, but instead demanded a new, more intensive investigation. The *Mossad*, however, informed Bauer through diplomatic channels that he would first have to disclose the source of his information, so that a thorough survey could be undertaken.

The Hesse Attorney General only disclosed the identity of his source with great reluctance. This turned out to be a long-retired half-Jew named Lothar Hermann, living in Argentina. He had meanwhile moved from the capital with his family and gone to Coronel Suarez, a provincial city more than four hours away by train from Buenos Aires.

Harel, who in his subsequent book *The House in Garibaldi Street* even had the temerity to claim that he had always believed in the Hermann story, still did not take the case seriously enough to send another agent to South America. He was waiting for the opportunity to combine this assignment with some other official mission. The chance came when Harel learned of the impending flight of a high-ranking, experienced police officer to an Interpol conference in South America.

Aharoni recalls: 'This was Efraim Hofstetter, Chief of the investigation department at police headquarters, a colleague and good friend of mine. Harel applied to the Inspector General of Police for his support. He agreed immediately. Hofstetter was to visit Hermann after his official mission as Israel's representative to Interpol was concluded. For support, he was assigned a *Mossad* man who happened to be in Argentina at the time: Efraim Ilani.

'Ilani, too, could look back on many successful missions. In Buenos Aires he was presently engaged in a personal project, and he readily agreed to accompany Hofstetter. Ilani not only spoke fluent Spanish, he had also mastered the local Castillano dialect.

'During the first week in March 1956, Hofstetter and Ilani took the train to the provincial capital of Coronel Suarez. After a brief search, they located the Hermann family house, where Hofstetter met Lothar Hermann. Shortly afterwards, his daughter Sylvia, the actual informant, returned home. The unannounced visitor did not introduce himself as an agent of the Israeli secret service but as Fritz Bauer's emissary. The State Attorney General, said Hofstetter, required further and more detailed information on Eichmann. At this first personal meeting, Hofstetter discovered a key fact that had not been known before: Hermann was blind.

'The following information from Hermann and his daughter comprised the kernel of Hofstetter's subsequent report to Isser Harel.

'Before moving to Coronel Suarez, Hermann and his family had lived in Olivos, a suburb of greater Buenos Aires. There, Sylvia had met a young German called Klaus Eichmann. The two became friends. Klaus came to visit the Hermanns several times without knowing that they were of Jewish extraction. Lothar Hermann's parents had been murdered by the Nazis. Klaus Eichmann did not mince matters and showed himself to be decidely anti-Semitic. On several occasions he declared that it was a pity Hitler had been prevented from fully achieving his objective, namely exterminating all the Jews.

'During one of these visits, young Eichmann was asked by Frau Hermann why, unusually, no trace of a local German dialect could be detected in his speech. Klaus declared that his father had been a high-ranking officer of the *Wehrmacht*. Therefore the family had moved many times during the war and had even lived in Poland.

'For a long time, Hermann's daughter Sylvia did not know where Klaus Eichmann lived, because he refused to give her his address. One day, however, when she happened to mention his name to a girl-friend she was visiting in Olivos, it turned out that the girl knew the address. Sylvia went to the house – No. 4261 Chacabuco Street – out of sheer curiosity.

'A corpulent woman had come to the door and introduced herself as Klaus's mother. She said he was not at home but away at work.

'At this moment, a middle-aged man with glasses had appeared. He had come to the door and lingered by the women for a time. Sylvia Hermann had asked in a friendly manner whether he was Klaus's father. The man had hesitated for quite some time, before he answered in the affirmative. The girl had smiled encouragingly, held out her hand to him and said: "So you are Herr Eichmann." He had neither answered nor shaken her hand, but had turned and left.

'The matter came full circle when Frau Hermann read about the war crimes trials in a German newspaper. The name Eichmann was mentioned quite frequently and very prominently. Now suddenly everything fell into place: the anti-Semitic remarks made by the boy, the lack of any regional dialect, the refusal to give an address, the strange behaviour of the father. All this made sense. The Hermanns therefore decided to report their observations to the German prosecutor, whose name had also been mentioned in the newspaper. When they received no reaction for some time, they were at first a little surprised and later on rather disappointed.

'Lothar Hermann indicated that he could obtain further information, if Hofstetter and his client were prepared to pay the necessary expenses: maybe even Eichmann's identity card, fingerprints and name, if he were using a false name, as well as detailed information about the other residents in his house. Hofstetter, who was much impressed by the Hermanns, left them a contact address in the United States and promised to reimburse all expenses as soon as further facts were produced. Then Hofstetter and Ilani, who had waited outside the apartment, returned to Buenos Aires.

'Before flying back to Tel Aviv, the police officer drove by Chacabuco Street. He came to the same spontaneous conclusion as his predecessor: an SS leader of the calibre of Adolf Eichmann simply could not be living in such a run-down area.

'What happened next is hard to understand. The reaction by Harel to Hofstetter's report was unbelievable, even grotesque. Despite the fact that Hofstetter shared the initial agent's doubts about the Eichmanns' living conditions in Chacabuco Street, he was able to report very favourably on Hermann and his daughter. This colleague from the Israeli police was a highly experienced investigator and had conducted many interrogations. His judgement on the credibility of witnesses therefore deserved to be trusted implicitly.

'Anyone would have thought that now things were going to happen. It would have been completely normal practice to send off a team of top agents in order to check both Hermann's story and all the residents of No. 4261 Chacabuco, and possibly even to prepare the conditions for a subsequent kidnapping. None of this occurred. Blind Lothar Hermann was left to collect further evidence. He was asked to bring proof that the strange German living in Chacabuco Street was in fact Adolf Eichmann. The great Isser Harel and his secret service, supposedly one of the best in the world, left the task to a blind pensioner living more than 250 miles away. It is difficult to believe, but this is what indeed happened. Harel's attitude was simple: Hermann claims to have located Eichmann. Very well, let him prove it!

'Hermann tried everything within his power, but it was not good enough for the nice man from New York (Hofstetter) who had taken everything so seriously and even promised to reimburse his expenses. Hermann tried to obtain further information on the tenants of No. 4261 Chacabuco. Handicapped as he was, he got nowhere. He was not able to produce the identity card he had promised, nor any fingerprints. Worst of all, he got himself entangled in contradictions.

'The final incentive for Harel to terminate all contact with Hermann was the information sent by the latter to Hofstetter that Eichmann was living at Chacabuco Street under the name of Francisco Schmidt – identity card No. 80,297. The existence of a Francisco Schmidt was easy to check with the help of a local contact. Schmidt turned out to be the owner of house No. 4261. The people who lived there were his tenants.

'At this point Harel lost confidence completely. The mighty Director of *Mossad* and *Shin Bet* gave the order to break off all contact with Hermann and to terminate all investigations concerning Chacabuco Street.

'The *Mossad* file on Eichmann was deposited in the archives. Even Bauer's attempts to have the case reopened did not help. In his subsequent statements, Harel naturally tried to sweep these unpleasant facts under the carpet. He never tired of recounting how, from its very inception, *Mossad* had meticulously pursued the trails of escaped Nazis throughout the world. However, too many former *Mossad* agents know the truth.

'A simple example shows Harel's real attitude towards the Chacabuco information. Hofstetter met Hermann in March of 1958. The blind man was given half a year to prove his statements. When he failed, Harel closed the whole case in September of that year.

'Six months later, on 9 March 1959, I, in my capacity as Chief of the interrogation department of *Shin Bet*, flew to Buenos Aires to conduct a highly secret investigation relating to a serious crime committed by an agent of the Israeli Military Intelligence Service. At this time, I had not heard anything about the Eichmann case, nor about Hermann or Chacabuco Street. As is usual in a professional secret service, each department worked completely sealed off from the others. Agents only received the information they needed to know for their current assignment. Everything else was kept secret. Therefore, I was totally unaware about the whole Bauer-Hermann-Chacabuco affair. I stayed in Buenos Aires for no less than thirty-eight days. When I had finally succeeded in fulfilling my mission, I flew back home.

'This little story goes further than a thousand words in demonstrating how uncompromisingly Harel had decided not to pursue the Hermann information any longer. Had he seen even the slightest chance, I would have been ordered to Chacabuco Street immediately. After all, I had been in Buenos Aires long enough to also clear up matters which were not directly related to my actual mission.

'In June 1960, *Stern* magazine printed a sensational series about "Eichmann's final years". The first part began with the following words: "Eichmann, the effective supplier of the gas chambers in Auschwitz, first lived in Germany and then in Argentina under a false name. But his sons lived, were educated and got married under the name of Eichmann. Despite this, the father remained undiscovered for ten years. It almost appears as if no one was looking for him." It hurt to have to read the truth.

'When we finally caught Eichmann in 1960, the chorus of famous and less famous Nazi-hunters who claimed the credit for having found him became louder and louder. Authors wrote about "the untiring search lasting fifteen years". I have little respect for these people. The sad truth is that Eichmann was discovered by a blind man and that *Mossad* needed more than two years to believe that blind man's story.'

'In the closing days of 1959, dramatic events were to bring the Chacabuco story back to life. Fritz Bauer, State Attorney General of Hesse, came to Israel at short notice to meet his colleague Chaim Cohen, the Israeli Attorney General and legal adviser to the government. Bauer was beside himself. He was convinced – and he made no bones about it – that *Mossad* had ignored a hot trail provided by him and his informants, and had completely botched an important investigation.

'Bauer went into detail and explained why he was so angry. Among the many bits of information provided by Hermann already in 1957 was the fact that there were two names on the electric meter of No. 4261 Chacabuco Street: Dagoto and Klement. A more recent tip, from a source that was completely independent of Hermann, had immediately electrified Bauer and made him travel to Jerusalem without delay. The new source claimed that nine years ago Adolf Eichmann had left Europe under the name of Ricardo Klement on a passport provided by the Vatican!

'Chaim Cohen called Harel and asked him to come to the Jerusalem offices of the State Prosecutor General. He was to meet with Bauer. Furthermore, Cohen suggested to the *Mossad* Chief that he bring me with him to the meeting. The nation's Chief Prosecutor had known me for years because I had been involved in all investigations in the areas of espionage, treason and high treason. I had had to brief him regularly on the state of such cases. Because of this, a close professional and personal friendship had developed between us.

'Harel must have felt how incensed the Prosecutor General was. He agreed immediately, but was still annoyed about Cohen's summons. After all, Cohen could not order him about: Harel took his orders exclusively and directly from the Prime Minister. But without a good reason, he could not very well refuse Cohen's request to come to Jerusalem and bring me with him. Cohen suggested to Harel that I, and no one else, should be sent to Buenos Aires to make a thorough investigation of the Chacabuco affair. And so I suddenly found myself smack in the middle of the Eichmann investigation.

'I was given a few hours to read the Eichmann file, particularly the final reports on the two previous actions. I had great difficulty to hide my surprise and disappointment over the fact that I had not been asked to check this address when I had been in Buenos Aires six months previously. Then I went to Jerusalem with Isser Harel and his chauffeur. The guest from Frankfurt was already waiting in Cohen's office on the second floor of the former Ministry of Justice in Jaffa Street. After a brief introduction, he told his story from beginning to end. Fritz Bauer was an impressive personality: a big man with grey, bushy eyebrows and a charming southern German accent.

'Bauer let everybody present feel his anger: "This is simply unbelievable! Here we have the name Klement. Two completely independent sources, who are strangers to each other, mention this name. Any second-class policeman would be able to follow such a lead. Just go and ask the nearest butcher or greengrocer and you will learn all there is to know about Klement."

'Chaim Cohen and Isser Harel did their best to calm down their visitor. They promised him they would send me to Argentina as soon as my commitments on current court cases were completed. I would then begin a comprehensive investigation based on the new information. We agreed that I would first study all the files in our archives and then meet Bauer in Frankfurt no later than in one month's time. There I was to be allowed to see the German Eichmann file. I could then copy all the data, photographs and documents and use them as a basis for my work in Argentina. We parted with a firm handshake.'

Later it transpired that it was not all that easy to copy files from the Frankurt Attorney General's office by daylight. In those days, diplomatic relations between Germany and Israel were still in their infancy and were highly sensitive. There was no mutual legal support on investigations. Furthermore, the Justice Department did not have a copying machine. Even so courageous a man as Fritz Bauer had to be circumspect, in order to continue to help in specific instances.

Given the situation, the Israeli Mission in Cologne sent photography student Michael Maor, a former paratrooper, to Frankfurt to photograph the Eichmann file in Bauer's personal office. Maor arrived at the venerable complex of buildings in the Gerichtsstrasse after office hours. The office of the State Attorney General was on the second floor. The all-important file lay on the left-hand desk. Maor was able to enter the building without problems. He had a key to Bauer's office. Just as he was about to begin his clandestine work, he heard steps. A cleaning woman, whom he had not reckoned with, stood on the other side of the door.

She decided, however, that she was not going to clean the office of the Chief on that particular day. The Israeli took a deep breath. His mission had almost failed. Now he could begin copying without interruption. He knew what he was doing – and he enjoyed doing it. A large part of his family had been murdered in the concentration camps. He had survived the Holocaust only because of a shipment of children to Palestine and now, in 1960, he was eager to help when the victims began to hit back.

Simon Wiesenthal had the same feelings when he again provided an important piece of information shortly before the beginning of the decisive months of 'Operation Eichmann'. On 22 April 1959, the Nazi-hunter by chance discovered an obituary in the *Oberösterreichische Nachrichten*, a newspaper published in Linz. Frau Maria Eichmann, the stepmother of the wanted Nazi criminal, had died. Among the names of the bereaved was Vera Eichmann. From this Wiesenthal concluded: 'One does not lie in an obituary. Veronika Liebl had gone back to using the name she now obviously regarded as being her only legitimate one. Wherever she was now, she was the wife of Adolf Eichmann.'

The hunting instinct of the famous survivor of the concentration camps had been reawakened. In the first week in February 1960, the well-to-do businessman Adolf Karl Eichmann – the father – also died. Again the observant Wiesenthal discovered the name of Vera among the names of the bereaved in the obituary. For a moment, the thought flashed through his mind that son Adolf might come for the funeral. This would have been conceivable, given his strong family ties.

He hired two photographers to take pictures of all the family members. When studying the photographs, he suddenly noticed a great resemblance between Adolf junior and his brother Otto. So, he thought, this is about what the *Obersturmbannführer* who had gone underground should look like today.

This time *Mossad* reacted somewhat more quickly and with more commitment than on previous missed occasions. After all, it was only a few months ago that autocrat Isser Harel had had to submit to the dressing-down by the German Jew Fritz Bauer. Two young men appeared 'in great haste' to collect from Wiesenthal the photographs taken at the cemetery.

CHAPTER 6
Garibaldi Street

'I am sorry. I have very bad news for you. All of our work to date has been in vain. We have been pursuing the wrong man.'

One of Aharoni's men

Aharoni's report: I left Israel on 26 February 1960 and was travelling on a diplomatic passport issued under a false name. According to it, I was from the accounts department of the Foreign Ministry in Jerusalem. My mission was naturally secret. Therefore neither the Ministry nor the Israeli embassy in Buenos Aires knew its true background. My cover: I was investigating current incidents of anti-Semitism in South America.

As is customary in such cases, I possessed a secret code that neither the encoders at the embassy nor the decoders in Tel Aviv knew. Only the recipients of my messages were able to understand their content. I recall that the house in Chacabuco Street was called 'orchard', and Eichmann 'the driver'. 'The driver is red' meant that I had found Klement and that there were good reasons to assume he was Eichmann; 'The driver is black', that there were no doubts about Klement being Eichmann. During this phase of the operation our only concern was to find Eichmann and to identify him. This had nothing at all to do with illegal activities. Therefore I was able to travel on a regular diplomatic passport.

I arrived in Buenos Aires in the evening hours of 1 March. I carried with me the files containing all the information on Eichmann from Tel Aviv and Frankfurt in a sealed diplomatic pouch. This included copies of the original SS personnel file, biographical details on Eichmann and his family, old photographs, a listing of his measurements and other specific identifying marks. In addition, there was all the information we had pointing to Eichmann's having gone underground in South America after the downfall of the Third *Reich*. There was the Hermann story in all its minute details, as well as the names of Argentinian companies in Buenos Aires and Tucuman that were suspected of having employed Eichmann at one time or another.

The only member of the Israeli embassy who knew my true mission – the security officer – picked me up at the airport. Even after so many years, I still cannot give his real name, even though I am convinced that the Argentinian authorities have known his true identity for a long time. Therefore, I will call him Yossef. We knew each other well, because we had worked in the same office years before in Tel Aviv. On top of that, his help had been of inestimable value during my secret mission the year before. He took me to the embassy where I deposited the Eichmann file in the safe. I briefed Yossef on the current state of developments in the case and discussed my initial steps in the Argentinian capital with him. I knew my way around Buenos Aires quite well. Local customs were not unfamiliar to me. I also spoke enough Castillano to be able to move about freely. However, we both knew that I would require help from locals. I could not go anywhere or approach anyone, without immediately being recognised as a foreigner. I therefore had to be very careful so as not to make our target become suspicious.

I knew I could not return to Tel Aviv without a conclusive answer. Yes or no! A 'maybe' or a 'possibly' were not enough. I therefore had to accept calculated risks. It was clear to me that Harel would never have approved certain steps had he been informed. But now I was on my own and I was my own boss. I carried full responsibility for all my decisions and manoeuvres.

My reasoning was based on the following: according to our information, Eichmann had now been living in Buenos Aires with his family for several years. In such a situation, one does not just run away or move the whole family, simply because something appears to be suspicious, for example, if one comes to believe one is under observation. Over time, one becomes accustomed to such things, one learns to live with such premonitions and moments of insecurity and submits to the inevitable. As it turned out later – very fortunately, because I was to make some quite serious mistakes – my evaluation had been correct.

Before he took me to my hotel, I also discussed the necessary local support with Yossef. To understand what I mean, one must know that all Israeli embassies can call on a number of local Jewish volunteers who are willing to follow the orders of their Israeli 'commanders' without asking too many questions or bargaining about being paid. Most of these forces stem from the ranks of organised Jewish defence against anti-Semitism.

In every embassy I ever visited, there was a hard core of young – and sometimes not so young – Jews, who were prepared to help by taking on confidential assignments at any time of the day or night. Whether one needed a car or a lorry for a surveillance job, or a house in a specific area to meet or observe people, everything was possible, without delays or unnecessary questions. It was only through such inestimably valuable help that we were able successfully to conclude this, and many another, operation. *

Before I begin to recount the events leading to the arrest of Eichmann, there is one further item to be mentioned: in addition to the Chacabuco information, I also had a number of tips and rumours from Hermann and other sources, all of which I needed to check on. These were names of people and also of companies. I tried to the best of my ability to follow up all of these leads personally.

What I was unable to do myself, I left to the voluntary helpers. Once I even travelled to Tucuman for three days in order to check out a former lead on Eichmann. In this instance, I had prepared the following cover story: I worked for a New York law firm and was looking for a man who had absconded with a large amount of money. I am not going to report on all of these sidelines of my investigations, because not one of them brought me closer to my objective. It is sufficient to describe the Chacabuco story in detail. It led us, after initial disappointments, to Eichmann's new place of residence and eventually set him on the road to the gallows.

I drove to Chacabuco Street for the first time on 3 March. It lies in a district called Vicente Lopez, which in turn is part of the large suburb of Olivos. I had rented a car, something that was not all that easy to do in those days. The day before, I had called on the Ambassador and the Military Attaché, who both knew my real background and were informed in general terms about the reason for my visit. Furthermore, I had met two Israelis who had been living in Argentina for many years and had excellent contacts with the local authorities. Without giving them an insight into my case, I had asked them to check on some of the names and companies from my secret file.

When I drove to Olivos I took along one of Yossef's helpers, a young man of about twenty. I shall call him Roberto. He was tall and thin and had a narrow black moustache. He, too, knew nothing at all about me or the real nature of the affair. However, he had been in the business long enough not to ask unnecessary questions.

With the help of a street map I had bought, we found Chacabuco without any problems. I drove by No. 4261 very slowly. I only stopped in a side street some 500 metres from the house. We went back on foot. Chacabuco was a nice, although untarred, street. There were trees and broad pavements. Within only a few hundred metres, the buildings changed from pretty, elegant villas to run-down two-storey apartments.

* The names of the voluntary helpers in Buenos Aires on the Eichmann case have all been changed.

No. 4261 belonged to the second category and stood somewhat back in a large neglected garden. The building made a very nondescript impression and blended in well with the neighbourhood. However, it was relatively far from the street so that we could not observe many details. We walked past it and then turned back.

By chance, I had a brand new picture postcard in my pocket. It was the sort of card one gets in aeroplanes. It showed a fantastic machine flying over even more fantastic tropical islands. I explained to Roberto what I wanted him to do next. Given his English and my Castillano, we got along quite well. Roberto wrote an invented name and a fictitious address in Buenos Aires on the card. As sender he put down: DAGOSTO, 4263 Chacabuco.

I chose the name Dagosto because it sounded similar to DAGOTO, which allegedly was the name on the electric meter of No. 4261. I chose 4263, a number that did not exist in Chacabuco Street, in order to have a reason to make direct enquiries of the tenants of No. 4261. The message on the card was very simple: *Have just returned. Best regards – George.*

I told Roberto that he could show the card to anyone who wished to see it. However, he was not to hand it over to anybody, otherwise they would be able to see that the card carried neither a stamp nor a postmark and was not even dated. Roberto was to enter the garden of No. 4261 and ask after the sender of the card. He should try to get inside the building in order to see who lived there. It was important to read the names on the doors, to find out as much as possible about the tenants and also whether they were locals or foreigners.

I waited in the car. Roberto returned after about twenty minutes. He was grinning and waving the postcard. He reported that he had spoken with a girl outside No. 4261 Chacabuco Street. The child had told him she knew all the people in the neighbourhood. However, none was called Dagosto. He had even succeeded in entering the grounds and inspecting the house at close quarters. A look through the windows on the ground floor had shown that the apartment was empty. There were painters at work in some of the rooms. I thanked him and we drove back to Buenos Aires.

I now concluded that the Klement/Eichmann family must have moved, assuming they had lived there at all. My ideas on the next step were simple. Were Eichmann actually living in the house in Chacabuco Street, I could not simply send someone to ask questions about Klement. But since to all appearances the house was empty and looked to be uninhabited, I considered it a justified risk to send someone over to ask directly about Klement and his new address.

I suddenly remembered something in the context of today's date, 3 March. According to my Eichmann file, it was the birthday of Klaus, the eldest of the sons. I therefore set out and bought a rather expensive cigarette lighter. One of the girls at the embassy had a fairly childlike, very feminine handwriting. She wrote a little birthday salutation for me in Spanish: *For my friend Nicki, in friendship, on his birthday*.

We deliberately left off any signature. The lighter was nicely wrapped. On the envelope of the greeting card the girl wrote: Nikolas Klement, Vicente Lopez, 4261 Chacabuco.

Since I did not want to send Roberto back to the building with a new story, I chose another young man from Yossef's group. He was a good-looking boy, had just turned eighteen, was slightly overweight and always seemed to be smiling. His name was Juan and he knew just as little about the operation as did his predecessor Roberto.

I asked Juan to drive to Vicente Lopez, to No. 4261 Chacabuco Street. He should tell everybody he met that he was required to bring something to a man called Nikolas Klement. This Klement was supposed to have lived here but had moved a short time ago. I made him understand that he was not to go to the new address under any circumstances if someone told him of it: not even if it were just across the street. He was first to come back so that we could decide together, whether and how the package was to be delivered.

If someone were to ask him where he had got the package from, then he was to say that a friend, who worked as a bell-boy in one of the bigger hotels in Buenos Aires, had been given the package and a handsome tip by a lady guest. The assignment had been to deliver the envelope to Vicente Lopez personally. The handover had already taken place yesterday (it was now 4 March, one day past the birthday), but the friend had been too busy to bring the package. Instead he had asked him, Juan, to do him this small favour. If he were to be asked what the young lady looked like or her name, he would be unable to reply, because he had never seen her himself.

I believed the risk entailed was calculable. If, after the present was delivered, Klement/Eichmann were to question his son about the sender and why he had given his name and address to a foreigner, it was doubtful whether the father would believe his son's claim, that he did not have the slightest idea who the present was from. He was more likely to assume that the son was having a little affair and did not want to talk about it. He would warn him. He would be angry, but he would hardly assume that the present came from the Israeli embassy.

After I had assured myself several times that Juan knew exactly what he was and was not to do, I wished him lots of luck. He then set off. When he came back, grinning as usual, he had a long story to tell me. I listened to him patiently and then asked him to write an exact report in Spanish, because every detail, no matter how minor, was important.

This is the translation of Juan's report: 'I was sent off to deliver a package to Mr Nikolas Klement in Vicente Lopez, No. 4261 Chacabuco Street. I had been instructed to find out his new address in case he no longer lived there and also as many details as possible about him and his family. I knew that if I needed help, a friend would be waiting for me four blocks further along in Parana Street.

'I went to the house. When I was not able to find a bell, I called as loudly as I could, which is quite usual here. When I still did not receive any answer, I went into the building. The doors and windows stood open, because there were painters working in the apartment. I was unable to find anybody. I therefore left the building again and went round to the back. Suddenly I saw a man of about thirty talking to a woman who was just cleaning something. She was standing next to a small hut made of red bricks that was not yet quite finished.

'I asked the man: "Excuse me please, but do you know whether Mr Klement lives here?"

The man: "Klement? Ah, Klement, yes, certainly..."

The woman: "Yes!"

The man: "You mean the Germans?"

Juan: "I don't know."

The man: "Do you mean the one with the three grown sons and the little son?"

Juan: "I don't know. I have a message for him. Where can I find him?"

The man: "These people used to live here, but now they have moved. I don't know exactly when. Maybe fifteen to twenty days ago."

Juan: "Where have they moved to?"

The man: "I don't know. You should ask the man who works in the house. He should know."

'He took me into the house. In a small room in the back we found one of the painters.

Juan: "I have a message for this gentleman" (I showed him the name on the piece of paper).

Man A: "He wants to know where he can find the man who moved away from here."

Man B: "Aha, the German..."

Juan: "Yes. Can you tell me where I can find him? I have a small package for him and I have to deliver it personally."

Man B: "I know that they moved to San Fernando. But you would not be able to find the place. I don't know the address either. You can take the minibus, the *collectivo* No. 60. But wait a minute. His son works here, only a few metres away." (Turns to man A): "Why don't you go with him and show him where the son works?"

Man A: "OK. Let's go then."

Juan: "Thank you."

'We crossed Chacabuco Street and went down to the corner. About twenty metres from Parana Street, we came to a small automobile repair shop. There were two or three mechanics working in the yard. The man pointed to a light Motonetta brand moped and said: That belongs to the son. I noted down the type: Siambretta 150 Sport. The man called a young man of about nineteen or twenty over. He had a German-looking face and was dressed like a mechanic. The German came over to us and the two of them shook hands.

'Man A: "This person would like to speak to your father."

Juan: "Look, I am supposed to deliver this letter to this gentleman" (I pointed to the card). "I was supposed to hand over the consignment, but now I learn that the intended recipient has moved away. Can you tell me where I can make the delivery?"

The German: "Look, we have just moved."

Juan: "Where to?"

The German: "To Don Torcuato."

Juan: "OK. Since you are the son, I can just as easily give you the package. But ... I'm not sure. It was given to me by a friend, who in turn was given it by someone in a hotel in Buenos Aires. It is to be delivered to Mr Klement. Because my friend was very busy, he asked me to make this delivery for him. I was not able to come yesterday, so I just came today."

The German: "OK, but I would like to know from whom you got that."

Juan: "I just told you everything I know."

Man A (addressing the German): "Look, someone gave him the message and asked him to deliver it. And because you have moved, I showed him where he could find you, where you work. But I think that it doesn't matter... He can just give the package to you."

The German: "OK, but I would still like to know who sent the package."

Juan: (pointed to the card).

The German: "OK, I'll take it. Maybe everything is explained inside."

Juan: "OK. Look, I have this (the card) and also this (the package) here in my pocket. Both are to go to Mr Klement. Can't you tell me the address?"

The German: "No, the street where we live does not have a name and no numbers."

Juan: "What should I do then? You are the son, aren't you?"

The German: "Yes, certainly, but I still would like to know more about your friend."

Juan: "What do you want to know? I have already told you everything. I was actually supposed to come yesterday. But then I had another job to do. I will give it to you and then I will say I delivered it to the house. It would therefore be better, if you were to give me the address."

Man A: "The streets in Don Torcuato don't have any names. So what name is he supposed to give you?"

Juan. "OK. Here, take this and this" (I gave him the card and the package).

The German: "Thank you. I am always here if you should need anything else." '

I thanked Juan and asked him whether he had time that afternoon to drive back again to Vicente Lopez with me. 'No problem,' he replied with his usual big grin. I asked him whether his companion had addressed the German boy by his first name. Juan frowned: 'Yes, he called him by a name. But it was difficult to understand. To me it sounded like Tito or Dito.' That was a piece of good news. I knew that Eichmann's third son, born on 29 March 1942, was named Dieter. The pieces suddenly seemed to fit.

I asked Yossef if he could put someone at my disposal for half a day. Someone who was a bit older and inspired more confidence. Someone who could pretend to be an insurance salesman. After half an hour, Lorenzo appeared. I was very pleased with him. He was tall, handsome, wore a coat and tie, and was about thirty-five, the perfect insurance salesman.

The three of us, Juan, Lorenzo and I, drove back to Olivos in my car. I had decided to try to do two more things that same day. First, I wanted to follow 'Dito' after work. He would probably ride home on his moped. Secondly, I wanted to have another try at obtaining Klement's address from the people in Chacabuco Street. I was worried that Klement – after having received this strange present in such an unusual way – would ensure the people in Chacabuco would not give a stranger his new address under any circumstances. I felt we should get to work quickly, before Klement had an opportunity to take precautions.

We sat in our car for over two hours, but 'Dito' did not appear. We had stationed ourselves strategically in Monteagudo Street, through which, according to Juan's and my opinion, every vehicle going from Parana to San Fernando and Don Torcuato had to pass. I had no fear that we would arouse the suspicion of any passer-by, because I had discovered that it was quite normal for the people here to sit in their cars, eat, read, talk or simply do nothing.

Juan had told us that the mechanics in the workshop would be work-ing till five o'clock, so we waited until six. Then we drove to the workshop and discovered that the moped had disappeared. There was nothing to do but to try again next day.

The next step was to ask Lorenzo to find out as much as possible about the house in Chacabuco Street. We deliberately waited until after six in order to be sure that Klement's son would no longer be around. We had to avoid friendly people again bringing Lorenzo across the street to see him. The fact that two different people were both looking for Klement on the same day had to be kept secret from him as far as possible. After Lorenzo returned, I had him write down even the most minute details.

This is the translation of Lorenzo's report: 'I visited the house at No. 4261 Chacabuco Street. There I met a man who spoke Castillano with a strong German accent. He and another man were at work painting the walls. I explained that I came from an insurance company and wished to see Mr Klement. He answered evasively. When I began to insist, he explained to me that Klement had moved from Chacabuco Street about three weeks ago and that he did not know his new address. All he knew was that it was in San Fernando. When I again insisted more strongly, he became obstinate and refused to answer further questions or just repeated his previous answers.

'He confirmed that Ricardo Klement had lived here. He was the father of three grown-up sons and a younger one. One of the sons was mar-ried, the second worked in the merchant marine and the third was employed by an automobile repair shop just a few houses away from here. The little one was eight.

'He said the easiest way to find Klement would be to ask the son in the workshop. But it was too late now anyway, because he normally only worked until five o'clock. Before I left, I again repeated my question about the new address in San Fernando. However, he stuck to his refusal. While we were still talking, two new clients came in. I decided to leave the house.'

I appreciated the importance of this information. The name Ricardo Klement had now been confirmed. He was German and he had three sons, which agreed with the information in my files. The only detail that did not fit was the younger, allegedly eight-year-old boy. According to my docu-ments, Vera Eichmann had only followed her husband to Argentina in 1953. If that were true, then the little boy could only be six at the most.

That the son from the workshop said he now lived in Don Torcuato, whereas we had heard from several people in Chacabuco Street that the fam-ily was now living in San Fernando, I attributed to the understandable attempt by the family to disguise their new address and to hinder possible

Adolf Eichmann.

One of the few pictures of Eichmann as a young man.

Already in 1933, Jewish stores were being boycotted, as here in Frankfurt.

1935 in Berlin: Jews wishing to emigrate, in the waiting room of the Society for the Aid of German Jews.

Approximately 30,000 men were arrested and dragged off to concentration camps during the pogroms on 9/10 November 1938.

Zvi Aharoni as an NCO in the
British Army.

Kurt Gerstein in SS uniform.

The 'Heckenholt Foundation'.

Isser Harel, Director of *Mossad*, 1952–63.

Present-day view of Garibaldi Street in San Fernando from the railway embankment. Eichmann's house has disappeared amongst other buildings (*above*). When Aharoni took a picture from the same angle in 1960, Eichmann's house (arrow) was all that was visible (*below*).

The pictures that Aharoni had a colleague take with the briefcase camera.

Eichmann, standing in front of his house and talking to the stranger, had no suspicions.

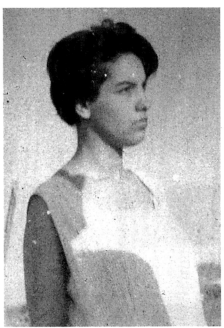

Also taken with the briefcase camera: Eichmann's son Dieter (*above*) and daughter-in-law Margarita, wife of Klaus Eichmann (*left*).

The Eichmann house in Garibaldi Street in 1995 (*top right*) and 1960 (*centre right*).

Hidden under the tarpaulin of this lorry (*right*), Zvi Aharoni observed Eichmann's house (*below*).

Eichmann as a prisoner. The thickly covered goggles were to prevent him being able to identify his kidnappers (*above*).

This picture of Eichmann was taken on 8 June 1960 in Israel (*right*).

The Trial. View of the courtroom in the 'People's House' in Jerusalem (*above*). Eichmann in a box of bulletproof glass on the opening day of the trial (*below*).

Zvi Aharoni (*right*) and Ricardo Eichmann.

investigations. According to my map, the distance from the centre of San Fernando to the middle of Don Torcuato was about five kilometres. I therefore believed it had to be a deliberate attempt at deception. Later on we were to discover that Eichmann's house stood on a piece of no-man's-land in an empty area between the two suburbs.

That evening I went to our embassy to send a coded message to *Mossad* headquarters in Tel Aviv:

THE DRIVER IS RED.

Isser Harel now knew that I had found Klement and there were grounds for assuming that he was Eichmann.

My message continued:

HE MOVED FROM THE ORCHARD THREE WEEKS AGO AND I AM TRYING TO FIND OUT THE NEW ADDRESS. WE HAVE SPOKEN TO A PERSON WHO ACCORDING TO APPEARANCE IS IDENTICAL WITH DANY (the third Eichmann son). I WILL TRY TO TAIL HIM AFTER WORK, ALTHOUGH POSSIBILITIES ARE LIMITED (NO WIRELESS COMMUNICATION, FEW CARS AND NO TRAINED HELPERS).

There was no doubt that the best and most obvious possibility of discovering the Klements' new address would be to follow Dieter home from Vicente Lopez. As 5 and 6 March were a weekend, his place of work was closed. We therefore had to wait till Monday for our next attempt. During these two days I was not idle but pursued other leads, unfortunately without any success.

On Monday 7 March, I again waited at the crossing of Avenida Santa Fé and Sarmiento Street together with Juan. Again, we had to give up our vigil when we had not been able to identify our target after three hours.

A new day came and we were waiting again on the same corner. Suddenly, around 1715, a moped approached from the direction of the workshop and turned left towards San Fernando. The driver was a dark-haired man in his mid-forties. He wore heavy, dark-rimmed glasses. Behind him sat a blond boy of about twenty, dressed in blue overalls. Juan believed he recognised the boy as the person he had spoken with in the workshop. However, he was not absolutely sure. Because the licence plate on the moped was quite dirty, we could not decipher it.

We followed the two men at a safe distance. From the Avenida Santa Fé, the moped turned left into Juan B. Justo and at the Beccar station left again, into a little alley called Haedo Beccar. The men stopped. While the older one remained seated on the moped, the young one went into a two-storey building on the north side of Haedo Beccar. In less than two minutes he returned. The two of them continued their drive in the direction of San Fernando. It was now 1725.

In the centre of San Fernando, near the main square, we lost the moped when we had to stop because of an endlessly long, enervatingly slow funeral procession. And since it never rains but it pours, our rented car broke down on the way back to the capital. We had a lot of trouble finding a repair shop. We were towed back to Buenos Aires and parked the car near the rental company. Next morning it turned out to be highly complicated to obtain a new car.

I was deliberating: under the given circumstances I was still not sure about the identity of the pillion passenger. He looked like 'Dito' but Juan was reluctant to commit himself. The fact that both men had driven to San Fernando on the moped spoke in favour of it being him. However, why had he been on the pillion and not driven his own moped himself? Question upon question. We would need to have another go.

With Yossef's help, I organised three observation teams for 9 March. Since it had rained all day, I feared 'Dito' might have left his moped at home and taken a bus. Therefore I stationed one of Yossef's people together with his 'girl-friend' on the corner of Chacabuco Street not far from the workshop, without a car. Their assignment was, if necessary, to take the same bus as 'Dito'.

I waited in Sarmiento Street in my new rented car as before. Juan, together with another local boy and his moped, were stationed on the market square in San Fernando where we had lost our target the evening before. When I had been unable to discover the moped we were looking for by six o'clock, I drove to San Fernando in the hope that Juan might have seen the target coming from a different direction. But the two boys had to pass as well. We gave up the search and drove back to Buenos Aires.

Next morning I met the young man who had waited together with his 'girl-friend' for 'Dito' near his place of work. He reported that a blond boy who fitted Juan's description had come out of the workshop and boarded a bus on the corner of Parana and Monteagudo. Our helper and his companion followed him. All three left the bus near the Martinez station. The target did not take the train to San Fernando at this point, but turned left into a side-street. The young couple, following my instructions, gave up the tail and went home.

On the afternoon of 10 March, we were more lucky. We were again waiting for our target at three different places. Juan was again on the main square in San Fernando, I was in my car on the corner of Monteagudo together with a young Israeli girl who had been living in Buenos Aires for several years. From experience gained in many similar cases, we knew that a parked car attracts less attention if at least one of the passengers is a woman.

I had asked Yossef to provide this companion and, as usual, he had 'delivered' promptly. Naturally, the girl was not initiated into our operation. All she knew was that I was collecting information on anti-Semitic activities in Argentina. She was happy to be able to help and did not ask any questions.

Another car with two local boys stood ready near Parana Street. We began our operation towards 1630. At 1750 our time finally came. The same moped with the same two people drove out of the workshop and turned into Parana Street. This time it was pulling a small trailer and therefore had to drive very slowly. To follow it was no problem. At the corner of Santa Fé I stopped briefly. The girl left my car and drove back to Buenos Aires with the other car. She had done her job and was not needed for the next stages. Together with one of the boys from the second car, I followed the moped.

The sequence of events of 8 March was repeated. The moped took the familiar route and the blond boy again went into the house on Haedo Beccar Street for about two minutes. The couple then drove via Sarmiento Street to the centre of San Fernando. On the main square there we picked up Juan, who had been sitting on a park bench waiting for us. As soon as he got in the car he excitedly told me that this time he had been able to have a good look at the moped and its two passengers. He was absolutely certain that it was 'Dito's' moped. However, the pillion passenger was definitely not 'Dito'.

Despite this new information, I decided to continue following the moped on its way through San Fernando. The men stopped for a moment at a kiosk near the market square. The younger one got off to buy something. During the next few minutes they took several turns into side-streets and it was difficult not to lose them. Finally, the moped continued its trip on Route 202, which leads to Bancalari and Don Torcuato. There was little traffic on the 202. Therefore, I had to increase the distance greatly between our car and the moped, so that the two men would not notice us. It was now 1830.

About 150 metres before the railway embankment and the big bridge, where Route 202 is crossed by the railway line, the moped again stopped beside a kiosk. When I saw this, I turned off the main road into an untarred road and stopped behind an obviously empty and almost derelict house. The three of us ran back towards the main street. The sun had already set and we could therefore no longer recognise many details. One of the two men was still sitting on the moped. He steered his vehicle off the 202 into Avellaneda Street, where he stopped outside a small wooden hut about 150 metres from the main road. In the meantime, his companion had disappeared somewhere in the vicinity of the kiosk. There was now nothing more we could do, so we returned to San Fernando for the time being.

About half an hour later, by when it had become pitch dark, we returned to the scene. From our former cover, we walked to the kiosk. That took about six to seven minutes. There was very little traffic on the 202 by this time, so we saw only two or three cars. We left the 202 and went down Avellaneda – a wide, straight and untarred street – past the wooden hut.

On our way, we encountered a group of workers who were obviously going to the kiosk to have a few drinks. On my whispered instructions, Juan stopped them and asked if they knew a man called Rodriguez who was supposed to live hereabouts. One of them pointed to a group of houses far to the north-west. He was not sure, but he believed a family of that name lived there. After another whispered remark from me, Juan asked if they knew who lived in the wooden hut. They did not know the name but said that it was a young man and his mother. There was no father. The young man owned a moped.

Unknowingly on that night we had walked past within about one hundred metres of Eichmann's house. One hundred metres past the kiosk and some fifty metres from the main road stood a solid, flat, one-storey brick house, unfinished, without rendering, but with massive doors and shutters. Eichmann had moved into this house with his family before I had arrived in Buenos Aires. On that dark evening, however, none of us paid the Eichmann house any particular attention.

This house in Garibaldi Street in San Fernando was later to become world famous. After Eichmann's abduction, *Stern* magazine wrote the history of its origin. After Eichmann's rabbit farm had gone bankrupt in mid-1958, the unemployed SS officer had taken advantage of his enforced idleness to make the 'dream of owning his own four walls' come true. With money he had saved, he bought a piece of swampy ground near Bancalari. He drained his new property with the help of his grown-up sons and began to build a house on it: not in the normal fashion of the country, but as if it were to last a thousand years. The foundations were 1.40m deep (40cm is normal), the walls 60cm thick (compared with the normal 20cm).

Before he began building, he prepared meticulously exact work-plans, with the same pedantic attention to detail he had practised when expediting transports to Auschwitz a decade and a half earlier. Weeks in advance, he wrote down exactly what he would do on each specific day: raise the western wall, install the door frames, or whatever else it might be.

By this time, the end of 1959, he must have felt that he was virtually safe. In any case, he no longer made any particular efforts to disguise his identity. The building material for the house was purchased by his wife, who also began to call herself by her right name. An invoice by the Cabora building material company was issued on 17 December 1958 under the name Señora Liebl de Eichmann.

In an interview with *Quick* magazine, Eichmann's son Klaus stated that the claim of 'bunker-like walls' was 'nonsense': 'Since there was a wave of inflation in Argentina, father believed we should have our own property. We bought 700 square metres in the suburb of San Fernando and paid 56,000 pesos. We built the house with our own hands. You should have seen our father then. He is so versatile, he could actually do anything, he took everything very seriously, he was correct, always correct. While building the house, we certainly worked like dogs.'

The house in Garibaldi Street, lot No. 14, was finished in early 1960 and the Eichmanns moved. Already the year before, the unemployed family man had noticed an advertisement by the Buenos Aires branch of Mercedes-Benz in a local newspaper and had applied. Ricardo Klement was offered a job as a welder. From 20 March 1959 on, the unobtrusive, slender man rode each morning to the DB plant in Gonzalez Catan, thirty kilometres to the southwest at kilometre No. 43 on the *Ruta Tres* (Highway No. 3) – two hours going, two hours returning.

The German showpiece company produced buses and lorries in Argentina. The bus was given the chassis of the lorry L 312 and therefore looked rather primitive. The sales manager at the time was David Filc, one of the few Jews in the company. In 1995 he recalled: 'The majority of the share capital of the company was held by Argentinian investors. They produced under licence from Germany. There were many Germans among the four to five hundred employees. Quite a few of them had been members of the SS in their former lives. The whole management of the company consisted of emigrants. Some of our people probably knew that Klement was Eichmann. However, nobody wanted to talk about it.'

Lucia Garibaldi worked in the company canteen for ten years. In an interview with Argentine journalist Jorge Camarasa, she reported on her meetings with co-worker Klement: 'He was very polite and pleasant. Every time he saw me, he said hello, and every evening when he left he said: see you tomorrow, Lucia! My family name caught his attention, because he lived in a street with the same name. I only learned that he was Eichmann when the Israelis took him.'

Contemporary witnesses report that Eichmann performed relatively simple work and stood closer to the lower end of the social scale. If what *Stern* magazine believes to have discovered about his income situation had been true ('Within only a few months he worked his way up to the top class of the middle management and was given three rises in quick succession'), then he would not have needed to live in a remote block resembling a prison, without electricity and running water.

Adolf Eichmann knew that he would never live in safety, that his pursuers could suddenly appear one day outside his door. Only with his family did he pretend that he was not worried by reports of the continuing hunt for Nazis . His son Klaus: 'In 1959 my wife heard on the radio in our apartment in Olivos that Adolf Eichmann was wanted by Interpol. My breath caught in my throat, because I knew that Interpol was only after major criminals. I rushed to San Fernando and shook father awake: "Interpol is after you!" This left him completely cold. All he said was: "Damn, and this is what you woke me in the middle of the night for? For this you could have waited until morning. Go home and sleep well." Even days later, he was cross and sour.'

Aharoni continues:

On 11 March 1960 I was still lurking near 'Dito's' place of work. I was now driving a new rented car, a Willys Station Wagon, as the little Fiat used previously had become too conspicuous and was therefore a security risk for me.

I was waiting in Monteagudo Street. At 1720 I noticed a blond boy who left the workshop on a black moped. The licence-plate was clearly recognisable: 118 111. The same night I passed it on to our police contact for the purpose of identifying the owner.

Juan and I followed the moped towards the Martinez station. In Ladislav-Martinez Street we observed him get off and go into a house on the south side. We slowly drove by the house and noticed that there was a dental surgery in the house. Juan took up position and had a look at the man from close-up. Juan was absolutely certain that he had never seen him before. Another day had passed without our having achieved a break-through.

Something simply had to be done to make progress. I was becoming uneasy that we had tried to follow 'Dito's' trail from the workshop to his home too often and with too many people. I saw no possibility of going on in this fashion. Either we discovered his address directly or we had to meet him again to have a close look at him. That was the only way we could make sure that we were trailing the right person.

I therefore ordered Juan to go back to No. 4261 Chacabuco Street once more and then possibly to the workshop to meet 'Dito'. He was to say that the sender of the package had complained. It had apparently never arrived. He had been asked either to bring back the consignment or to refund its value of 500 pesos. Juan was to try to find out the exact address, but in any case to take a very good look at 'Dito' so that at least we would know in future whether we were following the right man.

That evening I met Juan in a little café near our embassy. He looked tired and depressed and I felt sorry for him. 'What's the matter? Come on, let's have a drink.' He shook his head and sat down beside me. In his broken English he said: 'I'm sorry. I have bad news for you. All of our work so far has been in vain. We have been following the wrong man.'

'What do you mean by that?' I asked him. 'What wrong man?' Juan chose his words very carefully: 'Dito is not the man we are looking for. His name is not Klement. His name is Aitchman.' It took a great effort for me to remain calm. 'Never mind! Whether Klement or Aitchman, tell me the whole story.' He told me and I asked him to write it all down.

This is the translation of Juan's report: 'I was asked to go back to the house in Chacabuco Street in order to gather more information on the tenant who had recently moved from there. I arrived there at 1615 and enquired after the man who had told me on the previous occasion that the German's son worked in the automobile repair shop around the corner.

'I met him on the second floor where he was presently working. He remembered me, and also that I had brought something a week ago. I asked him for the new address of the former tenant and he told me that if I wanted to find him, I should first go to the station in San Fernando. From there I should take the *collectivo* (minibus) San Fernando No. 203 and buy a ticket for 4.50 pesos. I should ask the driver to tell me when we had reached Avellaneda Street.

'After getting off, I should cross the Avellaneda. There, on the corner, I would find a kiosk where someone could point out the German's house to me. If I preferred not to ask the people in the kiosk, I would only need to turn right. There was a brick house there with a flat roof and no rendering. That was where he lived, the German.

'I asked him whether he was absolutely certain. He said he was, because he had done some work in the new house and the German still owed him some money. In order to learn more, I asked him about the boy in the workshop who claimed to be the son of the German.

'The man answered that the boy's name was Tito but that he was not the son of the German. He added that the German only had one son, whereas Tito's mother had three or four children. Furthermore, he told me that Tito had two brothers. One was married and the other with the navy. He added, without my having asked him, that the German was only living with Tito's mother.

'I asked the man his name in case I had to come back again, but he did not want to tell me. He said: "What for? If you need me then simply ask after the carpenter. I live here on the second floor." The man is about fifty years old and has a heavy European accent. He also said that Tito does not actually own a moped, but drives to work with the moped of a neighbour.

'I left the house, went up the street and into the yard of the workshop. Inside I met Tito who recognised me immediately. As if it were a joke, he asked me whether I had come back because of the present and what it was that I wanted now. He also told me that he had received the envelope and read the address and immediately passed the present on to his brother. Because he, not his father, had celebrated his birthday on that day. He also added that the name Nikolas Klement could have meant either his father or his brother.

'I told him that the sender, whom I did not know at all, and who had given the present to my friend at the hotel for delivery, was now demanding 500 pesos in damages, because I had allegedly not passed the package on.

'He raised his voice and answered, highly excited: "How come? If she wanted to send it to my brother, why did she not write down my brother's correct name? Nikolas Aitchman!"

'I asked for his brother's address and he noted it down on a piece of paper: General Paz 30-30. Then I wanted to know where I could find Mr Klement in case the girl were to ask again and he repeated twice that Klement was in Tucuman on business. Before we ended our conversation, a second man, about thirty, nosed in from the side and asked Tito: "Where is your father?" And Tito said: "He is in Tucuman on business. Nobody knows when he will be back." I then drove back to Buenos Aires.'

I thanked Juan, who still looked unhappy and depressed. 'Don't worry,' I consoled him, 'you have done a fantastic job. Don't bother about the name. In the end we will get the right man and we will remember how much you helped us. Till then, if you still want to be helpful, don't talk to a living soul about this.' He promised me and we parted.

I now knew that I had found the Eichmanns and their new address between San Fernando and Don Torcuato. It also became clear to me that blind Hermann had been right all the time, when he had reported that Eichmann's son was living in Chacabuco Street under his right name. Finally, the report about a further Eichmann son, born to his wife Vera in Argentina, was also true.

Juan had been intentionally misinformed on two points, namely that Klement was not 'Tito's' father and that he was in Tucuman. At this time, however, I believed the story about Tucuman, because it fitted in with information we had received from another source. Maybe I would go to Tucuman and try to find him there. But before that, I wanted to discover more about the new house. Also about all the people who lived there. From my file I knew that the Eichmanns would be celebrating their silver wedding anniversary in about ten days' time on 21 March 1960. I assumed that Klement, if he were really Eichmann, would return from Tucuman to spend that day with his wife.

I had concluded an important stage of my investigations. Now I sent a further coded cable to Tel Aviv:

DANY, THE DRIVER'S THIRD SON IS DEFINITELY IDENTIFIED: LIVES HERE UNDER HIS REAL NAME OF BIRTH. LIVES WITH HIS MOTHER. ALSO THE NEW ADDRESS OF THE FAMILY HAS BEEN DISCOVERED. IT IS BEING CLAIMED THAT THE MOTHER HAS REMARRIED AND THAT THE STEPFATHER, NAMED KLEMENT, IS IN TUCUMAN, ALMOST 1600 KILOMETRES FROM BUENOS AIRES.

CHAPTER 7

Klement is Eichmann

'On this day I saw him for the first time. I saw Adolf Eichmann, the architect of the Endlösung!'

Zvi Aharoni

I had found the Eichmanns' new residence. The next step had to be to find out everything about the occupants and the ownership of the house. It was important to know the name under which these people had bought and registered their property.

During the late afternoon of 12 March, I drove slowly down Route 202. For the first time, I was able to take a good look at the house in daylight. I saw a single-storey, free-standing building with a flat roof, massively built with a heavy wooden door and shutters of the same material. It did not appear to be quite finished, since the masonry was still not rendered. The house, like the whole area, looked poor and run-down. Nowhere could I discover telephone or power lines. No fence marked the borders of the property.

When I was passing the house, at a distance of some fifty metres, I noticed a heavy-set, black-haired woman around fifty, standing on the unfinished terrace. She was of medium height and poorly dressed. Next to her stood a blond child of about five or six. I assumed I had before me Vera Eichmann and her fourth child, who had been born in Argentina. This assumption was soon to prove correct.

During the same night, I returned once more and left my car in a small road about 300 metres from the kiosk. I walked towards the brick house on a very narrow asphalt road running parallel to Route 202. Finally I passed it at the back, not more than fifteen metres from the outer wall. Despite the moonless night, I noticed for the first time that there was another brick house next to the building and obviously on the same property, which looked, however, more like a shed. Dim light, presumably from kerosene lamps, could be seen coming from both buildings. At some distance, I could hear dogs barking, but not a sound came from the Klements' house. I could assume that they did not own a dog. Even a sleepy house dog would have detected me as I walked along the totally deserted street and round the house twice at only a very short distance. That was reassuring. I returned to Buenos Aires quite satisfied.

During the next three days I was occupied with the Tucuman complex and other investigations on Eichmann. I had decided not to travel to Tucuman yet, even though at this point I believed the story of Eichmann being there. I wanted to wait out the week that separated Vera and Adolf Eichmann from their silver wedding anniversary. I wanted to see him as he came home to visit his wife. I wanted to see him with my own eyes!

On 16 March I again went to San Fernando at six o'clock in the morning. I walked by the house twice but did not detect a soul, neither in the house nor in the shed. An hour later, near the local district administration, I met a Jewish architect who had offered me his help. The man had emigrated to Argentina from Israel some years ago. He had come to join his family, who had established itself in the building industry. I gave him several letters of recommendation that came from friends in Tel Aviv. Like so many others, he helped me willingly without knowing the real reason for my investigations.

After we had studied all the building plans, drawings and maps of the district in question, we applied under false names for a list of the people living in the area of the kiosk. We spread the fairytale that we were engaged in a major project and wished to buy land. We were promised a detailed, written answer already for the very next day.

Towards nine o'clock we drove to the Klements' house. I had decided to take the direct way in order possibly to meet the woman I had seen on the terrace. I wanted to photograph her and compare the picture with an old photograph of Eichmann's wife from my files. My camera was hidden in a briefcase and I could activate it secretly.

We parked in a small side-road which led past the house in a right-hand curve to Route 202. The architect, who spoke Castillano like a native, called 'hello' in a loud voice. A middle-aged woman then came out of the little side-building. My friend asked her if she knew the name of the street we had parked in. She shook her head and answered that probably none of these small alleys had a name. My friend explained – we had agreed on the story beforehand – that we wished to buy more land for a big American company that had already purchased an initial piece of property. We asked whether her little house was for sale. She said yes.

Now our conversation was in full swing and so we continued to question her. Did she know who lived in the larger, more solid brick house next door? And was this also for sale? She told us the people came from Germany and had just moved in. The woman shrugged when we asked for the name of the neighbours. Nor did she seem to know anything at all about the new arrivals. Then, without our having to do anything, she suddenly approached the house and began to make her presence known.

A young woman, obviously a native and quite pretty, appeared in the door and asked us our business. Her tone was very aggressive. My friend approached her with a smile and told her our cover story. Since she was distracted, I triggered the shutter of my secret briefcase camera several times.

Her defensive manner slowly relaxed and the young woman told us that whereas she did not live in the house, her mother-in-law did. She stated adamantly that this house was not for sale. In a friendly way, we bade her ask her mother-in-law for the name of the little side-road. It was important for us to learn the name of the street, in order to be able to locate a piece of property purchased earlier. What we were secretly hoping was that Vera Eichmann would come out of the house. Then I could easily have taken a picture of her close-up.

The young woman prevented this happening. Her mother-in-law hardly spoke Spanish and could therefore not explain anything. She was now becoming angry again. When she heard that we spoke English with each other, she moved closer and addressed me directly in quite fluent English. I was not pleased, to put it mildly. Her English was good enough for her to be able to detect that I did not have a North American accent.

Suddenly she began to question our cover story in detail. She wanted to know the name of our employer and details of the sort of factory we were planning. She made no bones about the fact that she did not credit our explanations. The whole area was neither connected to the municipal water and electricity supply, nor to the telephone network or the sewerage system. She simply could not believe that a reputable company would be interested in such a location.

I decided in favour of a hasty retreat. In a loud voice, I told the architect that we had probably made a mistake and confused the area. Our property was more likely to be in a neighbouring zone, presumably on the other side of the railway line, but certainly not here. We said thank you, got into the car and disappeared as quickly as possible. We learned later that we had been speaking to Eichmann's daughter-in-law Margarita, the wife of his son Klaus.

Two months later, when Eichmann was in our hands and I was interrogating him, I asked him, among other things, whether he had noticed any suspicious occurrences during the preceding weeks and months. He mentioned various events which had aroused his suspicion. One of the examples had to do with a North American company that had been looking for property on which to build a factory. All the other cases he mentioned were simply imagined and had little to do with our activities. The company story, however, definitely had been a mistake.

In any case, it had stuck in Eichmann's memory. When, much later, he was being questioned by police officer Avner Less, he also mentioned it. He had detected that he 'had been surrounded by scouts' and that 'the circle around me was being tightened more and more'. Eichmann verbatim: 'First of all, there was the order from Israeli Prime Minister Ben Gurion, which I had read about in the newspaper, that I was to be looked for. And secondly, I learned that a task force had made enquiries directly in my neighbourhood, so to speak, about building a sewing-machine factory. But there was neither electricity nor fresh water there, and I had discovered that they, at least judging by their manner of speech, were North American Jews. At that time I would have had a marvellous opportunity to go underground once again.'

In the end, however, he decided to refrain 'from evading the accusation by fleeing'. Nothing more than a justification attempt from the standard repertoire of all prisoners. The fact remains, however, that already at this early stage of the *Mossad* operation, the family had been alarmed. Yet the threat from outside never really became tangible. This unseen Damocles' sword only led to the family moving closer together. Jointly they tried to face an ominous, latent danger – until it was too late.

In 1966, Klaus Eichmann recalled a further example: 'The day before the kidnapping he (my father) told us about a black limousine that had been standing near our house. The driver asked him the way to Buenos Aires. However, the driver should have known that, because the car carried a Buenos Aires number plate... My mother entreated him not to go to work next day. But he rejected this. Miss work, simply because of mere suspicion? He could not reconcile something like that with his sense of duty. Mother kept saying: stay at home!'

Klaus was mistaken as far as the black limousine was concerned. It had nothing to do with our operation. We had, however, made another mistake with the birthday present for Nikolas Klement. It was addressed to a person who did not exist under that name. Either we believed Hermann's story, and in that case the name should have read Nikolas Eichmann, or Hermann did not know what he was talking about and we were just wasting our time.

On the other hand, had the cigarette lighter been addressed to Nikolas Eichmann, then his brother Dieter would have given us Nikolas's address in Buenos Aires. This would have been absolutely counter-productive. Later on, by the way, it turned out that Eichmann senior had never been informed about the strange birthday present. Apparently Dieter had given his brother

Klaus the lighter and neither of them had told their father about this extra-ordinary incident. A further lucky break for us.

17 March. During one of my previous visits I had noticed a small plot of land south of Route 202 and about 600 metres from the Klements' house, that lay well away from any buildings and was overgrown with trees and thick bushes. This plot offered an ideal possibility of observing the house without being detected.

On that day, at about 0615 in the morning, I arrived with a brand new pair of binoculars and took up station behind a thick tree. Dieter came out of the door at 0715 and went to the kiosk. There was nobody else to be seen, either before or afterwards. I kept the house under constant observation until about 0825 when some workers arrived and began to dig a ditch, so that I had to retire.

During the late morning I visited the civil administration in San Fernando with my friend the architect to collect the results of our enquiry. A complete disappointment was waiting for us. An employee of the building office, who really seemed to want to help us, informed us that the whole area for about one kilometre around the kiosk was regarded as a sort of no-man's-land, at least as far as regulations and documentation by the local authorities were concerned. Every year, the whole area was inundated after any heavy rainfall. Only a very few people lived there and none of them had yet been registered. The community was not obliged to provide any services and had not yet collected any taxes from these 'settlers'. He could therefore not help us any further.

In order to be absolutely certain, we briefly visited the legal depart-ment of the administration. They confirmed the previous information. We would have to look elsewhere to find out under whose name the property had been purchased and registered. The architect was of the opinion that the only remaining possibility was now the GEOFINK company. It had bought up the whole area, partitioned off the lots and resold them. It was fortunate that the architect knew this development company well.

I also asked him whether he thought it would be possible to buy the little house next to the Klements. I had two things in mind. First, it was an ideal observation post for everything taking place around the target. We only needed to find a native we could trust, who would be willing to live in the shed. As a cover story he could say that he had been recently divorced and wished to be alone. We would then soon learn all about the circumstances next door.

The other idea was no less important. I was already thinking about the second stage of the operation, Eichmann's abduction. With the little house, we would have an ideal base and simultaneously keep potential witnesses away from the vicinity.

The architect explained we could undoubtedly buy the house for 500 to 1000 dollars. He would handle the whole deal, even using false identification papers, so that subsequent investigations by the police would lead to nothing. Furthermore, it would be possible for him to find a trustworthy person to live in the house and observe the Klements' activities. When we parted, the architect promised to continue the investigations at GEOFINK and report the results to Yossef at the embassy.

That same night I sent a long coded cable to Tel Aviv in which I explained the possibilities that the purchase of the little house next door would offer. The reply was not long in coming. It arrived at the embassy in less than twelve hours, early the following morning.

DO NOT BUY, REPEAT: NOT APPROVED.

18 March. I drove past the house twice. I again saw the little boy, who was playing on the unfinished terrace as usual. A blond child, about five years old, always dressed in an undershirt and underpants. On my way back, I again saw the woman. She wore a cheap summer dress and was hanging out washing.

In the afternoon, I met the architect in the embassy. From his smile I could see immediately that he had hit the jackpot. 'I have found out the registered owner of the house,' he proudly reported. 'It is registered in the name of the woman!' He waved a piece of paper in the air that he had received from his contact at the GEOFINK building company. The information concerned plot No. 14 and the owner was Veronica Catarina Liebl de Fichmann, No. 4251 Chacabuco, Olivos.

I was hard pressed not to show my excitement. Towards the architect I remained composed and friendly: 'I do not know how to thank you. That is exactly what I have been looking for.' 'Don't thank me,' he replied with satisfaction, 'just give me another job to do, I love to work with you. It gives me the feeling that I am doing something useful. I am already sick and tired of the real-estate business.'

'The next assignment I have for you is the most important of all,' I impressed upon him. 'Go home and forget everything you have done for me. If you promise to do that, maybe we will call upon you again some day.' He agreed with a laugh and we parted after a firm handshake.

I now knew that my search had come to an end. I had uncovered the most important piece of information to date. My files stated that the maiden name of Eichmann's wife was Vera Liebl. According to local custom, a woman used her maiden name as well as that of her husband. If, for example, Maria Lopez were to marry a man named Rodriguez, then she would subsequently be called Maria Lopez de Rodriguez. Therefore, the information from GEOFINK contained three exciting and most important facts:

1. I had definite proof that Eichmann's wife was the owner of the house in Garibaldi Street in San Fernando. The fact that her married name had been spelled with an F instead on an E was not important to me. It could be a spelling mistake by the person who had filled in the form, or deliberate misinformation to deceive anyone who was looking for Eichmann. The same naturally applied to the house number in Chacabuco Street. No. 4251 instead of the correct number – 4261 – had been registered.

2. Vera Liebl was not married to anybody but Adolf Eichmann. Otherwise she would have adopted the name of her new, second husband.

3. The fact that the house was registered under her name confirmed that her husband did not wish to appear on any official document.

I immediately sent a long coded message to Tel Aviv. I suggested I return without delay in order to report directly and enable the operations department to plan stage two: the abduction of Adolf Eichmann.

19 March. On this day I saw him for the first time. I saw Adolf Eichmann, the architect of the *Endlösung*! My patience and my decision, not to go looking for him in Tucuman but rather to wait for him in San Fernando, were rewarded. The silver wedding anniversary was approaching. Only two days separated us from the date. It was Saturday. Eichmann/Klement was at home. It was only later I realised that the reason he was at home was because most Argentinian companies did not work on weekends.

I was driving a five-year-old black De Soto, a car that was very popular in Buenos Aires in those days. The car belonged to a good friend, Menachem Barabash. Many years before, we had both been members of the same *kibbutz*, Alonim. I had learned with great joy that he was now in the Andean republic as the representative of the United Jewish Appeal. I had asked him to lend me his car. I had driven around in the vicinity of Garibaldi Street far too often in my rented Jeep. To keep changing rented cars was extremely difficult in Argentina in those days, because there were too few dependable cars.

In exchange I had offered Menachem the use of my Jeep and he had agreed without reservations. Naturally, he did not know what it was all about. He did know, however, that I worked for the Israeli secret service. Therefore he did not ask any questions. It was clear to him that he was lending me his car in a good cause.

On this trip to San Fernando, I was accompanied by a secretary from the embassy. It was actually her day off, but she nevertheless wanted to make herself useful. With her in the car, I felt more secure, simply because I attracted less attention.

I saw him at about two o'clock in the afternoon. As I was returning from Don Torcuato on Route 202 and driving past the house, I saw a man of medium size and build, about fifty years old, with a high forehead and partially bald, collecting the washing. He disappeared inside the house before I could use my hidden camera.

The girl noticed my excitement. 'What happened? Why are you so happy?' I laughed. 'Nothing's happened. I just remembered that today is my mother's birthday. Let's go and celebrate. I invite you to have the biggest *lomito* steak in the whole of Buenos Aires.' Astonished but pleased, she accepted the invitation.

That night I composed a new message to Tel Aviv headquarters:

A MAN HAS BEEN OBSERVED AT VERA EICHMANN'S HOUSE WHO DEFINITELY RESEMBLES EICHMANN. I HAD ASSUMED HE WOULD COME TODAY (SATURDAY), BECAUSE THE SILVER WEDDING ANNIVERSARY FALLS ON COMING MONDAY. ON MY PART THERE IS THEREFORE NO FURTHER DOUBT THAT KLEMENT IS EICHMANN. ANY FURTHER OBSERVATION OR INVESTIGATION COULD ENDANGER THE SUCCESS OF THE FORTHCOMING MAIN OPERATION. I ASSUME HE WILL RETURN TO HIS WORK IN TUCUMAN ON MONDAY. I WILL ALSO GO TO TUCUMAN, EVEN THOUGH IT WILL NOT BE EASY TO LOCATE HIM THERE. I RECOMMEND THAT I RETURN TO TEL AVIV IMMEDIATELY IN ORDER TO ASSIST IN THE PLANNING OF THE MAIN OPERATION. I AGAIN RECOMMEND TERMINATION OF ALL INVESTIGATION ACTIVITIES IN EUROPE.

The following day, Sunday, I decided to observe the Klements' house more closely and if possible, take a picture of the man whom I assumed was Eichmann. With Yossef's help I obtained an old pick-up truck for the day for this purpose. The small truck was delivered to the embassy on Saturday evening. It was an old Ford, the back part of which was covered with a heavy, dirty tarpaulin.

We began our preparations early in the morning. At the back of the truck I cut a small hole in the tarpaulin just above the level of the loading ramp. It was just large enough to accommodate my binoculars. In the coding room of the embassy, I found an old camp bed. We placed it on the loading platform. Lying on the bed, I was at exactly the right height. I could see everything by looking through the small hole and there was no danger of being observed from the outside.

The driver of the truck was given very precise instructions. First he was to drive to Don Torcuato. On the way back he was to park at the side of the road just short of the kiosk. The back of the little truck would then be pointing exactly in the direction of the house and offer me a good view through the hole in the tarpaulin. The driver was to go into the kiosk and have something to eat. He could take an hour and a half, in order to give me time to observe the house. At the same time, he would be near enough to chase away any nosy children who might insist on trying to discover what was hidden under the tarpaulin.

We reached our intended station towards eleven o'clock. After he had carefully parked, the driver disappeared inside the kiosk. I prepared myself for a lengthy observation. For a small eternity, the little boy was the only living being I could see. He was playing in the garden as usual.

Then, towards 1145, *he* appeared. I saw the same man who had taken the washing from the line the day before. He was approaching from the direction of the highway. Because the small hole in the tarpaulin only permitted me a narrow angle of view, I could not tell whether he had arrived by bus or by some other means. He did not turn into the side-road that led to the main entrance of the house, but walked straight across the field. The man briefly bent over, slipped under a wire that probably marked the border of the property and walked slowly towards the house. My carefully prepared observation post gave me a clear, unimpeded view of the subject who was so important to us. The man was dressed in a suit and tie. I estimated that he was about 1.70m tall. He was partially bald, had dark hair on both sides of his head, a high forehead, a large nose and wore glasses.

He stopped briefly to speak to the boy playing in the yard, stroked his hair and straightened his shirt and trousers. For the first time I saw the child decently dressed. That probably had something to do with it being Sunday. The man turned towards the main entrance. The woman opened the door for him. Before he entered the house, they both swatted at annoying flies. In less than two minutes he came back out and went to the small side-road on the other side of the house, which I could not observe. There was a horse-drawn cart standing there. The man bought two loaves of bread and went back into the house.

Ten minutes later he appeared again. This time he was wearing a white undershirt and pyjama trousers with white and blue stripes. He walked across the yard in the direction of my hideout and went into the small wooden shed. From there he fetched a large soda-siphon and returned to the house. Now his son Dieter arrived. He came from the direction of the wooden house where the owner of the moped lived. They exchanged a few words. Then the father and his two sons went back inside the house. It was 1205.

About thirty minutes later my driver had finished his lunch and came back. After he had received the agreed signal to leave, he drove off.

That evening I stayed in the embassy for a long time. I wrote a comprehensive, detailed report with invisible ink, which was to be sent to Tel Aviv next day with the diplomatic pouch. I believed it was time to give a summary of my activities to date. I felt it would be much too arduous to encode the whole text and send it by cable. That would have completely overstressed the poor encoding officers.

This is the translation of what I wrote: 'Vera Eichmann lives with Dieter and her youngest child, a son of about five, in a free-standing house about thirty kilometres from the centre of Buenos Aires. The house is registered under her real name. It consists of brick without rendering, has heavy shutters, barred windows and a heavy front door.

'By the same pouch I am sending several photographs that convey a good impression of the house and the surrounding terrain. With the exception of a small brick building that looks like a shed (to the right of the main house in the pictures), there are no other buildings in the vicinity. A local family lives in the small house on a lot of about 400 square metres.

'Up to last month, the Eichmann family lived in the house in Chacabuco Street in Olivos. I have already obtained the following information on Eichmann:

'From another tenant in Chacabuco (probably Francisco Schmidt) we learned that the tenant who moved one month ago was named Ricardo Klement. He is a German and Dieter, who works in a repair shop about one hundred metres further down, is his son.

'We learned that the son's name is Dieter Eichmann. The family moved into a new house on the border of San Fernando and the father works in the Tucuman area.

'When we tailed Dieter, we discovered the new house. Investigations with the company that sold the land disclosed that the house is registered in Vera's full name, i.e. her maiden name and her married name (in other words Eichmann). Such a combination of maiden and married names is customary here for all married women. There were no documents to be found on this area in the San Fernando administration offices. No local taxes are being collected in the whole area. There are also no public services. This area is regarded as no-man's-land. During every rainy season it is mostly under water.

'Yesterday and the day before, a man was observed near Vera's house. He showed a clear resemblance to photographs we have of Eichmann and his brothers. The name Ricardo Klement does not appear in police records in the greater Buenos Aires area. If Klement had emigrated to Argentina legally, he would have to be registered. The name does not appear in the local voters' register either. This leads to the conclusion that Klement must be Eichmann and that he came into the country illegally.

'In summary, I am of the opinion that we should now begin with the next phase of the operation. I have no doubts that I have seen Eichmann. The bread vendor confirmed that this man is married to Vera. The man caressed the little boy in the garden and changed clothes inside the house. If he is married to Vera but is not Eichmann, why was the house not registered in his real name? And why does Vera not carry his name?

'I believe we have enough information to plan the next stage. A final identification can only be made when the team is ready to go into action. Any steps that are too obvious could make him uneasy and he might then disappear. So far, his lack of sensitivity with regard to security and his carelessness have been astonishing. The whole family live here under their real names. Dieter revealed his real name as well as his new address (even though the house is difficult to locate) to a total stranger. These people made no effort at all to cover their tracks when they left Chacabuco Street.

'All this confirms that they do not fear any danger at the moment. This can change as soon as we make a wrong move. If we would have to wait for an operations team for weeks or months, the chances for a successful operation would decline.

'In my view there is little sense in chasing after him to Tucuman. Even if we were to be able to locate him there, which would not be easy, I do not believe in a successful operation. Tucuman is twenty-eight hours by train from Buenos Aires. I see no practical means of bringing him here from there. In my opinion, we must prepare everything here and then lie low until he comes back for a visit. I am awaiting instructions.'

I assumed that I would receive orders to return to Tel Aviv to brief and update the responsible people personally. However, that might take another week. On the one hand, my report had to arrive and be read at headquarters, on the other hand, all flights were completely booked. Before leaving, I therefore set myself two further tasks:

I needed a good photograph of Eichmann and I wanted to try to approach as near to the house as possible at night, in order to gain an impression of the interior through the lighted windows. That same night, I decided to go back to the house in Garibaldi Street and to undertake my second task.

This now posed a problem. How was I to get there? I did not want to take the bus. When buying a ticket, one has to state one's destination. What could I say? Everybody in the bus would have noticed that I was a foreigner. I would have to leave the bus near the Eichmann house. Next day, a neighbour could ask him by coincidence or out of curiosity, whether he had had a visitor the night before. I did not want to risk all that.

On the other hand, I did not want to go by myself in my rented Jeep. I felt it was not a good idea to park the off-roader near the house unattended for a longer period of time. Then I remembered that the safest method was to take a couple along. I had frequently observed vehicles with lovers parking for hours in the dark at various places between San Fernando and Don Torcuato. I would therefore need a man and a woman who would stay sitting in the Jeep while I tried to scout the house from close-up.

I finally talked one of the higher officials at the embassy into accompanying me together with his wife. Since, as with Yossef, I still cannot reveal his real name even today, let us simply call him Avi. We set out for San Fernando towards 2115 and arrived there half an hour later. I parked the car close to Avellaneda Street in the little side-road that led past the back of the Eichmann property. I asked Avi and his wife to remain seated in the car with the windows closed and not to answer any questions from inquisitive passers-by. We dared not be recognised as foreigners. Perish the thought of Eichmann learning that there were foreigners slinking around his house at night.

I set out on my little expedition. Three minutes later I was standing about fifteen metres away from the back of the house. I had actually intended to quit the road and to steal through the back garden to one of the windows. But it was dark inside the house and everything was still. Whoever lived here was apparently already asleep. We had probably come too late. Under these circumstances, I saw no reason why I should expose myself to the risk of being detected. I decided to try again on some other night but at an earlier hour, and turned back.

It was a moonless, cloudy night and visibility was almost nil. When I came back to the spot where I had parked the Jeep, it was gone. That confused me completely. I could not have gone wrong, because I had never left the little street that led to the house. To make sure, I went on for another few steps and then I saw the Jeep about ten to fifteen metres from where I had left it. The vehicle, however, was not standing on the road; no, it was lying in the ditch.

Then I noticed Avi and his wife who were cowering down on the ground close by. He apologised and tried to explain what had happened. He had only wanted to turn the Jeep around in order to be ready for the drive back to Buenos Aires. For the sake of security, he had manoeuvered without turning on the headlights. He had therefore not noticed that the road level was about one metre higher than the surrounding terrain. It had not been easy to turn the Jeep around on the narrow road. When the rear wheels had gone over the edge of the road, the vehicle had turned over almost without making a sound. Luckily, neither of them had been injured, except for a small bump on his wife's forehead. They had also been able to free themselves from the car without any problem.

I was angry and worried. What a mess we had got ourselves into! And how were we to get out again? Here we were, three Israelis, one hundred metres from Eichmann's house with an overturned Jeep. I had to think quickly, because somebody could come by at any moment and offer to help. Five or six men would probably have been able to set the Jeep right side up again. That, however, was something we dared not risk, because any native would have recognised us as foreigners immediately.

Even though this was highly risky, we had to get away from the car and leave it lying in the ditch. 'Let's go,' I said to my helpers, 'let's get the hell out of here!' 'Where to?' Avi asked me. 'Whom can we go to for help?' I did not know the answer. We walked down the Avellaneda in the direction of the kiosk. I turned to Avi: 'I know of only one man who can get us out of this: Vardi. If he can't, then no one else can either.' Avi agreed: 'You're right. I should have thought of him!'

Yitzhak Vardi was an Israeli banker who lived in Buenos Aires. Vardi was the head of the United Jewish Appeal for all of South America. I had been introduced to him by Yossef and later on had met him a few times. I had heard much good about him from several people. He seemed to be a man whose possibilities were unlimited. He knew my real background – it was difficult to keep something secret from Vardi – and, without our having talked about it, he surmised that I was on the trail of some important Nazi war criminal.

Suddenly we saw the bus from Don Torcuato approaching on the main road. I waved it down at the bus stop near the Avellaneda. A few minutes later we reached the station in San Fernando. It was already 2245. During our short ride, one question kept going through my mind: what would we do, if Vardi were not at home? But we were in luck, because Vardi was in and picked up the telephone himself.

By the tone of my voice, the banker recognised the urgency of the situation and did not ask any questions. When he learned that we needed a tow truck in order to pull a Jeep out of a ditch all he asked was: 'Where are you?' I explained and he answered briefly: 'Wait for me at the main entrance of San Fernando station. I will come in person.'

Less than forty-five minutes later he was there, followed by a tow truck from the Buenos Aires Automobile Association. We all got into Vardi's big Chevrolet and were standing just off the Avellaneda with the big rescue truck soon afterwards. The Jeep was still lying in the ditch, just as we had left it. As we approached, however, we saw that it had had a visitor in the meantime. One of the wheels was missing. It had been easy to remove the wheel, because the thief had not even needed a jack. The wheels were pointing at the sky.

With some difficulty, I managed to get the spare wheel out of the overturned Jeep. In order not to attract any attention, I worked in the dark, which did not exactly make my task any easier. Oil and petrol had run out and flowed all over the interior of the car.

By this time some neighbours, who had been attracted by the noise of the tow truck, came over. The driver calmed them down by assuring them that no one had been hurt and that everything was under control. I was relieved when I did not discover Dieter among the onlookers nor see any light from the nearby house. I finally succeeded in tightening the spare wheel by taking a nut from each of the three remaining wheels. By this time, I must have looked like a native mechanic and not like a foreign diplomat.

Minutes later the Jeep was back on the road standing on its own four wheels. To my surprise, the motor caught immediately, even though the petrol gauge stood at empty. I drove the Jeep to the nearest petrol station, followed by the others in Vardi's limousine. There I tanked up, topped up the oil and cleaned the oil smears from the driver's seat with some paper towels.

All's well that ends well. I thanked Vardi, Avi and his wife without shaking their hands, because I was far too dirty. Vardi grinned: 'It was a pleasure! Any time you get into trouble, just let me know!' I then returned to Buenos Aires.

Now it was 21 March, the long-awaited wedding day. All morning I was occupied with getting the Jeep back into its original condition. I had to prevent, at all costs, the car rental agency noticing anything about the mishap. I wanted to avoid them demanding details of the accident and maybe even bringing in the police.

With luck I managed to find a spare wheel that fitted the Jeep fairly well. I had the car washed inside and out. When I then took it back, no one asked awkward questions. That went a long way towards putting my mind back at ease. I obtained a new Jeep from another rental company, a grey one this time – the other one had been red.

The day had passed before I was able to return to San Fernando. This time I went alone. I drove past the target towards 2130. There was a dim light coming from a window on the side towards the main road. When I returned twenty minutes later, everything was silent and dark. So much for the festivities on the silver wedding anniversary in the Eichmann house.

22 March. During late afternoon, I drove my Jeep past the house and saw the woman and the little boy standing on the terrace. This time he was properly dressed. Ten minutes later, the little boy was gone. The woman was sitting alone in front of the house reading a book.

23/24 March. I travelled to Montevideo to work on my cover story. After all, my official reason for being in the area was to collect information on anti-Semitic activities and devise counter-measures.

25 March. I returned to Buenos Aires. Despite several attempts, I was not able to obtain a new rented car.

26 March. Now I again had a Jeep, a blue one this time. In the office of an Israeli friend, I met Yossef and his official contact with the Argentinian police. He was a tall man with a thick, bushy beard. Yossef had told me beforehand that the man was prepared to do anything, provided he was paid sufficiently.

Our contact showed us two files. They contained information on Klaus and Horst Eichmann, the two elder sons of Adolf Eichmann. With Yossef's help and some hard bargaining, the police official was talked into letting me keep the files for a few hours in order to study them more closely. None of us mentioned the word photocopying. That was not necessary, because everybody present understood anyway. I hurried to our embassy with the files, where I copied every single page. At the time agreed, I returned in order to hand back the material.

At six in the evening I again arrived back in San Fernando. Half an hour later I saw the man working in the little shed on the corner of his property. When I came by again ten minutes later he had disappeared.

27 March. When I scouted further afield in the San Fernando area, I discovered an ideal observation point on the other side of the Reconquista river on the way to the more northerly Tigre. It lay about 800 metres from the house and could not be seen from there. On my way back shortly after six o'clock, I noticed the man working in the front garden together with Dieter. Without stopping, I triggered the shutter on my hidden camera.

28 March. It rained cats and dogs. Together with Rendi, one of Yossef's boys, I again drove to San Fernando early in the morning. Rendi got out at the Avellaneda and went to the kiosk. He pretended to be seeking shelter from the rain and waiting for the bus. I myself only stopped the Jeep one and a half kilometres further along on the main road to San Fernando. We observed our target from eight o'clock until ten to nine but did

not see anybody. Rendi then returned to San Fernando by bus. There he waited for me.

29 March. I was keen to observe the man leaving the house in the morning. I thought that if we came earlier, we would have a better chance. I therefore arrived at the house with Rendi at 0655. By eight we had seen no one, not even Dieter. We broke off. In Buenos Aires I had to give up my Jeep again.

The following morning I flew to Tucuman with my friend Juan. For three days there, we followed up on all the leads that were in the Eichmann file. I pretended to be a lawyer from Germany. My job was to collect information on the CAPRI company, which had been founded by Germans in exile. In actual fact we met two people, independently of each other, who remembered a man called Klement who had worked for CAPRI years before. Both assured us that Klement had turned his back on Tucuman in 1953. After that he had been the owner of a laundry in Buenos Aires. We did not find any CAPRI office because the company had discontinued its activities in the Tucuman area years before.

For the first time I began to doubt Dieter's statement that his father worked in Tucuman. All the people we talked with stated credibly that they would certainly have learned of the return of any former CAPRI employees. By then I had observed the man, whom we took to be Dieter's father, near the house in San Fernando on five separate occasions. It slowly began to dawn on me that he probably did live and work in Buenos Aires after all. The Tucuman story was only being spread in order to obstruct investigations of Klement/Eichmann. To have been able to reach this conclusion made the trip to Tucuman worthwhile. On 1 April we returned to Buenos Aires.

2 April. I again drove to San Fernando in a new Willys station wagon. It was a good day for taking photographs. I took pictures of the house in Garibaldi Street from all sides. I finally even climbed up the nearby railway embankment which afforded an excellent view over the whole terrain and took a few panorama shots. Towards 1850 the man was again working in the garden.

I drove back to the outskirts of San Fernando and parked the car next to an old factory site. Then I walked back in the direction of the house. When I reached the kiosk, it was already completely dark. This time I had better luck. A dim light shone from the south-eastern window in the direction of the railway embankment. I came close enough to the house to be able to see the man sitting at a table. He was occupied with some sort of writing. The interior of the house, in contrast to its raw exterior, was clean, orderly and nicely furnished. The light came from a kerosene lamp in the shape of a lantern.

Next day, 3 April – a Sunday – I was determined finally to photograph this man from close-up. I was sure that if I were able to present a good photograph in Tel Aviv, this would be of great importance for the subsequent operation. I was also sure that my marching orders to return home would soon come and that the best and maybe the last chance to take pictures would be on a Sunday morning – the directive to return home did in fact arrive the following day.

Unfortunately, I was unable to do the job myself. To get a real good close-up shot from the briefcase camera, I needed to be near the subject, speaking to him. My Castillano was not good enough for this. Besides, there was always the danger that the young woman would be there again and recognise me from my previous visit. Therefore I had no choice but to rely on local helpers.

Again I needed two volunteers for the job. I regretfully had to decline Juan's offer to accompany me, because Dieter already knew him from his several visits to the workshop. I chose Rendi and Roberto, who both accepted immediately. I gave Rendi a crash course in the use of the briefcase camera. I adjusted the shutter speed and the likely distance and showed him the angle at which he had to hold the briefcase. After several attempts I was sure that he had understood. Furthermore, he was finally able to overcome the natural urge to look down at the briefcase when triggering the camera.

The three of us set out in a pick-up truck. We stopped under the Bancalari railway bridge and observed the house which was about 250 metres away. It was fairly dark under the bridge. I therefore assumed that from the house someone would only be able to see us as shadows, if at all.

I lay in the back and watched the house through my binoculars while Rendi and Roberto were busily fiddling around with the engine, as if something had broken down. My idea was to have Rendi go to the house and talk to the man about something. He could tell him, for example, that he was looking for this kind of a house to buy. While he was talking to the man, he should photograph him from several angles. To get a profile shot, I impressed upon him, was very important.

Naturally, there was the danger that Dieter or the young woman would come out when Rendi was standing at the gate and drawing attention to himself by calling out. In such a case, it would hardly be possible to ask to speak to the man himself. Rendi was therefore not to start out until we had seen our target at work in the garden or entering the little wooden shed.

Everything went according to plan. We had arrived under the bridge around 1030. Less than fifteen minutes later I saw the man come out of the house and go across the garden to the little shed. As agreed with Rendi, I gave a short whistle. My helper took the briefcase and hurried from the bridge towards the house. Two minutes later he crossed the field in a straight line, thus avoiding the main entrance as I had instructed him to do.

Near the wire that marked the boundary of the property, Rendi met Dieter and the man. The three of them talked for several minutes. Roberto and I were attentive and observant. We were prepared to rush to Rendi's aid should this become necessary. It was not. After two or three minutes, the man returned to the shed, while Rendi kept on chatting with Dieter.

Then Rendi left for the small brick building and talked to the people living there. After that he went to the kiosk and – following my instructions – took a bus to San Fernando. We picked him up at the station. He was quite enthusiastic that everything had gone so well. I congratulated and thanked him. I could hardly wait to see the photographs. Unfortunately, we had no means of developing the film at the embassy. It was only on the following morning that I was able to take it to a photography shop.

4 April. I took the valuable film to a large shop on one of the main streets in Buenos Aires. With some difficulty, I persuaded the assistants, in a mixture of languages, that all I needed was the negatives: no prints. In those days, there was no one-hour service such as we enjoy today. To enlarge the prints would have taken four to seven days. That was clearly far too long. Almost pleadingly, I explained to the assistants that I was leaving Buenos Aires in two days' time and therefore needed the negatives in twenty-four hours.

My reasons were simple. I had to be sure that I had at least one good shot of the man before I returned home. It is not easy to use a briefcase camera, particularly if one is not experienced and labouring under the stress of an on-going operation. I had to be sure that Rendi had not mistakenly cut out the man's head when photographing. However, I had to avoid, under all circumstances, anyone else seeing the pictures. With the minimal odds of a million to one, they just might fall into the hands of someone who knew Eichmann and who would ask him, by some freak coincidence, what they were. I did not want to run any risk at all. It was almost certain that no one would recognise him from the negatives.

The photography shop promised me my negatives for next morning. I accepted an extra charge of one hundred per cent for express treatment. I then went to the embassy, where I found the following cable waiting for me:

IN ORDER TO ENABLE YOUR GIVING US A COMPLETE REPORT AND TO PREPARE A DETAILED PLAN FOR THE MAIN OPERATION, WE REQUEST YOU TO RETURN AS QUICKLY AS POSSIBLE.

I set out again to book a flight. The earliest reservation I could obtain was with *Aerolineas Argentinas* via Paris on 8 April.

On Tuesday 5 April, I went to pick up my negatives. An assistant greeted me with the apology that the prints were not yet ready.

'What prints? Who asked for prints? I want my negatives and I want them now! I am leaving Buenos Aires tonight and I need my film!'

A noisy argument started, half in English, half in Castillano. As far as I was able to understand, the film had been sent to a distant laboratory to be developed and have prints made. I became very agitated and started to imagine all sorts of dark machinations. I demanded that the man call the laboratory and have the film brought by taxi by the shortest possible route. Either the assistant could not understand my excited words or – and that was more likely – he did not want to.

He telephoned several times. Half an hour went by without anything happening. I now lost my composure.

'Why is it so difficult to ask the man to take a taxi? I will pay! I have to have the film before I leave!'

A further telephone call and a further meaningless excuse.

I had had enough. 'Give me the address and I will drive there myself to pick up my film.'

'You will not find the place. The streets where the man lives do not have any names.'

Now where had I heard that before? More and more I was coming to the conclusion that I had fallen into a trap set by one of Eichmann's friends. Then, just as I was ready to beat a retreat, a boy arrived on a moped. From a shoulder pouch he pulled a large envelope with my negatives – and my prints.

When I saw the pictures, my fears evaporated. Without prior experience, Rendi had managed to take four fantastic shots of Dieter and his father from every possible angle. I now realised that the whole scene at the photography shop had only been enacted in order to fleece a stupid foreigner. I paid for the pictures and also gave the courier with the moped a generous tip.

My mission was concluded. I could now return to Tel Aviv. I used the final three days to gather as much information as possible about the port and the airport in Buenos Aires. After all, we had to devise various methods of getting our target out of the country once he was in our hands. I even organised a boat trip around the harbour for all the Israelis who had helped me on my case. Officially, it was to thank them all. In actual fact, I wanted to check out whether it was possible to charter a boat with which to bring a 'sick' passenger to a ship anchored far outside the harbour.

I also said goodbye to all the local helpers. I knew that I would never see them again. None of the locals would be permitted to take part in the main operation in any way. It is one thing to look for a man, collect information about him and take pictures of him. None of this is punishable under the law. To kidnap an Argentinian citizen and to smuggle him out of the country is another matter entirely. That can only be done by professionals and none of them would carry an Argentinian, or even an authentic, passport.

On 7 April I returned my last rented car and the following day I flew from Buenos Aires to Paris. During the long trip home my thoughts kept returning to the question of whether I would be taking part in the next phase of the operation. I knew the *Mossad* operations department inside-out. It was a tightly welded team and did not trust any outsider. I was almost certain that I would be allowed to report and explain everything. Then, however, the professionals would take over and proceed to abduct this man. I would have to stay at home and return to my interrogations. How unfair!

To my great relief I soon learned that my anxiety had been unfounded. By pure coincidence I met Isser Harel on the aeroplane from Paris to Tel Aviv. At this point, he was not interested in any details. Harel only asked me one question: 'Are you absolutely sure that he is our man?'

I took a photograph from Rendi's series out of my case and showed it to Harel. Simultaneously I answered: 'I have not the slightest doubt!' I was flattered to what extent Isser Harel trusted my judgement. He glanced at the picture and then looked at me: 'In that case we will go and get him.'

I could not help myself, I had to ask him: 'Will I be part of the team for the main operation?' Harel laughed. 'Have you any reason not to take part? We need you. I have already told Rafi to include you as a member of his team.' That made me feel very happy. Rafi Eitan, chief of the *Mossad* operations department, was an old friend of mine.

We landed in Tel Aviv during the evening of 9 April. Exactly two weeks later, on 23 April, I was again to fly to Buenos Aires. That was when our actual 'Operation Eichmann' began.

CHAPTER 8

Eleventh May,
Nineteen Hundred and Sixty

'All honours should go to Zvi! Without him we would not be sitting here'

Isser Harel

On 24 April I again arrived in Buenos Aires. This time, however, I was not an Israeli diplomat, but a German businessman. My passport carried a different name, I was wearing different clothes, had let my hair grow longer and had stopped shaving my upper lip. I avoided hotels, restaurants and car rentals where someone might remember me and made a wide detour around the Israeli Embassy.

I was part of the four-man advance guard. We were to check out the situation on the spot and find out if the circumstances for the main operation – the abduction of Eichmann – were favourable. The other members of the team, including Isser Harel and the actual leader of the operation, Rafi Eitan, were making final preparations in Tel Aviv.

One of the men in the advance party was Rafi Eitan's deputy – not only during this operation but also in the corresponding department at *Shin Bet* – Avraham Shalom, formerly Bendor. The operations department to which they both belonged had been created by Isser Harel and was there to serve the internal service as well as *Mossad*. The department was the pride of the *Memuneh*. In it he had concentrated the best agents in the Israeli services.

Shalom was a veteran of the *Palmach* and had worked his way up in the *Shabak*. He had been born in Vienna in 1929. His mother came from South Tyrol, his father from Bulgaria. In 1939, between the *Reichskristall-nacht* and the start of the war, the family emigrated to Palestine via Italy. In Tel Aviv the father founded a textile company. Avraham Shalom and I had led similar lives and knew each other from numerous cases handled by the internal service. We got along well together. Avraham Shalom was also travelling under the cover of a German passport.

The third man was Yaakov Gat, called Yankele, a man for the practical side of the operation. Also included was Efraim Ilani, who had lived in Buenos Aires for several years and knew the giant city inside out. As already mentioned, he had been involved in the Eichmann case two years previously.

Ilani and Efraim Hofstetter, the police officer from Israel, had visited blind Lothar Hermann and his family in Coronel Suarez and questioned them about the people living in Chacabuco Street in Olivos.

Ilani was the only one of us who was travelling on an Israeli passport. He was to be our contact man to the embassy. That was an immensely important role, because we were not allowed to go near the embassy, not even to call it on the telephone. Naturally we needed a man who could, for example, send and receive cables. That was Ilani. Before leaving Tel Aviv, the two of us had worked out a very detailed and meticulous plan, with meeting points. Each of us had been assigned an hotel with a second one as an alternative. So we did not have to worry about bumping into another member of the team if we had to change hotels. Each of us had a list of cafés, restaurants and street corners for each day of the week, with additional alternative places in case contact could not be made on the first attempt.

On 25 April I was able to contact both Ilani and Yankele with the aid of this list. Together with Yankele, I set out to find a rented car. However, we were unable to find one that suited, but we were promised one for the following morning. We finished the first day with juicy, oversized Argentinian steaks and then gave ourselves over to jet-lag. In other words, we slept long and deeply.

After things had worked out with the rented car, we went to find Avraham at one of the agreed meeting points, a café in Corrientes Street. Since he was a man of deeds and not of big words, he immediately announced his first decision: 'Let's get in the car and go have a look at the house.' I expressed doubts: 'It is winter. By the time we get there, it will long be dark. It would be better to go tomorrow morning.' Avraham, however, had his way and so I drove the car through the heavy rush-hour traffic in the direction of San Fernando. When we finally set course for the kiosk on Route 202, the sun had long gone down.

Suddenly, it happened. Somewhere between the bus stop and the little side-street that led to Eichmann's house. There we saw him walking on the left-hand side of the street on his way home. Avraham was the first to notice the man. 'There he goes,' he hissed excitedly. We drove past him and there was no doubt. This was our man. I stopped the car a few hundred metres further on. I had braked far too suddenly and far too hard, according to Avraham. I got out and lifted the bonnet, which is always the best excuse if one stops in the middle of nowhere. Avraham and Yankele kept the man under observation, who at this moment had left the main road and was walking along the side-street to his house.

I put the bonnet down again. We drove a few kilometres further on and then back to the city. We excitedly discussed the situation. We all agreed that we now had the green light and were justified to call in the rest of the team. Obviously the man lived and worked in Buenos Aires and not in Tucuman. That we had seen him near his house on the very first day was all we needed at this point.

On 27 April we met Ilani at the agreed meeting point, where Avraham gave him a cable for Tel Aviv. The decisive phase of the operation had begun. Bit by bit, the rest of the team was sent over. The first to arrive was Yitzhak Nesher. He was capable of playing the rôle of the German businessman to perfection. Yitzhak came from *Mossad* and his job was to rent safe houses and large, dependable cars. That same day Avraham, Yankele and I were again in San Fernando around six in the evening. We left the car about one and a half kilometres from the house and walked along Route 202 in order to find a good observation point. We hoped to see our man again coming home. The light was already fading when we took up position halfway up the railway embankment. From there we had an excellent view of the house and the traffic.

And indeed, at 1940, at exactly the same time as the day before, a bus from San Fernando stopped near the kiosk. A single passenger got off – our man. He crossed the street and walked slowly toward his house. It was still early days to draw final conclusions, but we had now twice seen him coming home at the same time. At the thought of the deserted stretch of road that he had to walk along on his way home, we suddenly had lots of ideas. We considered the situation to be absolutely ideal.

We therefore decided that at least two of us, sometimes all three, should be here every evening at 1940 in order to keep watch on the situation. That worked very well. Only once did some railway workers come near us, so that we quickly had to leave our place on the embankment. In the succeeding four days, our man always arrived punctually at 1940. Twice we observed him use a small flashlight that blinked white in front and red at the back when cars approached. Furthermore, on several occasions he took a turn around the house before going inside. At first we believed he did this for reasons of security. Later on we found out that he was just inspecting his vegetable garden.

The rest of the task force arrived between 29 April and 4 May. In total there were ten of us, including the doctor. We had known from the beginning that we would need a doctor on the team. In the course of the operation it might become necessary to put our target to sleep, even if only for a brief time. Therefore we needed our own medical expert to take care of him. His wellbeing was of great concern to us. We could not permit his possibly dying of a heart attack. For obvious reasons, I cannot disclose the name of the doctor even today. I will therefore simply call him doctor.

Isser Harel arrived on 1 May. It was clear that he would not take part in the operation directly, but always remain in the background. Because of the enormous importance of the operation, however, his would always be the final decision and he would have to approve each of our steps. Every morning he met a member of the team, received a detailed report on our activities, and gave directives.

Isser also wanted to see the house in San Fernando, the whole area and all the approaches. On 3 May I took him for a trip around. I showed him all the roads leading to San Fernando and finally drove past the house on Route 202. I could sense that the cool, impenetrable Harel was deeply impressed. However, he did not utter a word, not even when we saw the house from close up. Unfortunately, there was no member of the family in sight just then.

The last to arrive were Rafi Eitan, who had been held up in Europe by an upset stomach and overbooked flights, and Zvi Malchin, called Zvika. Zvika was the strong man on the team. He was to grab Eichmann and not let go. He was to put him out of action, but not to harm a hair on his head. That was not so easy for someone who had lost relatives in the Holocaust.

Polish-born Malchin had escaped the industrialised destruction of the Jews and emigrated to Palestine with his family in 1934 at the age of four and a half. He had joined the *Haganah* as a teenager and subsequently Isser Harel's secret organisation. His speciality was the safe use of explosives. During his initial years in the service, he trained the personnel of the Israeli embassies in dealing with letter bombs. He was now travelling on a German passport under the name of Maxim Nolte.

The physically small Rafi Eitan was a clever organiser and an absolutely sovereign leader, a man of action in the true sense of the word. His parents stemmed from Russia and had decided – independently of each other – to emigrate to Palestine in 1917. On the way to the Promised Land, they met at a pioneer camp of the Young Zionists in Odessa, and married shortly afterwards. It was only in 1922 that they reached their destination and Rafi was born four years later. He attended a first-class school and in the summer of 1944 was recruited by the *Palmach*, the élite unit of *Haganah*.

Rafi Eitan moved rapidly up the officers' ladder and directed early commando operations against the British. His unit blew up a radar station on Mount Carmel and freed immigrants from the prison cells of the Mandate power. During the war of independence, Eitan was in command of a company at the age of twenty-one. After recovering from a wound, he turned to the career of intelligence officer. He reached the position of Deputy Intelligence Chief of Command South.

His proximity to the secret services determined his further career. In 1951 Eitan joined *Shin Bet*, which in those days only employed a few hundred people. After only a short time, he reached a key position in the operations department.

In 1955, Rafi Eitan took a three-year unpaid leave of absence. In his words: 'Towards the end of 1958 a letter from Amos Manor, then Director of *Shin Bet*, arrived. He wrote: "I will wait for you for two months. You will come back as Chief of the operations department. If not, someone else will get the job." I came back.'

The logical consequence was that Rafi Eitan led the operation in Buenos Aires. For this, he slipped into the role of a British businessman. In the first few days after his arrival there was hectic activity. The team was still trying to find out as much as possible about Adolf Eichmann's daily routine. From the sum of this data, the kidnapping plan was to be developed. Agents Yitzhak Nesher and Zeev Keren were permanently criss-crossing the city in search of 'safe' apartments and houses. In addition, they had the task of providing two large, dependable American limousines that should look 'official'.

I was mainly occupied in finding out everything about Eichmann's daily routine. As an outcome of our daily surveillance, we had been able to observe his return home always at the same time, evening after evening. In fact, we observed him arriving punctually with bus No. 203 from San Fernando nine days in a row, except for weekends when he did not go to work, and once when he arrived twenty-five minutes late. On Sunday 1 May, we saw him working in his garden. There was no longer any doubt possible, he was permanently living in this house.

The team tried several times to find out where Eichmann boarded bus No. 203, which brought him home every evening. This could possibly have provided an alternative for the snatch. Only once, on 4 May, when I boarded the bus in Karupa about seven or eight stops before San Fernando, did I see Eichmann, who was sitting around the middle of the passenger section. I gave the driver four pesos and hoped that he would not ask me anything. He did not.

I sat down on the only empty seat and found myself directly behind Eichmann. I must admit that the thought of being so close to the man who had been in charge of the destruction of my people agitated me considerably. I got off at the San Fernando station. There was no reason to follow him to his house. Finally, we gave up trying to discover where he was coming from and where he boarded the bus. The conditions for kidnapping him near his house were very favourable and therefore we decided there was no sense in looking further. We began to work out our plan.

We needed at least two large 'safe houses' as well as two or three apartments in Buenos Aires. We required a secure place where we could meet in the evening, report the important events of the day and discuss the next steps of the operation. We had to store our technical equipment, which we were bringing into the country through diplomatic channels. Our expert – or rather our genius – in false documents needed a place where he could work in peace.

His name was Shalom Dany. He came from *Mossad* and in the past had earned considerable renown by secretly smuggling Moroccan Jews into Israel. Himself a survivor of the Holocaust, hollow-cheeked and rather melancholy in appearance, Shalom Dany had no rivals in his field. He always travelled with large quantities of baggage, including the tools of the trade for his cover profession: artist.

Dany was a man with a golden touch. Always calm and reserved, he could put any desired date and visa stamp on passports, and deliver a driving licence or diplomatic passport overnight. His handwriting was always clearer and more exact than the original document. If there was anyone on the team who was indispensable, it was Shalom Dany. The apartments were quickly found and Shalom installed his workshop.

The search for houses proved to be more complicated. We needed at least one alternative in order to be able to move our prisoner should a problem arise. We would probably have to house him for a total of five or six days. It should be a free-standing villa with a large garden, where five to six men could live without difficulty. A direct entry into the house from the street through the garage would be a particular advantage. After all, we would have to be able to unload our man without being observed by the neighbours. The houses should be at least ten kilometres from San Fernando and offer a good connection to the airport. Finally, there should be neither a janitor or gardener, nor any cleaning staff.

This was precisely where our efforts threatened to fail time and again. Regardless of whether we wanted to rent a house on the open market or to accept the offers by local Jewish businessmen to use their weekend houses, there was always staff involved. The better the house, the more it seemed to involve gardeners, chauffeurs, maids and cleaning women. It was always a major problem when we had to refuse these generous offers without arousing too much suspicion.

Finally we did find two appropriate houses, and Lithuanian-born Zeev Keren took them over. Zeev, too, had the golden touch, his, however, in the area of arts and crafts. Within only a few days he built a small room with a hidden door in one of the houses, where we could hide our captive for a short period if a cursory search of the house were to occur. Zeev also quickly prepared two-sided number plates. In no time at all the registration numbers of our cars could now be changed.

Furthermore, he was a big man with strong arms and hands. During the war he had been in Italy with the Jewish Brigade and immediately afterwards had formed a kind of death squad, together with other Jewish activists, which had specialised in searching for Nazis that had gone underground. Together, they combed all of central Europe. The operation was said to have been highly successful. The experiences Zeev had gained from this could be very useful for the kidnapping team, which was another reason why he was here.

The last area that caused us a serious problem was finding a large, dependable and imposing limousine. Such a limousine, which in New York at that time cost 5000–6000 dollars, cost 25,000 dollars in Buenos Aires. It was therefore virtually impossible to rent such a car. At best, these cars were half a dozen years old and had several hundred thousand kilometres on their backs. Normally, the tyres were completely worn down and the battery almost dead. Frequently, there were problems with the starter. How could one depend on such a "highway junk-heap" when planning a kidnapping in open terrain? Even for a test drive, one had to put down a deposit of no less than 5000 dollars in cash. Anybody running around with so much money was bound to attract attention.

All of the cars we rented during the preparatory stages of the kidnapping had grotesque deficiencies. On one Jeep, for example, the reverse gear did not work. On one occasion, when Rafi – who was very shortsighted – was driving the Jeep, he took a wrong turning despite my warning shout and was stopped by a policeman in the middle of a road junction. Rafi was ordered by the cop to reverse the Jeep out of the junction. We had no choice: three of us jumped out and pushed the Jeep out of the crossing.

Finally Yitzhak Nesher found a large, four-year-old Buick limousine and rented it. The car was black and looked impressive – at least from the outside. Yitzhak immediately took the car to a repair shop recommended by Ilani. There the Buick was thoroughly checked out and 'renovated'. Many small defects were set right at our expense. We even had to replace two wheels. Avraham Shalom found the second car, a black Chevrolet. It, too, received the same special service in our repair shop.

We were now ready to plan the details of the actual abduction. It had been clear from the beginning that Zvika Malchin and Zeev Keren, our two strong men, would be in the first car. They were to overpower Eichmann and drag him on to the back seat. Rafi, the team leader, would also be in the first car. The only remaining question was discussed endlessly. Who would drive the car? Both Rafi and his deputy Avraham were hot candidates for the job. I objected violently to either solution and brought all my powers of persuasion into play, until Isser Harel himself decided that I should drive the car.

My reasoning was clear and convincing. I knew Buenos Aires far better than did Rafi or Avraham. I knew enough Castillano to get around and spoke fluent German and English. I could pretend to be a diplomat accredited in Argentina – which is what I then did. My strongest argument, however, was Rafi's thick glasses. At night he could not see very well at all. Once, during darkness, he had almost run into a road barrier that was blocking the street. He had simply not seen it.

Finally all was accepted and agreed. There would be four men in the kidnap car and I would be the driver. After lengthy discussions, we decided that we would wait for Adolf Eichmann between the bus stop and the house. As soon as he walked past our car, we would grab him and pull him inside. We rejected the idea of waiting on the main road because the risk, despite the relatively light traffic, was still too great. It was unthinkable to pull Eichmann into our car in the glare of the headlights of an approaching car.

I was therefore to drive the heavy limousine into the narrow side-road and stop some twenty-five metres from the highway. We would then wait, with the bonnet up, for our man. The car was to stand on the right side of the roadway and leave a free space of about two metres on the left. Eichmann's house would then be about thirty to forty metres away. I was to start the engine as soon as our man had approached to within ten metres. The motor had to be running in order to drown out possible sounds of a scuffle. Furthermore, we would then be in a position to drive off immediately the target was on the back seat. We also assumed it would put the man more at ease if the driver were seen to be trying to get his broken-down car going. It would be much more alarming for him to see several people just sitting quietly inside a dark car.

At the moment of the snatch he would only be able to see two of our people: Zvika standing next to the open driver's window and possibly me as driver. We had to avoid alarming him by the presence of too many men. Zeev was to stand at the front of the car, bending down under the bonnet. Since the car would be standing with the front end away from the main road, the man would not be able to see Zeev.

Rafi was to lie down on the floor in the back. As soon as Zvika and Zeev had overpowered Eichmann, he would open the back door and help pull our captive inside. We then intended to tie him up and hide him under a blanket. After that, the run to the 'safe house' could begin.

The plan was simple and logical, but it was still not easy to convince all those involved. Isser Harel, in particular, voiced doubts. What would happen if the man got the wind up as soon as he saw the car and took a different route? How could we prevent him taking the shorter route across the field instead of his normal way along the road? We had to admit that that could happen. In the end, however, we succeeded in convincing Isser of our plan and obtaining his blessing.

Our concept was the lesser evil compared to any other variation. If the man were suddenly to walk across the field, then we would have to do the same. We would race over the field, try to catch him and drag him to our car. If he were to reach the house before we caught up with him, then all we could do was to break down the door and bring him out by force, even if this meant putting the rest of the inhabitants out of action.

Avraham was to drive the second car. His two passengers were to be Yankele Gat and the doctor. Should we have a breakdown or an accident, then the second car would get us out of the mess. Avraham was to park near the railway bridge and turn on his lights as soon as Eichmann got off the bus. That would blind him and make it more difficult for him to detect the first car and its passengers. At the same time, other drivers who happened to be driving past would also be blinded and less likely to observe the scene clearly.

Now all that was left was to set the date for the operation. It was a bit of luck that Argentina was just celebrating the 150th anniversary of its independence. Delegations from all over the world had been invited for the occasion. Israel intended to send one under the leadership of the then Foreign Minister Abba Eban. To everyone's surprise – including the minister's – the Prime Minister's Office approved a special flight by *El Al*, the state airline. *El Al* normally did not fly to South America, but the occasion was officially to be used to examine the possibilities of establishing regular flight services.

Originally the plan was to have the *El Al* special flight arrive in Argentina on 12 May. The delegation would stay for eight to ten days and take part in the festivities. The Britannia aircraft, however, would return to Israel after the compulsory twenty-four hour rest period for the crew. Nobody, not even an Abba Eban, expected *El Al* to do without one of its most modern aeroplanes for almost two weeks during the main travel season.

After the return flight had been set for 13 May, we agreed for our operation to take place on 10 May. Naturally, there should be as short a timespan as possible between the kidnapping and the flight to Israel. Every additional day might only create new dangers. The task of holding Eichmann, guarding him, feeding him, was arduous enough as it was.

On the other hand, we could not afford to set the kidnapping for the last day before the arrival of the plane. What if the operation were to fall through, if, for example, he were not to come home on that evening? What if he had gone sick or taken a vacation? We had to plan everything so that we had at least two or three days to try again in case things did not work at the first attempt.

In the event, the flight from Tel Aviv only arrived in Buenos Aires on 19 May, because the Protocol Department of the Foreign Ministry had suddenly asked to delay the arrival of the delegation to that date. We decided to postpone the date of the operation by only one day, from 10 May, as originally planned, to 11 May. We did not want to delay the action for any longer period. All the men were tired and tense. It had to go ahead, come what might. 11 May was to be the last day as a free man in the life of former *Obersturmbannführer* Adolf Eichmann.

Everything was prepared. We had two big cars, both with easily changeable number plates. We had two suitable 'safe houses'. One of them had been made ready to take in our unwilling guest. The other was available as an alternative. Furthermore, we had three rented apartments at our disposal.

We had all already checked out of our hotels on 9 May and officially 'left' Buenos Aires. This was intended to cover our tracks. Six of us moved into house No. 1 and began to prepare for the arrival of our prisoner. Besides the doctor, agent Judith Nesiyahu was also included in this team. She had just arrived in Buenos Aires.

Harel had decided to include a woman in the team because her presence in the villa would indicate that the occupants were leading a normal family life. The nosy neighbourhood was more likely to accept this than a house full only of men. Her tasks included keeping house. She had to cook for half a dozen people and that was quite some job. The orthodox Jewess was a *Mossad* agent of long experience. Unfortunately, she was not a good cook. This constantly led to complaints. The rest of the team moved into the apartments. Now everything was set.

On 10 May, late in the evening, we all met in one of our 'safe' apartments for a last-minute 'dress-rehearsal'. Every step and alternative was discussed and every member of the team had his task explained to him in detail.

Isser Harel opened the meeting with a remark of the kind that none of us had ever heard him make before or since. He glanced in my direction and said something like: 'All honours should go to Zvi Aharoni. Without him we would not be sitting here.' I was deeply embarrassed and did not know where to look. We were not used to hearing compliments from the Old Man.

We discussed one of the worst possible scenarios. We had Eichmann in our power. We were driving towards house No. 1. Suddenly the police were after us. What would we do? First of all, we would obviously try to shake off the guardians of the law, even if we had to break every single Argentinian traffic regulation. If necessary, the second car would even ram the police car.

In the worst case, after everything was lost and we had been stopped by an overwhelming number of policemen, one of us was to chain himself to Eichmann with a pair of handcuffs. The key was to be 'lost'. Whoever was attached to Eichmann was to declare that his companion was one of the most infamous war criminals of all time. He was not prepared to let the man go. A high-ranking police officer had to guarantee that the man would be detained and the whole case investigated. If we were to be arrested, we were to claim that we were all Jewish volunteers who had discovered Eichmann and wanted to be sure that he would be brought to justice.

The morning of 11 May passed in making final preparations. I picked up car No. 1 where Yitzhak had parked it for me and found that despite all our technical efforts, the battery was almost flat. I was lucky and found a repair shop that sold me a new one at a horrendous black-market price.

During the afternoon we checked all the roads leading from and to San Fernando and to our house. We did not want to encounter any unwelcome surprises in the evening. Over the past few weeks, we had experienced quite frequently that streets were suddenly and unexpectedly blocked by construction work or police controls. Innumerable railway crossings and railway lines were constantly being repaired, which also led to occasional closing of streets. We wanted to run a last-minute check that our main route, as well as the alternative routes, from San Fernando were clear. We did not find anything unusual.

As planned, I drove past the kiosk at exactly 1925 and turned into the side-street that led to Eichmann's house. I wore a suit and tie in order to look like a respectable foreign diplomat. I stopped the car about twenty-five metres from the main road and turned off the engine. I released the catch on the bonnet. Zvika and Zeev got out. Zeev lifted the bonnet and bent over the motor with his upper body. From that instant he was invisible to anybody observing us from the main road. Zvika took up his agreed position at the front end of the car and bent over the engine from the left side. Rafi lay in the back.

It was a dark evening, but we could clearly recognise our second car, which was parked near the bridge, by the lights of passing cars. Nobody said anything. Everything had already been said.

About ten minutes after our arrival, a boy of fifteen or sixteen approached on a bicycle. He was obviously curious and wanted to know if we had a problem. He very politely offered his help. In my best possible Castillano I said to him: 'Thank you! We do not need you. Please get lost!'

He understood immediately and rode on. We continued our silent watch. Two to three minutes past the scheduled time of 1940, a bus approached from the direction of San Fernando. To our disappointment, the bus did not stop at the kiosk but continued on its way to Don Torcuato. The minutes dragged on. The next bus was slow in coming. During our discussions, we had decided that we would stay until eight o'clock and then try the operation anew the following day. We believed we would attract too much attention if we were to stand in front of the Eichmann house for longer than half an hour.

When the eight o'clock deadline had actually passed, I whispered to Rafi: 'Do we leave or continue to wait?'

His order was short but firm: 'We wait!'

At the same moment I saw Avraham, who had left his car and was coming towards us. It was 2005 and he, too, obviously wanted to consult with Rafi. At that exact instant, a bus stopped near the kiosk.

I saw a man get off, cross the road and walk in our direction. Even a look through the binoculars was not able to tell us with certainty who this was. Then Avraham – who had hurried back to his car – switched on his lights and I could see him clearly. It was our man. In a whisper, I informed Rafi and naturally also alerted Zvika. As I was watching the man through my binoculars, I saw him put his left hand in his pocket. My first thought was: 'A pistol!' For the moment, I did not know what to do.

I asked Rafi: 'Should I warn Zvika?'

'Yes. Tell him to watch the hand!'

I leaned out of the window and whispered to Zvika: 'He has a hand in his pocket. Watch out for a weapon.'

At this moment the man turned the corner and came towards us. When he was still some ten metres away, I started the engine. Three seconds later he went past my window and Zvika went into action. He turned around and blocked the man's path. 'Momentito,' he barked.

Zvika had an astonishingly poor and almost grotesque sense for any sort of foreign language. Countless times we had tried to teach him a few words in Spanish, with which he should address the man before pouncing on him. It had been a hopeless endeavour. Even simple phrases like 'Excuse me, please', or 'Can you tell me what time it is?' went far beyond the limits of Zvi Malchin's language abilities and so we had finally agreed on 'momen-tito', which means 'Just a moment'.

The man stopped as if rooted to the ground. In that instant, Zvika jumped towards him.

I later regretted that I had mentioned my initial suspicion about a pistol. This turned a well-planned and carefully exercised operation into an unholy mess. Instead of grabbing the man by the neck, Zvika now tried to push down both his arms. The man backed away. Both of them lost their balance and, before Zeev could intervene, were rolling together in the ditch.

During the whole time, the man howled and screamed. I gunned the engine but the howling went on and was clearly audible despite the loud noise from the car. Zeev had jumped down into the ditch with the other two and was trying to help Zvika by holding the man's legs. However, the man kept on screaming and kicking out. The whole thing seemed to be taking forever.

According to our plan, I was not supposed to leave the driver's seat, not even for an instant. But what about Rafi? He was still lying in the back of the car, even though there was now no longer any reason to remain hidden. Instinctively, I shouted in Hebrew: 'Go and help them!'

That made him move. He opened the door of the car, jumped into the ditch and within moments the three of them had dragged the man to his feet and pulled him into the Buick. Zeev slammed the door, ran around the car, shut the bonnet and got in beside me. I stepped on the gas and tore off.

I steered left, circled the house and then drove right on Avellaneda Street towards the centre of Buenos Aires. Even though our place of refuge lay in the north-west of the capital, I drove south as our carefully laid plan intended. Had there been a witness to the kidnapping after all, he would send the police in the wrong direction. Our second car followed a short distance behind.

After a few seconds of silence I called to our captive in German: 'Do not move and no one will hurt you. If you resist, you will be shot!'

There was no answer, no reaction at all. I raised my voice and repeated what I had said.

Still no answer. I now shouted: 'Can you hear me? Do you understand me? What language do you speak?' I also repeated this in Spanish.

Still no answer. For a moment I thought that he had already given up the ghost. Then I heard him suddenly say with a clear voice in perfect German: 'I have already accepted my fate!'

That was highly reassuring. First of all it meant that he was still alive, that he was OK under the circumstances and that he could hear me. Furthermore, he was German and obviously knew what this was all about. He had 'accepted his fate'. That pointed to the context of our operation. We had obviously got the right man.

At this point and only as a note: none of us in the car had a pistol. We had not thought that we would need one. It would only have complicated matters, had we been caught. As we soon found out, Eichmann had not been armed either when we took him.

After about 800 metres on the Avellaneda, I turned left and stopped at a deserted spot that we had scouted earlier. Zeev jumped out and switched the number plates. Before, we had been driving with black and white number plates: we were now using blue ones, such as the diplomatic corps did. That was also part of our tactics. Under any circumstances it was safer to drive a 'diplomatic car'. This reduced the danger of being stopped, let alone searched. If we were to be stopped anywhere despite this, I would only speak German. I carried perfect forgeries of Austrian diplomatic papers with me.

Naturally there was a good reason for not using the diplomatic number plates from the very start of the operation. We had not wanted to be seen with them near the Eichmann house. Unwelcome witnesses could easily have remembered the unusual number plates. The police would then have set out to look for a diplomatic car.

The rest of the drive to our house in the suburb of Kilmes went off without incident. We were now heading north. Twice we had to wait at a railway crossing. The prisoner lay under a blanket at the feet of Rafi and Zvika. He did not move or make a sound. When we had to stop again, the second car pulled up beside us. I lifted my hand a bit and gave the 'V' for victory sign. The doctor on the front passenger seat stared straight ahead and completely ignored my friendly gesture. I admired his composure.

The gates went up and we continued on our way. Ten minutes later we reached the vicinity of our 'safe house'. Exactly according to plan, I stopped again less than a kilometre from our destination. Zeev jumped out of the car and once more changed the number plates. Now we were back to a set of normal black and white number plates . We wished to avoid someone seeing us near our house with diplomatic number plates. And obviously we did not again want to use the same plates with which we had parked in front of Eichmann's house for over half an hour.

Yitzhak was already waiting for us. He had been the one who had rented the property, and was therefore now 'proprietor' and 'host'. He opened the gate and I drove the car straight into the garage. The door was closed behind us. The man got out of the car. He appeared to be intimidated but was able to walk with Zvika's support. He had to be led, because his eyes were covered by a pair of large motorcycle goggles. The goggles were covered with adhesive tape. He was not to see any of his guards until the day we would leave for Tel Aviv. Should something go wrong, he was not to be able to identify any member of our team.

There was a door directly connecting the garage with the kitchen. We led our 'guest' to a small bedroom which had been prepared for him on the second floor. There was a heavy iron bedstead with a plain mattress standing in the middle of the room. The two small windows had been sound-proofed with thick mattresses. The rest of the furniture consisted of a small table and two plain chairs.

He was made to lie down on the bed and undressed. I can still recall exactly how I was touched, even a bit disgusted, when I saw his shabby clothing, particularly his underwear. I could not help it and asked myself spontaneously: is this really the great Eichmann, the man who decided the fate of millions of my people?

The doctor examined him. He searched his body and the inside of his mouth for hidden poison capsules. He also looked for scars, which he compared with the information contained in Bauer's files. Everything matched our files to the last detail. On the left upper arm we found a small scar. This must have been the former tattoo with his SS number. As he told me later, he had tried to burn it off with a cigarette in an American prisoner-of-war camp shortly after the German capitulation.

We dressed him in a set of pyjamas and attached his left leg to the frame of the bed with a pair of handcuffs. I had insisted we do that. We had had an argument on this point.

'Who needs handcuffs? Someone will be in the room with him day and night. Furthermore, the room will constantly be kept locked. Why should we manacle him?'

I had objected. I was the only member of our team with police and prison experience. I knew of cases where prisoners had been under special guard round the clock and had still managed to escape. The most attentive and dedicated watchman can drop off sometimes. If this was really Eichmann, then he would be desperate. What had he left to lose? I insisted on handcuffs and the others finally agreed with me.

My first interrogation began at 2115. It had been a clear decision, and everybody on the team knew Isser Harel's directive, that I was to be the only one who spoke with the prisoner. German was my mother tongue. I was experienced in interrogations and had all the details on Eichmann in my file, most of them in my head. Furthermore, the man was not to be able to recognise any other member of the team by his voice if there were eventually to be problems.

Before leaving Tel Aviv I had received exact instructions from Attorney General Chaim Cohen. I had asked him if it were necessary for the future court proceedings against Eichmann to obtain a statement or a confession while still on Argentinian territory? Should he admit his guilt in connection with the Third Reich immediately? Should I demand a written statement from him?

Cohen had replied that there was no need for any of that. What was important, however, was a written statement by the man that he was actually Adolf Eichmann. Nothing else mattered. From the very beginning of my interrogations I therefore concentrated on this objective.

I have read time and again what Eichmann is supposed to have told me after being captured. These were really astonishing stories. Allegedly he spoke some Hebrew and started repeating the holy Jewish prayer *Shmah Israel*... Or he asked me for a glass of red wine. He knew from the first that we came from *Mossad*. And so on, and so on. I do not know who invented all these stories. I assume it was Zvika Malchin, who later wrote a book about the 'Eichmann Operation'.

In this he describes his alleged conversations with the prisoner Eichmann in detail. Malchin was a member of the five-man guard team. Had he really talked with Eichmann at length, then this would have been a direct breach of Isser Harel's orders. It would not surprise me, because Malchin was the one member of the team for whom the word discipline had always been without meaning. One could not depend upon his reports. It was always more important to him to tell a good story and crack jokes than to adhere to the bare facts.

Rafi and Isser had included him in the team mainly because of his physical strength and his ability to improvise. In the course of time, however, it became increasingly clear that Zvika was more of a liability than an asset. He even failed at his most important job. When he was supposed to grab Eichmann and push him into the car that stood less than a metre away, the puny, weak man slipped through his hands. Both of them rolled around in the ditch for minutes. Eichmann howled like a wild animal. Two other members of the team had to rush to his aid.

Later, Zvika accused me of having warned him unnecessarily of a nonexistent weapon. He knew very well, however, that I had been following an order from Rafi. He was never willing to accept any blame himself.

As far as Zvika's alleged conversations with Eichmann are concerned, ninety per cent of them are just figments of his imagination. The moving and heartrending descriptions of the confrontations between the Jewish kidnapper and the Nazi prisoner were freely invented by Malchin. It would hardly have escaped the attention of the other members of the team if Zvika and Eichmann had constantly been putting their heads together. On top of that, he forgets to mention that he and Eichmann had no common language. Zvika's Yiddish – that was the closest he came to speaking German – was good enough to give Eichmann simple orders and to allow him to use the toilet. It was not sufficient for profound dialogues about the Holocaust. Eichmann, on the other hand, understood neither Hebrew nor Yiddish.

What I find particularly absurd and hard to understand is, that in his detailed report on the Eichmann operation, even Isser Harel was not above putting the most crazy words into the man's mouth. This is inexcusable, because Isser – unlike other authors – questioned all the participants in the operation personally and had access to all secret files. His version should actually have been the true, official history of this operation. It is not.

This, therefore, is the real, initial interrogation of Adolf Eichmann. I portray it faithfully according to my own notes.

'What is your name?'

'Ricardo Klement.'

'What were you called before?'

'Otto Heninger.'

At this point I became somewhat uneasy. He was replying in a calm and factual tone of voice and did not appear to be the least bit nervous or excited. At this time I was not aware that Eichmann had used several names during the post-war years in Germany. I therefore did not know that his answers had been absolutely correct so far. I assumed that the man – whoever he might be – would never admit directly that he was Adolf Eichmann. I therefore took an indirect approach in order to achieve the same result.

'How tall are you?'

'One metre seventy-seven.'

'What size shoes do you wear?'

'Forty-two.'

'What size clothing?'

'Forty-four.'

So far, so good. Everything fitted in perfectly with the content of my files. Now I went at it directly.

'What was your membership number in the NSDAP?'

'899 895.'

'What was your number in the SS?'

'45 326.'

The answers agreed with my information. I could already see the light at the end of the tunnel.

'What is your date of birth?'

'19 March 1906.'

'Place of birth?'

'Solingen.'

'Under what name were you born?'

'Adolf Eichmann.'

We had come out of the tunnel. Bright sunshine! Eichmann lay on the bed. I was standing on one side and Avraham on the other. When I heard the name Adolf Eichmann, the tensions of a long and difficult operation dissolved. I had to show my joy. I therefore stretched my hand out across the bed. Avraham shook it. We were happy.

I continued my questioning and concentrated on his and his immediate family's biographical details. I wanted to know the dates and places of birth of his parents, brothers, wife and sons. I asked him about the addresses of his relatives in Austria and the various places where he himself had lived.

The reason for these precise questions was simple: should the man claim at some point in the future that he was not Adolf Eichmann at all, and that this confession had been beaten out of him, the sheer mass of information that only Eichmann could possess would refute him. This is what the continuing interrogation concentrated upon.

Time flew. It was already ten o'clock and we had not yet informed Isser about our success. Furthermore, we had to get rid of the Buick. We did not want to run any further risk. While I had been questioning Eichmann, Zeev had been taking care of the car. He had exchanged it for the second car. The intended escape car, in other words car No. 2, now stood in the garage. All fingerprints and the mechanism for switching licence plates had been removed from the kidnap car. It could now be returned to the car rental.

Avraham and I took the car back to Buenos Aires and parked it at a previously agreed spot. Yitzhak was to pick it up next morning and return it. We again wiped the interior clear of fingerprints and then took a taxi to the café where we knew Isser would be waiting. The main job of the Director of *Mossad* during the past few days had been to compile a list of cafés and restaurants where he could be found at any given hour. He met one of us every evening and gave him the list for the following day. We always knew where we could find him and ask him for advice.

When we now looked for him, he was just about to change from the eleven o'clock meeting point, the Café Opera, to the midnight meeting point. We sat down at a table and Avraham gave a brief report on the historic events of the evening. Isser listened stiffly and without comment. He did not even smile, did not deign to utter a single word of praise. He appeared to be very tense. I attributed this to his long wait, but the way he acted still felt like a dash of cold water. All he eventually said was something like: 'I knew everything must have gone well, because otherwise I would not have had to hang around for so long. Had you come sooner, I would have been disappointed.' After briefly making an appointment for the following day, we parted and each of us went his own way. I was very tired. Bit by bit, however, I began to feel content. The task had been concluded successfully. That was all that mattered.

In January 1966, in a long statement in *Quick* magazine, Klaus Eichmann described what had happened in the family the following day, how they had coped with the loss of the father, how they had wanted to avenge him:

'On 12 May I was standing in an elevator shaft in a new building with a screwdriver in my hand. I was working on a control panel. Suddenly my brother Dieter came into the building, out of breath: "The Old Man is gone." I dropped the screwdriver. My first reaction: the Israelis! Dieter and I rushed across Buenos Aires to San Fernando. On the way, we alerted an SS leader whose name I cannot disclose. He was father's best friend. He forced us to start thinking objectively.

'There were three possibilities. Father had been arrested by a police patrol for some infringement of the law or booked because he had been drunk. He had had an accident and had been taken to a hospital injured or to a morgue as a corpse. Or else the Israelis had him. For two days we searched police stations, hospitals and morgues. In vain. What was left was the realisation: they had him.

'Our feeling of bitterness grew. The wildest plans were discussed. The leader of the youth group finally suggested: "Let's kidnap the Israeli ambassador and take him out of the city! We will torture him until your father is back home safe." The plan was rejected. Somebody else suggested blowing up the Israeli Embassy. This plan too was rejected.'

CHAPTER 9

The Prisoner

'One day I asked him a question that threw him off balance. I asked him if he were prepared to come to Israel and face a judge for his crimes.'

Zvi Aharoni

The year 1960 was a turbulent, exciting year. For the first time, the Soviets brought an American U-2 spy plane, formerly considered to be invulnerable, down from the sky over Sverdlovsk. The pilot, Gary Powers, survived the crash, was taken prisoner on 7 May and subsequently sentenced to hard labour. Nikita Khrushchev, the strong man in Moscow, attacked the Americans from the rostrum of the UN. In Paris, he let the summit meeting of the four victorious powers over Hitler collapse. The losers did not obtain a peace treaty and the status of Berlin remained undecided for the time being. The world stared at Germany's contradictions with horror. Here, anti-Semitic excesses, there satisfied consumers of the new world of the *Witschaftswunder* (economic miracle, i.e. Germany's rapid post-war recovery). Carlo Schmidt, one of the great men of the *SPD* (*Sozialdemokratische Partei Deutschlands* or German Social Democratic Party) deplored 'the evil that is still at work here and there among our people'.

It was the year of the Africans. Seventeen nations on the black continent achieved their independence. The Congo immediately drowned in chaos. In Algeria, the war of independence continued to rage. At Sharpeville in South Africa, demonstrating blacks were massacred. France, a colonial power and still present, exploded its first atom bomb in the Sahara. The Cold War was in full swing.

The new man in Havana, Fidel Castro, had all US property in his island confiscated. US President Eisenhower sent the Marines to the Caribbean as a gesture of intimidation. In South Vietnam, Ngo Dinh Diem came back to power. Thereupon the forces of the Vietcong began to assemble. The winners of the US presidential elections, John F. Kennedy and Lyndon B. Johnson, would soon become embroiled in a major war there. On the other side of the world, however, in Geneva, the first East-West disarmament conference convened.

The heart pacemaker was developed, the laser, weather satellites, the contraceptive pill. The Beatles went on stage in Hamburg. Cinemas showed *Exodus*, the film portraying the tragic circumstances of Jewish emigration to Palestine. It was a year of important films and great directors: John Huston, Jean-Luc Godard, Louis Malle, Alfred Hitchcock, Federico Fellini. One of the non-fictional best-sellers of the year: *The Rise and Fall of the Third Reich* by William Shirer. The women of the year were Maria Callas, Marlene Dietrich, Farah Diba. Among the stars who died in 1960 were Clark Gable and Hans Albers.

The capture of Adolf Eichmann was one of the biggest, top-ranking news items of the year. It caused as much sensation as the global political movements and crises of those tension-filled months. 'Operation Eichmann' was a welcome blow for the damaged self-confidence of the Jews. On 11 May 1960, the architect of the *Endlösung* had been kidnapped by a commando of the *Mossad*. However, another twelve long, enervating days were to go by before Israeli Prime Minister David Ben Gurion would be able to announce the success of the operation in Parliament in Jerusalem.

Aharoni continues:

Our team in Buenos Aires was involved in hectic activities, taking care of the prisoner and arranging his forthcoming transport to Israel, 15,000 kilometres away. My principal task consisted of interrogating Eichmann. Harel had ordered that I should be the only one permitted to speak with him. One reason was that he should not to be able to identify anyone, not even by voice, in case of a sudden attack on our villa by the police. The other, that it was my profession to interrogate suspects.

Eichmann wore his thickly taped pair of goggles day and night. He was not allowed to remove them even when going to the toilet or at mealtimes. During the following ten days, he therefore did not see any of his guards. The only voice he knew was mine. I questioned him for several hours each day. During this he always lay on the bed with his left leg chained to the frame. He never refused an answer. He never raised his voice. In the course of those ten days a sort of feeling of mutual respect developed between us. Without his ever admitting it, I could clearly sense that he looked forward to our daily meetings. They broke the monotony of captivity.

The only task of this former high-ranking SS officer of the Third Reich had been to plan and supervise the systematic destruction of my people. He never asked who we were. He seemed to know this already. Instinctively he accepted and respected our method of operation. He knew that his life now had as little value as the life of one of his victims who, squeezed like sardines, had ridden to the extermination camp. Eichmann never complained and made no requests. Only once did he ask to have the manacle removed from his leg. He said he had difficulty sleeping, because the iron hampered his movements and that he believed he had already had a heart attack at night. I assured him that it was beyond my control to have him freed from the handcuffs. The doctor examined him, but did not detect anything unusual in his heartbeat.

Adolf Eichmann told me in detail what had happened to him since the end of the Hitler *Reich*. He began with the closing days of the war in Budapest and described his escape and disappointing meeting with his former chief and protector Ernst Kaltenbrunner, who had sent him on his way because he did not wish to be caught in his company. The fervid follower of Hitler was never able to forgive this. His whole world collapsed and he felt real fear for the first time. Eichmann maintained that he had never committed a wrong, but had only carried out the orders of his superiors throughout the whole of his official life.

Our prisoner described his time in the American camps, his interrogations by the Counter Intelligence Corps (CIC) and the constant fear of attracting attention through verifiable untruths or contradictions. Eichmann described his life as Adolf Barth, Otto Eckmann, as Otto Heninger and finally as Ricardo Klement.

He organised his voyage to South America with the help of old comrades from Celle, the district town in Lower Saxony. By means of carefully coded advertisements in the local press, he had managed to make contact with an organisation of former SS men. His contact was called Günther – the surname was never mentioned – who passed him on to the God-fearing people from the Vatican who helped fugitives. This is how he came to Argentina in 1950.

He had corresponded with his wife in Austria for a whole year and a half before she followed him across the Atlantic with the children. Nobody – neither the secret services nor any of the many 'Nazi-hunters' – had noticed the extensive exchange of letters at the time. When he was finally reunited with his family, his name was Klement; the others, however, were known as Eichmann. This had turned out to be a capital mistake.

He had not known how to obtain documents for his wife and sons under the false name of Klement. This had been beyond his range of possibilities. Therefore, he had constantly instructed the members of his family to invent stories about themselves and lie to people. Otherwise things would probably have turned out differently. If his sons had called themselves Klement, then neither blind Hermann nor his daughter Sylvia would ever have become suspicious. Eichmann could possibly still be living in his house in San Fernando today.

The Israeli secret service had not hunted Eichmann intensively for years, because our limited resources had initially been directed against hostile neighbouring countries and their armies. The second priority had been the secret organisation of our self defence and the immigration of Jews from Islamic states. This pushed the search for war criminals into the background for many years. Then, too, there was personal failure. As mentioned, Isser Harel had given the order to close the file containing Eichmann's real address. He mistrusted the information from Lothar Hermann.

Eichmann and his family lived in the apartment on the second floor of No. 4261 Chacabuco Street for more than six years. He told me about his desperate attempts to build up a normal, civilian existence. In Olivos he tried his hand as the owner of a steam laundry. Soon he had to admit that he could not keep pace with the local, mostly Chinese, competition. He sold the business at a loss. After the free and relatively carefree life in the solitude of Tucuman, he was no longer able to adjust to a multi-million city like Buenos Aires.

This was why he gladly accepted the job as manager of a rabbit farm in the country. However, he suffered from only seeing his family on weekends. When the fourth son, Ricardo Francisco, was born in 1955, he had returned home.

I asked Eichmann why he had moved into the desolate area between Don Torcuato and San Fernando. In the rented apartment, he told me, he had not felt safe even for a single day. He had had to share the house in Chacabuco Street with other tenants. He wanted to have his own house at all costs – one which could not be observed from across the street, one with no neighbours. In the spring of 1958, he had heard about the remote and undeveloped area to the north of San Fernando. He bought the long-desired property under the name of his wife.

I wanted to know whether the entry 'Liebl de Fichmann' had been an error. Smiling, Eichmann replied that it had been his idea to make a deliberate spelling mistake. He did not want the name 'Eichmann' to appear in an official document. They had worked at building the house for one and a half years, because they could not afford to hire workmen. Any stranger wanted to be paid immediately and the Eichmanns were always on the brink of insolvency. Vera had not been enthusiastic about moving into a house without electricity and running water. However, she had given in. Apart from the parents, only Ricardo and Dieter lived in San Fernando. Klaus had married a local girl and shared her apartment. Horst, the second son, had found a job with the Argentinian merchant marine.

Naturally I did not tell him that the site of his new house had been almost ideal from our point of view, in any case far more favourable than the building in Chacabuco Street. Everything had worked in our favour – the railway embankment as an observation point, the absence of inquisitive passers-by, the lack of street lighting, no neighbours to be alerted by cries for help. At the former residence, our surveillance would constantly have been hampered. The kidnapping itself would also have been much more difficult.

Besides his personal history, I also had to question him about more far-reaching topics. These included his knowledge of what had become of other Nazi war criminals, Hitler's secretary Martin Bormann, for example, or the man responsible for the unspeakable human experiments at Auschwitz, Josef Mengele. Months before, we had received the information from Germany that Mengele was probably living in Buenos Aires under his real name. In those days, hardly a member of our team knew the name Mengele, Isser Harel least of all. He had only learned of it just before his trip to Argentina.

This came about in the following way. In 1960 *Shin Bet* was headed by the brilliant survivor of Auschwitz, Amos Manor. Harel was Manor's direct supervisor since he coordinated the two civilian services. Manor knew Mengele because he had met him face to face in Auschwitz. In the course of a conversation, Manor and Harel came to talk about the *Todesengel*. The director of *Shin Bet* made a great impression on Harel, telling him about the unbelievable cruelties committed by the camp doctor. Harel came to Buenos Aires with the firm conviction that we should also try to find Mengele. If we had the moral right to abduct Eichmann from a neutral, friendly country by force, then this would apply even more to a devil like Mengele.

Harel kept the topic of Mengele under wraps until after the successful kidnapping of Eichmann. He obviously did not want to distract anybody on the team from their primary objective. However, after Eichmann was detained in our 'safe house', he began to talk about Mengele. He ordered the search for the doctor to be given new, highest priority. Harel assured us that he would make every effort to bring him to Tel Aviv, together with Eichmann, on the same plane.

If necessary, he would order a commando action, in an extreme case even hours before the departure of the *El Al* aircraft. Should this become necessary, our men were to force entry into Mengele's house and break any resistance with fire from automatic weapons. Harel issued a directive to the operations department to send over two more men on the aircraft as reserves.

None of us showed any enthusiasm for the Mengele operation. This certainly had nothing to do with a lack of courage. We only feared that such a questionable double-Rambo action would endanger the success of 'Operation

Eichmann'. We believed – and Rafi stated it plainly to Harel in my presence – that we should first bring Eichmann safely home. Any further operation, no matter how justified it might be, should only be started thereafter. Rafi and Isser had a real argument. Then Rafi tried to wind up the discussion with a grin and a Hebrew saying: 'Try to catch a lot – and you will catch nothing.'

Harel stubbornly held to his opinion and, quite unimpressed, ordered the search for Mengele to continue. I was required to question Eichmann about him. To begin with, our prisoner denied any knowledge at all about the SS doctor. Besides, he said, he would rather die than betray a comrade from the SS. I assured him that we had unlimited time to wait for his constructive answers. In addition, I began to debate with him the ideology of the SS. I told him that I could understand he did not want to deliver a real comrade to the knife. Mengele, however, was someone who had dragged the flag and the good reputation of the SS into the dirt. Inhuman experiments on women and little children could surely not have been part of the ideals of the SS.

After two or three days of arguments, Eichmann finally admitted having met Mengele some time previously in Buenos Aires – in a restaurant in the city centre – purely by coincidence. Mengele had offered him medical care, but had not disclosed his exact address. Eichmann believed he recalled that he had spoken about a guest-house that belonged to a German woman, somewhere in Olivos. Mengele was living there under his real name. But Eichmann was not sure whether Mengele was still in Argentina at all.

I knew that we could soften Eichmann up primarily by means of the time factor. He was housed in a small, windowless and sound-proofed room, which gave him no indication as to whether it was day or night. The man lay on a bed the whole time and one of his legs was manacled to it. He could not anticipate that we were waiting for an aircraft which would take him to Tel Aviv. Therefore he might well stay chained to this bed for months. I took care to provide him with no inkling of the exact time schedule that we had to meet under all circumstances. Even though this was never expressed between us, he certainly assumed that his uncomfortable situation would improve after his interrogation was over.

As far as Mengele was concerned, I did not doubt Eichmann's statements. Harel, however, refused to believe this. Impatiently he insisted on increasing the pressure on Eichmann: 'He is lying to you! He knows exactly where Mengele is.' Harel seemed possessed. He was already imagining himself getting off the plane in Tel Aviv with not one, but two of the greatest war criminals.

Only years later were we able to find out that Mengele actually had lived in a guest-house in Vicente Lopez until September 1959 and had practised under his real name. The house was run by a German woman named Jurmann. Mengele disappeared a few days after the German embassy had received the extradition papers for delivery to the proper authorities. He now lived in Asuncion in neighbouring Paraguay again under his real name. Only the day he heard of Eichmann's capture, he went underground and lived under various false names. It was to take almost two years before I was able to pick up his track in Brazil with a new team.

At that time we had already searched for Mengele in Uruguay, Brazil, Bolivia and Chile when, in 1962, we received help from an unexpected source. By means of sweet pursuasion – and 5000 dollars a month – I was able to talk the old Nazi Willem Sassen into helping us with the search for Mengele. He pointed out a man in São Paulo who was in contact with and providing shelter for Mengele. His name was Wolfgang Gerhard. We did not know at the time how close we already were to our target. I had established the fact that Gerhard owned a farm in some remote forest area about forty kilometres from São Paulo. One day, when scouting the area between the farm and the main road, together with two local Jewish helpers, we met on a jungle path a group of three men. One looked like a European and the other two like local guards. Today I am almost certain that I had seen Mengele face to face, especially after having seen the pictures that were published after his death.

At the time I thought the time had now come to put together a team for the abduction of Mengele. But I was mistaken. Suddenly we were all called back in order to participate in one of Isser Harel's surprise projects. An eight-year-old boy named Yossele Schuhmacher had been smuggled out of Israel in girl's clothing by a group of religious extremists. Since this was in breach of a court order and furthermore was of political importance, we had to search for him on Harel's orders.

Forty men took part in this generously endowed 'Operation Tiger'. We finally found Yossele in New York and brought him back to his mother. After that, no member of our team was sent back to South America again to look for Mengele. That is the true reason why the doctor of Auschwitz died while swimming in the ocean and not on the gallows in Ramleh prison.

It was understandable that Eichmann had no social contacts at all with Mengele, even though both of them lived in Buenos Aires. They each belonged to completely different social strata. The Eichmann family lived from hand to mouth. Mengele was well-off. He practised as a doctor and had a decent income. In addition, he was generously supported by his family, who owned a large factory in Günzburg in Bavaria producing agricultural machines.

In May 1960 none of us knew any of these details. That is why the frantic search for the doctor went on right up to the departure of the aircraft carrying Eichmann. But since Mengele was no longer living in Buenos Aires, we naturally did not find him and so were spared a Wild West commando action.

Questions to Eichmann about other war criminals were not fruitful either. He had really lived a very withdrawn life and always tried to avoid any contacts with other people. He felt safer that way. When in doubt, he preferred to read a book.

Following Chaim Cohen's directives, I asked him a question one day that threw him completely off-balance. I asked him whether he was prepared to come to Israel and face a judge for his crimes. His initial reaction was violent and negative. 'I have not committed any crimes and I am not prepared to go anywhere with you.'

'Think about it,' I said to him, 'we have plenty of time.'

The following day I repeated my question. He told me that he had lain awake for half the night and thought about it.

'And what do you think now?' I wanted to know.

Hesitantly and choosing his words carefully, he replied in a very low voice, almost in a whisper: 'I am prepared to face a court and I will prove to the whole world that I only obeyed orders and never committed any crimes. But not in Israel. I do not owe Israel anything. If at all, I owe an accounting to Germany and Argentina, where I am a citizen. I am prepared to face a court in one of these two countries.'

'You can't be serious. You insult my intelligence. You know very well that we can never accept such a suggestion. Fifteen years after the war neither of these two countries has the slightest interest in a court case against you. Your suggestion sounds like a direct refusal.'

'How about Austria?' he interrupted me. 'My family lives in Austria and I lived there myself for many years.'

'Stop insulting me! It will either be in Israel or not at all. Either you agree or you refuse. But do not try to cloud the issue. Think about it carefully. We have lots of time.' I tried to calm him down. 'You should not gain any false impressions. It will be a fair trial before the world and the media. You may choose your own defence lawyer. If you have committed no wrong, then you have nothing to fear. Think about it.'

The very next day he returned to this topic without my having to mention it. He said that he had carefully considered every aspect and come to a decision. He was prepared to come to Israel.

'Would you give me that in writing?'

Eichmann agreed. I took his goggles off and gave him a ballpoint pen and paper. Together, we formulated his confirming statement in German. I dictated my draft. Where he had no objections, he wrote it down slowly sentence by sentence, just as if he were deep in thought. The final sentence was his alone. He insisted on this additional clause. Since the events that were obviously to be the subject of the proceedings had taken place almost twenty years ago, he needed to ask the German and Israeli governments to provide him with documents to enable him to refresh his memory. I assured him that there was nothing standing in the way of this request being granted.

As he signed, he asked me for the date. He had obviously lost all sense of time. That was fine with us. We wanted this to remain that way, as one factor in the psychological pressure we were exerting.

I said to him: 'Just write Buenos Aires, May 1960, that will be enough.'

He did so and handed me the letter with a faint smile. His expression seemed to be saying: 'Now my fate is sealed. But surely anything else will be better than spending the rest of my life chained to a bedstead.'

I put his goggles back on him and said in a deliberately matter-of-fact manner: 'We will now arrange your transport to Israel and we expect your full cooperation.' He nodded in agreement.

His written statement verbatim (in translation) read:

'I, Adolf Eichmann, the undersigned, declare herewith of my own free will:

'Since my true identity is now known, I recognise that there is no sense in attempting to evade justice any longer. I declare myself willing to go to Israel and face proceedings there before a competent court.

'It goes without saying that I will receive legal defence and I will try to put the facts of my final years in office in Germany into the record without any embellishments, so that posterity will be given a true picture. I am making this declaration of my own free will. No promises were made to me, nor was I threatened in any way. I wish finally to find peace of mind again. Since I cannot recall all of the details and tend to confuse or mix things up, I request that I receive help in my desire to find the truth by having documents and testimony put at my disposal.

(signed) Adolf Eichmann
Buenos Aires, May 1960'

That same evening I handed Eichmann's letter over to Harel. I translated the statement from German into Hebrew. We only spoke a few words together, but both recognised that this was a milestone in 'Operation Eichmann'. We could not guess at this point in time that less than three weeks later, the letter would be on the front pages of newspapers all over the world.

On the flight back to Tel Aviv, I gave the ballpoint pen with which this confirmation had been written to Yankele Gat as a souvenir. I can easily imagine that he has kept it to this very day.

During these fateful days I had taken on two further duties. I supplied the house and its seven inmates with food, toiletries, reading material and whatever else was necessary. This task fell to me because I had to come and go every day anyway. It was important to us that not too many strange faces be seen in the neighbourhood. In those days there were no supermarkets where one could buy everything in any quantity without arousing suspicion. I therefore had to visit butchers and bakers, greengrocers and dairies in several different city districts. As far as possible, I avoided visiting the same store twice. That made things quite complicated. In the worst case, if the police were already looking for us, I did not want to give any shop-owner the chance to report us and then simply wait for my next shopping visit.

The same applied to the removal of rubbish. Since the daily accumulation of waste matter was far more than for a normal family, we removed it ourselves. I bought several large plastic bags and transported them full of rubbish to far distant places. In this way, I regularly spent many hours shopping and disposing of waste. This may sound banal, but it was an important task.

Now Isser Harel, Rafi Eitan, Avraham Shalom and I sat together every evening in order to discuss the next step: the transport of Eichmann out of Argentina. After endless discussion, we worked out five or six different possibilities.

The first plan was the simplest, most direct and also fairly uncomplicated. From among our men in Tel Aviv we had selected one who resembled Eichmann in build, age and general appearance. He was to arrive in Buenos Aires on 19 May aboard the *El Al* flight. The man would be travelling under the cover of an *El Al* steward. Later on, Eichmann was to take the flight back in his stead as a member of the crew. He would be wearing the steward's uniform and carrying his papers. The 'double' would stay behind in Argentina and receive a set of false papers from Shalom Dany. With a perfectly forged European passport, including all the necessary entry stamps, he would depart for Chile in the guise of a tourist one day after the take-off of our plane.

Eichmann himself would therefore travel as a member of the *El Al* crew. All Shalom had to do was to photograph him and then exchange the pictures in the Israeli passport and the airline identity card. Our doctor would give Eichmann a small injection that would be strong enough to render him quite helpless. He should, however, still have sufficient control over his body to be able to sit upright in the car and to walk the few steps from the car to the aircraft and up the gangway with the help of two 'colleagues from *El Al'*.

Our doctor, who was one of the most experienced anaesthetists at one of Israel's major hospitals, told us that he would be able to control the strength of the medication exactly. Eichmann would then be incapable of calling for help, but still be able to use his legs. Any eyewitness would gain the impression that two *El Al* people were helping a drunk or sick colleague into the aircraft.

The plan was simple and uncomplicated. Despite this, we were well aware that two conditions had to be met. First, that neither the police nor the secret service were already informed about Adolf Eichmann's disappearance. If they were, then they would certainly assume we were going to use our aircraft to smuggle Adolf Eichmann out of the country. They would erect roadblocks and search every car on the way to Ezeiza airport. In any case, they would surround the suspicious aeroplane with a heavy cordon of guards and watch it day and night. Only by doing this could they prevent unauthorised persons boarding the plane.

The second requirement for the success of our plan was a very negligent, superficial passport control of the crew by the Argentinian authorities. Isser voiced many objections to our simple strategy. How could we be sure that the police were not alerted even on the last day? How could we be certain that Eichmann would even be given permission to board the plane in his semi-conscious condition? Maybe the Argentinians would classify him as being in need of medical help and therefore unfit to fly.

Again and again I tried to dispel Isser's objections. It was highly unlikely that Eichmann's family would have gone to the police. There were actually only two possibilities. If the police were to be given a missing person's report for a Ricardo Klement, they would not react too rigorously. The guardians of the law would perhaps look through the accident reports, check out the hospitals and morgues, add a Señor Klement to a long list of missing persons. That would be of little avail to the Eichmanns. The only way they could really get the police to move would be to report the disappearance of one of the greatest war criminals of all time, in other words, Adolf Eichmann. They would have to explain that he had come to Argentina under false papers and was living here illegally. The family, so I assured our boss, would never dare take such a step. 'I know the Germans and I have had the family under observation for weeks. In their eyes, this would only make the situation even worse.'

Sometimes I would really have liked to know what was happening on the other side, with the Eichmanns and their friends. The flow of information was cut off since we were no longer observing the house. Nor did we have an informer who could help us further.

It is doubtful whether Klaus Eichmann's statements to *Quick* magazine are accurate in every detail, or whether they are to be taken seriously at all. According to what he said in 1966, there was feverish activity to find the missing father. His mother and little brother Ricardo were sheltered in the house of a former SS man.

Klaus Eichmann: 'Another friend of my father's, also an SS man, organised an observation network over all the seaports and airports. No airport, no harbour, no major railway station, no important crossroads that was not being watched by our people.'

The family feared that Vera and her son Ricardo could also be abducted. A tip from old SS comrades said that Eichmann was being hidden away in the cellar of a synagogue in Buenos Aires. This turned out to be a false lead. Klaus Eichmann: 'My brother Dieter, eighteen at the time, and I, twenty-four, hardly slept. We were on guard duty day and night. Each of us on a four-hour shift. For many days we did this by ourselves. Then a Perónist youth organisation joined us. While our Argentinian friends were minding the house, we tried to find father. We knew with certainty that he had not yet left Argentina.'

The brothers were very self-confident: 'We tried to provoke the other side into some sort of action. We simply spread the news that an Israeli special military commando had kidnapped our father. This alerted the Argentinian army.' However – in absolute contradiction to the statements by the sons – no one on the official side was looking for the missing man.

Aharoni continues:

The strategy discussions at *Mossad* continued. The other weak point, the passport control for departing crew members, should not worry us either. By now I was familiar with Argentina and its administration. All we needed, I argued with Isser, were one or two senior representatives from *El Al* as an advance guard a week before the arrival of the aircraft. They should thoroughly inspect the airport, strike up friendships with the local staff, distribute cigarettes and drinks with a lavish hand. They would need to learn all the routines and to become known as representatives of *El Al*. At the time of departure, they would accompany our crew with Eichmann in the middle and, without any doubt, be waved through without any formalities.

Isser was still unconvinced. He demanded further alternatives. We should be prepared, for example, for the police to be guarding our aircraft round the clock simply for reasons of security. That would make it more difficult to bring Eichmann on board. We should be prepared for the emergency situation that *El Al* would have to take off without the prisoner and that all that would remain for us would be the way out by sea.

Therefore we now began preparations of alternative plans. We persuaded an Israeli, who happened to be in Argentina as a tourist, to move into a hospital for a few days as a patient. We had checked him out and believed he was loyal. He did not know what it was all about, but he wanted to be helpful to his country. Our doctor briefed him thoroughly in his role as the victim of an accident.

As he then claimed, in the emergency department of a large hospital, he had been involved in a collision with two cars. The symptoms he described were clear and the doctors accepted his presumed concussion of the brain. He was to be released on the day of departure of the special flight – just in time to hand over his identity documents to us. In this case we would use the documents for Eichmann as the 'patient'. Had we used this variation, Eichmann would have been carried into the aircraft on a stretcher.

From a carpenter who had already worked for the Israeli embassy on prior occasions, we ordered a massive wooden crate, large enough to transport a grown man in a sitting position. Our doctor assured us that he could knock Eichmann out for a period of about four hours without any danger. He did admit, however, that there was a certain risk involved. For a healthy adult, however, this was minimal.

When the doctor saw the finished crate, he immediately detected a fundamental problem. It did not have any air-holes. The inmate had to be able to breathe freely. We could not take the crate back to the carpenter without arousing his suspicion. Therefore we did the job ourselves. Four millimetres, we believed, was the maximum diameter. Larger holes would attract unnecessary attention. The doctor recommended we drill at least fifty holes. Otherwise there would not be enough oxygen. We borrowed a small pick-up truck from Yossef's friends and collected the crate from the carpenter. We then brought it to the cellar of the embassy.

We screwed four heavy straps of leather to the inside, two each on the left and right. They were to be used to tie Eichmann's arms fast and keep him in a sitting position. He should not slide around inside the crate. Then we drilled twenty symmetrical holes each through both side walls and through the top. Most of the holes were located where his head would later be resting. On the cover we stencilled in large letters:

DIPLOMATIC POST
FROM: ISRAELI EMBASSY, BUENOS AIRES
TO: FOREIGN MINISTRY JERUSALEM

We left the crate ready for collection in the embassy cellar.

The next alternative plan, with which I was personally occupied, required the use of a small boat. We had to consider how we could bring Eichmann to an Israeli ship outside Argentinian territorial waters. For this purpose, we bought sea charts and undertook trips around the harbour and its vicinity. On our charts we marked down deserted beaches, which could serve to put Eichmann on board a boat. We studied the possibilities of renting a large speedboat for water skiing. One day we did this and went far out into the 300-kilometre-wide estuary of the Rio de la Plata. The open sea posed no problem. Except on stormy days, according to our findings, it could easily be negotiated in a speedboat.

We knew that transporting Eichmann by the sea route would have been our very last possibility and almost an act of desperation. A glance at the schedules of the official Israeli ship line *ZIM* showed us that there was no scheduled freighter to Argentina or Uruguay during the next few months. In an emergency, we would therefore have had to redirect a ship from its regular run to Brazil or Central America. That would not only have been extremely expensive but also very time-consuming. An Israeli ship could not have been in our vicinity before the end of June or the beginning of July at the earliest. Eichmann would therefore have been in our custody for a further six weeks. This idea did not suit us at all. We would also not have been able to prevent many people suddenly learning that a freighter had been diverted and an unknown person put aboard on the high seas. Nonetheless, in order also to be prepared for this worst contingency, we collected all the information necessary for a sea voyage.

However, we did not lose sight of plan No. 1, to put Eichmann aboard in an *El Al* uniform in plain sight. We spent many hours at all times of day driving along all the roads leading to Ezeiza, and were particularly on the lookout for possible police roadblocks. Even though the 150th anniversary celebrations had already begun and delegations from all over the world were arriving, there were no unusual security measures to be detected.

Every day we studied the local Spanish- and German-language press. We were relieved, time and again, that no indication of the disappearance of Klement or Eichmann appeared.

Eichmann now also began to notice that something was going on. We dressed him in a white shirt and a black tie. This resembled the *El Al* uniform. Zvika, who was good at make-up, prepared the prisoner and Shalom Dany photographed him. With these passport photos, our master forger prepared a regular Israeli passport and an airline identity card. Without being asked, Eichmann asserted repeatedly that he would offer no resistance and would cooperate with us in every way. However, Isser and I were in agreement that we should not rely blindly on such promises.

Now two high-ranking officials from *El Al* arrived in Buenos Aires to make all necessary preparations for the planned special flight. They arrived from New York and Tel Aviv six days before the expected arrival of the aircraft. Both of them quickly learned the operational routine at Ezeiza. Within a short time, they struck up many friendships, not only with the technical staff, but also with the customs people, the police and the security department.

It was decided that during the twenty-four-hour rest period of the crew, the *El Al* aircraft was to be parked on an area reserved for *Aerolineas Argentinas*, the state airline. This was to be preferred for reasons of security. Furthermore, the area was in a favourable location for bringing our 'guest' on board before the plane was towed to the take-off position. As the planned arrival date of the special flight approached, we became more and more convinced that nothing would distract us from plan No. 1. We began to work out the details. We planned to collect Eichmann from the house about three hours before take-off and arrive at the airport with him one hour later. The genuine crew had to arrive in their minibus at precisely the same moment.

We decided to take Eichmann to the airport in an official car from the embassy, marked with diplomatic number plates. Yankele and the doctor would be in the car. They would all be wearing *El Al* uniforms. A second car would follow the first – in order to be able to intervene in case of an incident. The question remained: who would drive the car? Again, as on the night of the kidnapping, I convinced Isser that he should choose me. Eichmann knew me and trusted me. He had promised me repeatedly that he would offer no resistance. But even in a state of semi-consciousness, we had to watch him all the time. Furthermore, I already knew the roads to the airport inside and out, including alternative secondary routes.

We did not know if we could rely on the regular embassy staff in an emergency. At this critical point of the operation, we did not want to run any risks. Isser therefore accepted my suggestion. Avraham was to drive the second car.

Next we cleared up the point of who was to return to Israel on the aircraft. We could not take the whole team as an oversized *El Al* crew. Furthermore, some had to stay behind in order to clean up the tracks left by the operation. In the days following, the cars, houses and apartments had to be cleaned and returned to their owners. Then the rest of the people would take the train over the Andes to Chile and fly back to Europe from there.

Apart from Isser Harel and the doctor, both of whom doubtlessly had to be aboard, only two more of us would come along to reinforce the crew and guard the prisoner. Isser suggested that I should take the trip over the mountains. 'You have earned this reward and need a rest,' he said. 'Take it easy and see the remainder of the trip as a vacation.'

I objected to the Old Man: 'I started this job and I want to finish it. Eichmann knows me and has grown accustomed to me. I believe I should stay close to him all the way.'

Finally Isser agreed. However, I could not board the special flight to Tel Aviv under my cover story as a German businessman. I had to transform myself into a diplomatic courier, drive the car in this capacity and take care of the diplomatic mail. So Shalom Dany went to work again. He produced a complete set of new papers for me, which identified me as an Israeli diplomat. The stamps in my passport showed that I had just arrived in Buenos Aires two days ago.

CHAPTER 10

In the Name
of the Jewish People

'Mass murder on a large scale requires someone who is socially adjusted as a murderer.'

Simon Wiesenthal

El Al special flight No 4X-AGE, a turbo-prop Bristol Britannia, landed on the runway of Ezeiza airport at 1752 on 19 May 1960. According to schedule, it should already have arrived three hours earlier. The official reception committee from the Argentinian Foreign Ministry had come on time and had been waiting since then. The aircraft had been delayed because it had been temporarily refused permission to take off after refuelling in Recife, Brazil.

Air traffic control had said something about permission to fly over Brazilian territory being missing. That could not have been the true reason, because the paper-work had already been taken care of six days before. We shall probably never learn the real reason.

When the plane finally landed, Avraham Shalom and I were at Ezeiza. We had scheduled one of our routine checks on the road to the airport in such a manner that we would be able to see the *El Al* and the Israeli delegation. Because of a traffic accident and the ensuing traffic block, we had almost arrived too late.

The Britannia taxied to a stop in the twilight. She was the newest, quietest and most comfortable aeroplane in the *El Al* fleet. More importantly, she had the longest range for non-stop flights: a worthy means of transport for the delegation, at whose head stood Foreign Minister Abba Eban. The Israelis gathered near the aircraft. Host and guest made the customary short speeches of welcome. Inside the terminal, the heads of the Jewish community were already waiting. We were following the event from a distance. All we were actually interested in was observing how the Britannia was towed into the parking area of *Aerolineas Argentinas*.

We were to meet the new arrivals from *Mossad* that same night at a place agreed long before. Therefore, there was no reason to attract unnecessary attention at the airport. After all, no member of the official delegation, including the Foreign Minister, knew the real reason for this special flight. No one knew of our presence.

In the evening, all the members of our team who were not on duty guarding Eichmann met in one of our apartments for a final briefing. The two new agents were welcomed. They were given a short introduction to the situation and learned what they were required to do.

We were under the impression that nothing stood in the way of our plan No. 1. The streets were clear. We had never observed a roadblock or a traffic control on the route to Ezeiza. The aircraft was parked favourably. Eichmann was cooperative. Nobody seemed to be looking for him. The exact time plan for the final phase of the operation was fixed. Everyone knew his job. Step by step. Minute by minute.

During the night, Isser met the *El Al* representatives and informed them about the details of plan No. 1. The movements of the crew were synchronised with the activities of our team, because Eichmann was to board together with the *El Al* crew. Despite the late hour and the long distance, I drove from the centre of the capital to our 'safe house' and informed the rest of the team about the time schedule for next day.

All of them were happy and noticeably excited. They were overjoyed that everything had worked perfectly so far and that they were now to be allowed to return home. The nine days and nights during which they had guarded Eichmann, prepared his food and taken care of his physical needs, had left their marks on all of the people on the team. The nerves of some were stretched to breaking point. There simply could not be any further delay.

Next morning I packed my small case. I reached for a suit and tie, because I had to slip into the role of a diplomat again one hour hence. I returned my rented car, a small Fiat, and took a taxi to the embassy. There Yossef gave me the keys to a shining, impressive-looking Chevrolet limousine with diplomatic plates. Shalom Dany handed me my documents as a diplomat. In exchange, I gave him my German passport, the international driving licence and other documents.

Now I was no longer a German businessman, but a member of the South America desk in the Israeli Foreign Ministry. I had come to Buenos Aires on a short visit and was taking advantage of the special flight to return home. Simultaneously, I was taking care of two sacks of diplomatic mail that were destined for Jerusalem. This made sense and was a part of normal routine. The official courier only came to Argentina once a month. In the interim, the mail was carried by any visitor with a diplomatic passport.

In Argentina I mistrusted any car and therefore I first took the new Chevrolet to a filling station. I checked oil, water, tyre pressure, battery and brake fluid and filled the tank. Then I once again checked the route to the airport. Traffic was flowing normally and undisturbed.

I arrived at Eichmann's hideout towards four in the afternoon. I told him we would be leaving for Israel that same evening. I warned him to remember his promise to cooperate. Eichmann calmly replied: 'You have nothing to fear. I am going with you voluntarily and will keep my promise.'

Then I instructed the others to be ready by eight o'clock and returned to the airport. There I met Isser, who had moved his official 'command post' to Ezeiza in the meantime. I reported clear roads and from the embassy the information came in that the afternoon papers had again not reported anything about the disappearance of Adolf Eichmann. Isser now decided to execute plan No. 1. At 1930 he sent me off.

Fifty minutes later I arrived at the 'safe house', followed by Avraham in the second car. Everybody was ready. Feelings ran high. Eichmann, the doctor and Yankele were wearing *El Al* uniforms. However, our prisoner's jacket was missing. He told me immediately that he too should have a jacket so as not to attract attention. At first I could not decide whether he was just pretending or whether he really meant it. He appeared, however, to be quite serious. Was it fear of being shot if complications were to arise or simply the submission of the vanquished?

He was quickly made to understand that there was a very simple reason for him to be travelling in his shirt. The doctor had to be able to reach his arm and a vein at any time. He would inject his patient with a certain amount of medication and then leave the needle sticking in the vein. In that way, he could increase the dose at any time. The shirt would hide the needle but not hamper the doctor. This would be much harder with a jacket.

In the kitchen, we asked Eichmann to sit down and put his right arm on the table. While the doctor was preparing the injection, Eichmann again assured us that he would obey instructions. We did not have to put him under drugs. I talked to him: 'This is only a sedative that will make you relax. You have a very long journey ahead of you. This medication will help you to overcome all the strain.' He stretched out his arm. A moment later the doctor felt his patient's pulse and stated: 'We are ready to travel.'

It was now approaching nine o'clock. Yankele and the doctor each took an arm and pulled him to his feet. He was incapable of speech, but seemed to be fully conscious and was able to control his movements. With the help of the two 'crew members', Eichmann slowly walked out of the kitchen and into the garage. I opened the door of the car and he was helped on to the rear seat. The doctor sat down next to him on his right. I drove the car and Yankele sat next to me. Eichmann seemed to perceive everything that was going on around him. However, when I asked him how he felt, there was no answer.

Our little convoy set off. Out of care for our prisoner, I drove very slowly. The doctor had warned me. Were I to brake suddenly or take a corner too fast, Eichmann could fall over and injure himself with the needle in his vein. Furthermore, there was another reason not to rush. I had to arrive simultaneously with the bus of the *El Al* crew and that was exactly at 2230.

The ride to the airport passed without incident. At the gate, we were waved through because of our diplomatic number plates. Avraham, who was driving a normal rented car, parked outside. I steered for the sector of *Aerolineas Argentinas*. Nobody interfered with us. We saw only a few people, because there were no further flights scheduled for that night. Two minutes later the crew bus appeared beside us and stopped. Isser now gave the order to take Eichmann on board according to plan No. 1. It was Yankele who came over from the main passenger hall with those instructions.

The bus and my car stopped only a few steps from the gangway of the Britannia. The captain and two other crew members got out, exchanged a few words with the *El Al* guards and disappeared inside the cockpit. In under one minute, one of them appeared again in the doorway and gave the signal to board.

Yankele opened the rear door of the car. He and the doctor pulled Eichmann out and supported him on either side. Slowly they mounted the steps to the entry door of the plane. The rest of the crew followed a short distance behind. The whole group screened the conspicuous trio from curious eyes, even though this was not necessary in this remote place. When Eichmann had disappeared inside the plane, I drew a deep breath. Taking quick steps, I hastened after him and checked on the situation. He was already sitting belted up on an aisle seat in first-class. The doctor was in the row behind him. I could readily understand that no one on the team was interested in spending the next twenty hours elbow to elbow with Adolf Eichmann. The prisoner still had the needle in his arm. The doctor would only remove it after take-off. He seemed to be taking everything in and his eyes were wide open. This time, too, he did not react when I spoke to him, although he could obviously hear me. After I told him, 'Try to get a bit of sleep and you surely will feel better,' he closed his eyes and leaned back.

I left the aircraft and handed over my car to two men from the embassy in the diplomatic parking area. With my case and two sealed courier bags I went to the departure hall. Isser Harel was already waiting for me. I reported the successful conclusion. It was almost eleven o'clock.

The hour that followed was by far the most difficult and nerve-wracking of the whole operation. We had nothing left to do, except to wait for take-off. The two *El Al* officials and five of our men, Isser and I included, sat in the lounge. After about ten minutes a member of the crew appeared and reported that the plane was in its take-off position. We even had permission for take-off. Only the officials from passport control were keeping us waiting.

Every minute seemed to last for an hour. We were tense and indescribably nervous. Our final success was so close and now we had to sit around here senselessly. As time passed, all sorts of horrific thoughts quite naturally went through our minds. Was it only negligence on the part of the officials or was there something ominous in the offing? Had someone smelled a rat? Had somebody seen a sick crew member being dragged on to the plane? Was the aircraft being searched? Should we ask the captain to take off without further delay and leave us behind?

Suddenly, only a few minutes before midnight, relief appeared in the guise of a big, bearded emigration officer. With a wide, slightly embarrassed smile, he waved us through the exit door.

'Please excuse me! I am sorry! Never mind!'

Without looking, he stamped our passports. A loud *'Bon viaje'* and we were on the way to the aircraft. We still could not credit our enormous luck. Even after the doors of the plane had been closed and the engines started, I was still unable to relax. Then the aircraft began to move. The runway was clear. At the end of the runway, the Britannia lifted off. It was four minutes past midnight. We had made it! One of the stewardesses asked me if I wanted something to eat. I gratefully declined but asked for a double whisky. That helped.

Eichmann had returned to full consciousness. The doctor had checked his heart and his breathing and found that he had come through the long period of semi-consciousness without harm. Eichmann quietly sat in his seat. After the medication had worn off, we put his prepared goggles back on. He slept for most of the time. Whenever he asked for something to eat, he was given small portions, which had been prepared according to the instructions by our doctor, who wanted to be sure that he could knock him out again at any time without endangering his health.

After the uncomfortable experience during the stop-over in Recife, we wanted to make every effort to avoid Brazil this time. Captain Zvi Tohar, Chief Pilot of *El Al*, came to the conclusion that we could make the thirteen-hour flight to Dakar in the Senegal without stop-over. He was to be proved right. With the last remaining fuel, we landed on the other side of the Atlantic. Since we had reached Dakar, we could also make the remaining ten and a half hours to Tel Aviv non-stop.

Over the whole of the long 15,000-kilometre stretch we were extremely lucky and had a favourable wind. Sometime between two and three o'clock in the morning, we flew over the Straits of Gibraltar. From there it was straight across the Mediterranean. At 0720, we saw the first strip of the Israeli coastline. Fifteen minutes later, the plane taxied to a stop on the runway of Lydda airport. One of those cloudless, hot summer days awaited us. It was the 22 of May 1960 – eighty-three days after I had first flown out to hunt for Adolf Eichmann. The most sensational operation in which I took part during my long years with the secret service was already history.

Our plane taxied to a parking position out of sight of the passenger building. Besides two high-ranking *El Al* officials, a leading officer of *Shin Bet* came on board. Moshe Drori had been in charge of the necessary logistics for 'Operation Eichmann' in Israel. He greeted Isser Harel and congratulated him on his great success.

Isser thanked him and asked: 'Where are we going to take him now?'

'I don't know,' answered Drori, still smiling.

Isser reacted with disbelief and assumed the other man had not understood the question. He repeated it: 'Where are we going to take Eichmann from here? What preparations have you made?'

The smile disappeared. 'I have not made any preparations. I have been waiting for you and your instructions.'

Isser Harel turned pale. He was completely beside himself and bit his lips to avoid making a cutting rejoinder. He left the plane together with Drori. We waited for his return. It took over two hours before a windowless minibus pulled up beside the airplane. It was followed by a large car with oversized antennae. The occupants belonged to the operations department of *Shin Bet*. They temporarily took Eichmann to a small, secret detention centre of the internal service not far from Jaffa. There the police were later to take him over.

Then came 23 May, an historic date. Together with Isser Harel and other colleagues, I had been invited to attend a session of the *Knesset*. For the first time in my life, I was visiting the parliament building. I was impressed by its size and architecture.

Seventy-four-year-old David Ben Gurion, Prime Minister and founder of Israel, stepped up to the rostrum. His statement was brief: 'I have to inform the *Knesset* that some time ago Israeli security forces found one of the greatest Nazi criminals, Adolf Eichmann, who together with other Nazi leaders, is responsible for what they termed the *Endlösung* of the Jewish question, in other words, the extermination of six million European Jews.

Adolf Eichmann is already in this country under arrest and will shortly be brought to trial here under the law of the year 1950 covering the punishment of Nazis and their helpers.'

There was a breathless silence in the chamber. I could not believe it, was surprised and disappointed. What had I expected? Pandemonium? Thundering applause? An ear-splitting scream from the delegates? It was obviously taking some time for the unexpected news to penetrate people's heads. I recall individual shouts of surprise. Two or three reporters ran to the telephones. Shortly thereafter we left the *Knesset* and drove back to Tel Aviv.

Ben Gurion's statement had quite a dramatic effect on my private life. Many times before I had been out of the country on secret missions. My family and my friends had never known the reason I had gone abroad nor where to. Not even my wife had been informed. She had long grown accustomed to my life as a secret agent and did not ask any questions. She knew that in an emergency she could call my office and ask for help. Some day I always turned up again. Even then, she would not ask any questions. Sometimes she could tell, from the presents I brought back for her and the children, from which country or continent I had just returned. That was all.

This time it was different. The same evening my brother Yochanan, the archaeologist, called and welcomed me back. I asked in surprise: 'How did you know I was back?' 'Don't be naive. I knew that you were away for over two months and I heard Ben Gurion on the radio. I can add two and two together. Or can't I? Well done!' What could I say? I neither confirmed, nor did I deny. Understandably, I was proud.

I returned to my office in Jaffa. On the stairs, I ran into one of our secretaries. Without warning, she wrapped her arms around my neck and kissed me on both cheeks. I was speechless, I hardly knew the girl. Before I could react, I noticed that she was crying. I did not have to ask her why. The girl had lost many relatives in Eichmann's extermination camps. It was her way of showing gratitude.

Israel is a small country. To my great astonishment, everybody I met during the ensuing days and weeks seemed to be in the know. Even the director of *Shin Bet*, Amos Manor, who was normally an absolute fiend for secrecy, called me 'architect of the success' in public. But life went on.

On 23 May, Eichmann was taken before the court. The prisoner stood at attention. The charges against him were read and translated into German. After he had satisfied himself as to Eichmann's identity, the judge remanded him into custody for fourteen days.

On 24 May a telegram from the documentation centre *Yad Vashem* in Jerusalem arrived in Linz for Nazi-hunter Simon Wiesenthal: 'Heartiest congratulations on your brilliant success.'

During the following days, international public opinion raised the question of whether Israel could be objective enough to hold court on a man such as Adolf Eichmann. David Ben Gurion answered on 27 May in the newspaper *Dawar*: The 'history of the Jewish catastrophe' had to be unfolded before an Israeli court 'so that the younger generation growing up and being educated in Israel, which has only a pale idea of the unthinkable cruelties committed, can learn what really happened'. In a letter to Nahum Goldmann, Ben Gurion spoke of an 'act of historic justice'.

Within only a few days, *Time* magazine published an exclusive article on the circumstances of Eichmann's kidnapping. It said he had been found in Buenos Aires by Israeli agents and arrested. This was a sensational piece of news, because Israel had not announced the place of the abduction.

On 1 June, the Israeli ambassador to Argentina, Arieh Levavi, was called to the Foreign Ministry and asked for a comprehensive statement. The Argentinian police declared officially that Adolf Eichmann was Ricardo Klement. Many details from his life history were published, few of them true. In the police statement, it was claimed that Eichmann had also lived alternately in Paraguay, Bolivia and Brazil.

The warrant to hold Eichmann was extended for a further two weeks. The Israeli police evacuated a huge police station in Jelame near Haifa called Camp Iyar and housed the country's most prominent prisoner there. On 29 May, Eichmann met police captain Avner Less, born in Berlin, and his superior, Colonel Efraim Hofstetter, for the first time. An interrogation marathon lasting 270 hours began. Less questioned Eichmann ninety times – until 2 February 1961. The prisoner was now in the hands of Police Department 06. It consisted of thirty men and was divided into five sections. The investigators compiled documents, questioned witnesses, evaluated the material and prepared the indictment.

Arieh Levavi, the Israeli ambassador in Buenos Aires, came under pressure. On 4 June he replied to Argentine Foreign Minister Diogenes Taboada by handing over a *note verbale*. The note was published two days later in Buenos Aires and Tel Aviv. In fact, it was so naive and far from the actual events, that it is difficult to understand how anyone in the Israeli Foreign Ministry could have hoped to end the delicate affair in such a way.

The key arguments in the note were as follows:

✡   The Israeli Government had had no knowledge of the operation against Adolf Eichmann, because it was not informed in time by its secret services.

✪   After the Second World War, Jewish volunteers (including several Israelis) had begun to search for the war criminal. For fifteen years they had not been successful. Some months ago they had learned that Eichmann was living in Buenos Aires, supported by other Nazis but unknown to the Argentinian authorities.

✪   A renewed search had begun. The group of volunteers had found the fugitive and asked him whether he was prepared to come to Israel to stand trial. Eichmann had admitted his identity when he recognised that he no longer had a chance against his pursuers. After twenty-four hours' time for reflection, he had agreed to travel to Israel and face the court.

✪   The activists had brought him out of Argentina and delivered him to the Israeli secret service.

✪   It had informed the Government. The police and the State Attorney General had been instructed to prepare proceedings.

✪   Attached to the note was a translation of Eichmann's letter, in which he announced that he would go to Israel voluntarily. The note ends:

✪   Should the group of volunteers have broken Argentinian law or violated the sovereign rights of Argentina, the Government of Israel expresses its regrets. The Government of Israel requests that consideration be given to the extraordinary fact that now a person can finally be brought to trial, who is responsible for the murder of millions of people of our nation. Furthermore, it requests the Argentinian Govenment to consider that these volunteers, who are themselves survivors of the Holocaust, only put their historic mission ahead of any other consideration. The Government of Israel is convinced that the Government of Argentina will appreciate these historic and moral values.

Except for the fact, mentioned in the sixth paragraph of the note, that the Government of Israel (read: Israeli Foreign Office) was only informed on 23 May that Eichmann had arrived in Israel, and the fact that he had given his agreement in writing to stand trial in Israel, all other facts mentioned in the note were pure fiction, and it really should not have surprised anyone that the Argentine Government strongly rejected the note.

On 8 June, the Argentinians indeed rejected the Israeli excuses in a harshly worded statement. They demanded 'appropriate damages' – Eichmann's immediate return to Buenos Aires and punishment of the 'volunteers'. This letter crossed with a personal message from Ben Gurion to Arturo Frondizi, President of Argentina.

Ben Gurion in his memoirs: 'In the closing paragraph of the letter I asked the President to conscientiously consider all of the circumstances. He himself had fought against dictatorship and proved his appreciation of human values. I hoped that he would accept our regrets for the violation of the laws of his country, which were only committed out of the dictates of conscience.'

World opinion supported Argentina and massively attacked Israel. The Jewish state, however, remained steadfast and did not give in to the demand to return Eichmann. Thereupon Argentina took the case before the Security Council of the United Nations on 15 June 1960. In a statement from Buenos Aires, it said that the abduction of Adolf Eichmann to Israel had created an atmosphere of insecurity and mistrust, which could not be reconciled with the efforts to maintain international peace.

After a long and controversial debate, a resolution was passed which condemned Eichmann's abduction as a violation of Argentinian sovereignty. Argentina had the right to demand damages. The traditionally pro-Israeli Americans tried to mediate between the two contestants. However, on 25 June Argentina declared Israel's apology to be insufficient and rejected it. The same day Ben Gurion again stated that Eichmann would not be allowed to return to Buenos Aires.

Israel's offer of 'expressions of sincere regrets' was resolutely rejected by Argentina, which demanded 'appropriate reparations'. Only after weeks of negotiations and numerous exchanges of notes between the two governments, a compromise solution was accepted by Argentina. Israel's ambassador, Arieh Levavi, was declared 'persona non grata' and recalled to Israel.

On 3 August, both governments published a joint statement in which they assured each other of mutual sympathy. 'Actions by citizens of Israel', which had 'violated fundamental rights of the state of Argentina' were condemned. Former *Mossad* Chief Isser Harel ('After I had brought Eichmann to Israel, I lost interest in this case') is still incensed today about the political manoeuvres at the time: 'Our government declared, out of stupidity, that the operation had been carried out by Jewish volunteers and not by the secret service. Despite this, we were not able to avoid the conflict with Argentina. But the government had now committed itself to a certain version and had to stick with it for many years.' This had wounded the professional pride of the agency chief.

The preliminary investigation of the Eichmann case took eight months. In the end, the interrogations alone were documented on 3564 pages. Eichmann's statements always ended with the claim that he had formerly only been 'a minor recipient of orders'. The guilt, so he kept assuring his interrogator Avner Less, had lain only with his superiors. He himself had done nothing evil. Less: 'He obviously believed he could escape the gallows if he were able to convince us all of his unimportance.' What most enraged the slightly built, patient Less was 'that Eichmann obviously had no sense at all of the immensity of his crimes and that he did not feel the slightest trace of remorse'.

Adolf Eichmann only received one visit by someone from the *Mossad* team. Rafi Eitan had himself been shown the prisoner and his new living conditions by his friend Avner Less. Less: 'Eichmann's cell measured about three by four metres. It only contained a narrow bed, a table and a chair. During darkness there was always an electric light on. The cell and the shower room in front of it were cleaned daily by Eichmann himself. He did this thoroughly and with dedication. There was a guard sitting inside the cell round the clock and a second guard outside the door, who watched his colleague sitting inside through a spyhole in order to ensure that no contacts developed between prisoner and guard in the cell. This second guard was watched in turn by a third guard who sat behind the next door, the exit.' The guards' constant concern was that their prisoner might commit suicide.

The sensational trial of fifty-four-year-old Adolf Eichmann – file No. 40/61 – lasted from 11 April to 14 August 1961. For four months, the eyes of the world were on the 'House of the People' in Jerusalem. Simon Wiesenthal arrived on the first day of the proceedings and saw 'a weak, colourless, shabby fellow in a glass cell between two Israeli police officers; they looked more interesting and remarkable than he did... There was nothing demonic about him; he looked like an accountant who was afraid to ask for a rise in salary.' The Nazi-hunter from Austria suddenly realised why this Eichmann looked so terribly stolid: 'He wore a cheap, dark suit and presented the picture of an empty, two-dimensional cardboard figure.' He lacked the black uniform with the death's-head insignia. Wiesenthal suggested to the prosecutor, Senior District Attorney Gideon Hausner, that Eichmann be dressed in an authentic uniform. Hausner objected. It was sufficient for him to 'represent six millions, whose voices had been smothered and whose ashes had been blown away by the wind' without any theatricals at all.

The indictment, which contained fifteen separate points, accused Eichmann of 'having committed crimes against the Jewish people' by having instigated 'together with others, in the period between 1939 and 1945, the killing of millions of Jews'. Fifteen times, the man in the glass box declared himself to be 'not guilty as charged'. Many witnesses and documents proved the contrary. In the final analysis, it was also important to prove Eichmann's personal guilt. Not only had he received orders from higher up and passed them on down, but he had destroyed individual Jewish lives directly and meticulously, with sadistic pleasure.

He was always informed and took care of every single detail personally. When the Argentinian government had wanted to discover the fate of one of its citizens, Gerson Millner from Lemberg, from the Foreign Office in Berlin, the German diplomats had approached Himmler. The relations between Germany and Argentina should be taken into consideration and the man not put into a concentration camp. Eichmann's cynical reply was that the Jew in question had died of a weak heart, despite the excellent care he had been given.

When Eichmann learned that a Jew named Golub, from the French camp in Drancy, was to be granted the citizenship of a Latin American country and would therefore be able to emigrate, he ordered *Gestapo* headquarters in Paris to have Golub sent to Auschwitz as quickly as possible. Andreas Michaelis, who was married to a Swiss woman, was to be allowed to emigrate into Switzerland on the advice of the Foreign Ministry. His father-in-law was a member of the pro-German lobby in Switzerland. Eichmann sent a personal reply: 'As a matter of principle, I am not able to let the stateless Jew Michaelis emigrate to Switzerland.'

The *Obersturmbannführer*, in a similar letter of 2 December 1942 to the Foreign Ministry: 'Subject: former French prisoner of war and Jew Roger Masse, born in Besançon 13.12.1884... The above-named Jew was sent to the east (Auschwitz) from Compiègne on 5.6.1942. I cannot agree his return for reasons of principle. Please take note.'

Only a few examples of many, showing that Eichmann also took decisions on life and death in individual cases. He had whole-heartedly dedicated himself to the industrialised extermination of the Jews.

Aharoni recalls: 'I attended the trial on one occasion to have a look at the proceedings in court and to gain a first-hand impression of the whole atmosphere... I had been invited by the Chief of *Shin Bet* in Jerusalem. We sat in the front row for visitors. I do not know what I had expected. I recall very well, however, that I found the factual, legalistic situation to be very sobering. If I had expected 'fireworks', I would have been disappointed. I am not sure whether Eichmann recognised me. He looked directly at us several times, but did not give any sign that he knew who I was.'

On 11 December 1961, the Chairman of the court, Moshe Landau, who was of German origin, announced the verdict: death by hanging. It was the first and only death sentence in the history of the state of Israel. Eichmann delivered his final statement in what Avner Less called 'Austrian-Berliner bureaucratic Nazi German':

'In my hope for justice, I see myself disappointed. I cannot accept the verdict of guilty... I had the bad luck to have become involved in these acts of horror. But these crimes did not occur of my volition. It was not my will to kill people. The mass murder is solely the fault of the political leaders.'

His only guilt, said Eichmann, had been unconditional obedience. Under the conditions of the time, he had not been able to withhold it. At the end of the trial he appeared exhausted and burned out. His striking features seemed to have changed into a rigid mask. The appeal to the Supreme Court was hopeless from the start and only delayed the execution of the sentence. Ben Zvi, President of Israel, also rejected Eichmann's appeal for clemency.

On 1 June 1962, a few minutes before midnight, Adolf Eichmann was executed. Rafi Eitan recalls: 'I was sitting at home. The Director of Ramleh prison called up and said, "We will hang Eichmann in one hour!" He asked me to come. I jumped into my car and rushed to Ramleh. I was taken to the director's office. The priest had already left. Then I met Eichmann. He looked at me, I looked at him. We were about ten metres apart. He said something in German. It sounded like: "I hope very much, that it will be your turn soon after mine!" Later on he repeated the sentence again and he seemed to mean all of us. We were six or seven people. Eichmann stayed very calm and again asked for a glass of wine. Then he walked straight to the gallows.'

Rudolf Küstermeier, the correspondent of the German Press Agency in Israel, was one of the four accredited journalists. He reported how calmly and composedly Eichmann went to meet his death. He wore brown trousers and a brown shirt. He refused the black cloth mask offered him by the hangman. When he was already standing on the trap-door he suddenly said in a calm, but firm voice: 'Long live Germany. Long live Austria. Long live Argentina. Those are the three countries to which I had the closest ties. I will not forget them. I greet my wife, my family and my friends. I was required to obey the laws of war and of my flag. I am prepared.' The noose was put around Eichmann's neck. He no longer looked at anybody.

Witness Rudolf Küstermeier: 'The click of the suddenly opening trap-door on which Adolf Eichmann had been standing was the only sound we then heard. Within a fraction of a second, the body of the man who had just been standing upright before us had disappeared. The opening which had swallowed him up yawned darkly. Below us, one storey down, the body hung from a swaying rope.' Eichmann's corpse was burned and the ashes were scattered in the Mediterranean Sea.

Aharoni recalls: 'I had also been invited to the execution. Fortunately I was spared the dilemma of deciding whether to accept or to decline out of principle. In fact, on this very day, I was back again in South America, this time in search of Josef Mengele. I was breaking the strict order by Harel never again to enter Argentina. But I was not there of my own free choice. I was on a plane to Montevideo, the capital of Uruguay, but bad weather conditions prevented the plane from landing. We were diverted to the nearest alternative, just across the La Plata estuary: Buenos Aires. It was late evening and no more flights were leaving that day. I had no choice but to stay overnight in Buenos Aires. The next morning all local papers carried huge headlines: Eichmann had been executed.

'Eichmann was now dead. Somehow, I believe, he had been prepared for this. He had waited for us for fifteen years. His first words in the darkened car, barely a minute after he had been overpowered, had been: "I have already resigned myself to my fate." He knew there was no escape. And somehow it seemed that he felt a kind of relief that the long years as a fugitive and the endless tension were over. From the moment of his capture, he knew he would die and he submitted.'

Simon Wiesenthal, in his analysis of the four months at Jerusalem, which brought the long forgotten Holocaust back to life and unearthed many things that the victims had meanwhile suppressed, commented: 'The Eichmann trial conveyed the essential, deep understanding of the Nazi murder machine and its most important representatives. Since that time, the world understands the term *Schreibtischmörder* (literally "killer behind the desk", i.e., the person giving the orders without getting his own hands dirty). We know that one need not be a fanatic, a sadist or mentally deranged, in order to commit murder by the millions; it is enough to be a loyal follower, one who is avid to perform his duty for a leader, and that mass murderers need not be the least bit anti-social – in fact cannot be. Mass murder on a large scale requires someone who is socially adjusted as a murderer.'

CHAPTER 11
How It All Ended

'I feel nothing towards my father. No emotions. I cannot find any words to describe the terrible things he did during the war.'

Ricardo Eichmann

Mossad's 'Operation Eichmann' kindled a wave of anti-Semitic acts of violence in South America. A whole continent felt its honour wounded. Right-wing machos devastated Jewish cemeteries, set fire to schools, fired on Jewish restaurants with heavy calibre rifles and laid bombs in synagogues. Fascist youth groups marched through the streets of the big cities. In Colombia, the Nazi criminals executed in Nuremberg were mourned in public.

In Buenos Aires, two young women fell victim to the Nazi mob. One of them, Graciella Sirota, was alleged to be the daughter of the man who had rented *Mossad* the 'safe house'. She was kidnapped, violated and tortured. The culprits burned a swastika into her breast. The other, Merta Penjerek, was accused of having supplied the *Mossad* team with food. She was found dead.

The life of the Eichmanns changed. Soon after the abduction of her husband, Vera Eichmann and her son Ricardo moved to Germany. They found a place to stay with grandmother Liebl in North Baden. Ricardo started school at the age of six. His three brothers stayed in Buenos Aires for the time being, working at technical trades. Vera Eichmann met her husband one more time in Israeli captivity in May 1962. This was reported by the news agencies one day after his execution.

She was somehow unable to adjust to life in the new Germany. When Ricardo had completed the first grade in primary school, his mother returned with him to Argentina – to Garibaldi Street in San Fernando. But three years later, mother and son were again drawn back to Germany, this time for good. Young Eichmann attended the *Gymnasium* (secondary school) in Osterburken and was drafted into the *Bundesluftwaffe* (German Air Force). He was stationed in the Eifel and in Munich-Neubiberg, where he reached the rank of corporal.

Ricardo, who even today still appears youthful and debonair, never had an easy time with the family into which he was born. His brothers were ten to fifteen years older than he was, of a totally different generation. For a long time no one explained the importance of his father to him. 'My mother only talked about father with my brothers. When I happened to join them, they clammed up. If I asked her directly, she evaded me. There was something there that one did not talk about. The question marks remained.'

Ricardo Eichmann cannot recall his father. The pieces of the puzzle are too small to make sense. In the beginning, he was only 'my mother's husband' or 'uncle Ricardo', and then suddenly he was gone. He was to encounter him again during military service, when the room in which gas masks were tried on was dubbed 'Eichmann's hobby shop'. Eventually, Ricardo quit the *Bundeswehr* (German Armed Forces). He prefers to think in pacifist terms anyway.

He saw his father in books that describe the whole horror of the Third *Reich*. He was not mentioned during history lessons. He was absent from the family. The fathers of classmates, for example, had died in accidents or from illness. Ricardo had no story to tell the others about his father; yet his classmates often knew more than he did.

The name Eichmann is a heavy burden for Ricardo, whereas his three elder brothers carry it almost with reverence. Horst still lives in Buenos Aires. He has, however, gone under cover. His small transport business is run under the name of his wife. In files of the secret police from 1965, he is listed as the presumed leader of a neo-Nazi group. Argentinian journalist Raul M. Kollmann investigated him intensively: 'It was in the early Sixties. Horst wanted to kidnap somebody in order to exchange him for his father. He was therefore arrested by the police. The corrupt officials let him go again for a large sum of money. The German embassy also made efforts on his behalf at the time.' Statements that cannot be verified objectively, because the family maintains silence.

The other sons, Dieter and Klaus, today live on Lake Constance. Dieter, now fifty-three, is the family archivist. He collects everything that is shown or written about the father. On the telephone, he presents himself as the defender of a father he last saw when he was eighteen. 'My father has had so much dirt thrown at him. So much has been written about him that is false. If I were to tell the truth, I would have to leave Germany again anyway.'

He talks in riddles and metaphors. He refused a meeting to talk things over. His few words indicate a conviction that his father Adolf was more or less innocent and was punished as a scapegoat for others. Brother Klaus, today sixty years old, was already making brazen comparisons in his interview with *Quick* magazine in 1966: 'He is just as much guilty or innocent as a bomber pilot who opens the bomb bay of his plane and lets bombs fall on defenceless people... My father was an officer. He obeyed orders.' The elder Eichmann sons are very different from the children of other Nazi celebrities – for example Niklas Frank – who have made it their life's work to call their fathers to account.

Youngest brother Ricardo belongs to a different epoch in every respect. He studied anthropology and prehistory in Heidelberg from 1976 to 1984 and specialised in archaeology of the Near East, classical archaeology and Egyptology. Eventually he obtained his doctor's degree with a thesis on the subject of 'The Aspects of Practical Foundation Lay-out as found in the Near East'. After completing his studies, he found a job as scientific assistant with the *Deutsche Archäologische Institut* (German Archaeological Institute) in Berlin. On 1 April 1995, he accepted a professorship in Tübingen. At the time, he decided to practise active public relations for several weeks and to talk about his family name with selected journalists.

One of his key statements was: 'I am not happy that my father was executed, but in the case of Adolf Eichmann the verdict was just. If he had not run away in 1945, he would have been brought to trial in Nuremberg. Had he been innocent, he would not have had to flee to South America.' He says this in such a soft voice that one has to listen very closely.

Such statements infuriate his brother Dieter: 'I do not agree with what Ricardo says. School is much to blame for his stance. He was indoctrinated in Germany.'

Their mother Vera can no longer be questioned. She died in 1993 at the age of eighty-four. Ricardo: 'She never got over the fact that Adolf Eichmann was executed.' Adolf Eichmann! He enunciates the name of this 'historic figure' with great detachment. In letters, he sometimes abbreviates it simply as 'E'.

Isser Harel, possibly the best known former chief of a secret service in the world, was not to enjoy his success. Inspired by the Eichmann case, he formed a special unit that occupied itself exclusively with Nazi criminals who had disappeared. The intensive hunt now began for Müller, Bormann, Mengele and others. The task force was stationed in Paris, as sub-tenants in *Mossad's* European central office. It was run by Aharoni ('suddenly this business was quite in vogue'), after having been transferred to *Mossad*, on loan from *Shin Bet*. The operation continued until 1964.

During these years Aharoni was more in South America than in Paris. Despite large investments, however, the Eichmann success could never be repeated.

Harel the crusader soon discovered a new and equally exciting topic. With something like hysterical obsession, he went in pursuit of German technicians and their families who were working on a rocket project in the enemy country of Egypt. 'Operation Damocles' was also to end Harel's own career. *Mossad* sent letter-bombs, hired the former Nazi officer Otto Skorzeny and became more and more of a state within the state. Harel was practising foreign policy without first agreeing it with his boss, Prime Minister David Ben Gurion. When he then joined Ben Gurion's political adversaries, he went completely out of control. On 25 March 1963, Harel tendered his resignation in the hope that the Prime Minister would not accept it. He had miscalculated.

Since then, he lives in seclusion and profound bitterness in his house in northern Tel Aviv. Occasionally he appears on television, instructs *Mossad* trainees or writes a book. The latest major controversy involving Harel has to do with Simon Wiesenthal. The two octogenarians began attacking each other in 1989, shortly after the (temporarily) latest volume of Wiesenthal's memoirs was published – and misinterpreted. As so many times before, the historians again attributed the lion's share in the successful kidnapping of Eichmann to the Nazi-hunter from Vienna. Harel made himself heard from Tel Aviv, breathing fire and brimstone and eager to fight: 'Wiesenthal has not the slightest thing to do with this operation, nothing at all!'

In 1991, Harel compiled a 278-page thick documentation which was intended to prove exactly this claim. To this very day the work has not been published, because Harel wishes to keep back a 'secret weapon' in the war against Wiesenthal. The latter, however, keeps a low profile: 'I have never claimed that I was involved in the operation in Argentina. But for over ten years I did do everything possible to find Eichmann and to bring him to justice. The *Mossad* knows this. I have kept all the questions to my former reports asked by Harel's office. In my view, he is sick.'

Rafi Eitan, the team leader in Buenos Aires, began his victory march through a succession of organisations. During the past thirty-five years he has not had a moment's rest. Following the Eichmann operation, he also moved from *Shin Bet* to *Mossad* and went to Europe. From 1964 to 1970 he was the Chief Resident for Europe, for one year in parallel with his *Mossad* colleague Yitzhak Shamir, who later became Prime Minister. Eitan: 'After Harel came Meir Amit. He turned the service inside out. I was sent out to implement these changes.'

Rafi Eitan, though shortsighted and almost deaf in one ear, is an extremely clever tactician who went on to become Deputy Head of the

Mossad operations department. When he was refused the position of Director, he resigned. His friend Ariel Sharon became Security Adviser to Prime Minister Yitzhak Rabin and Eitan followed him as his assistant. In 1976 he was fired by Shimon Peres, who had been in office as Minister of Defence since 1974.

Two years later he returned to the field of secret service as anti-terror adviser to Prime Minister Menachem Begin. At the time, *Mossad* blew up Arafat confidant Ali Hassan Salameh, code name 'Red Prince', alleged to have planned the attack on the Israeli team at the Olympic Games in Munich. It was the end of an extremely elaborate operation lasting seven years.

Rafi Eitan followed Ariel Sharon to the Ministry of Defence and took over the highly secret technology service *Lakam* in 1981. In 1984, Eitan met a civilian employee of the United States Navy named Jonathan Pollard. The pro-Israeli Pollard entangled himself in Eitan's closely knit net and for seventeen months he delivered most secret Pentagon material, more than one thousand sensitive documents, among them many satellite photographs. It was a goldmine of intelligence information. With this operation, however, Rafi Eitan overstepped the invisible line in the dealings between friendly secret services. When Pollard was exposed, this led to probably the worst crisis in American-Israeli relations. For diplomatic reasons, *Lakam* was disbanded immediately.

Eichmann-hunter Eitan switched over to the chair of Director General of the Israeli chemical industry. He grins when he looks back today: 'That is where I learned how to make money.' The next step was to go into business. In the real estate market in Berlin, he paid beginner's fees, only subsequently to land one successful deal after the other in the commodity trade. Now sixty-nine, Eitan has meanwhile become one of the most important newcomers to this business.

Zvika Malchin left the world of secret service in 1976. His last position had been that of Chief of Operations. As he admits, he then fell into a deep hole: 'I still felt young, but became more and more aware that others no longer saw me as such.' Malchin tried his hand at many different things, but always failed. Then he began to write a book about his Eichmann experience (*Eichmann in My Hands*), a book more about himself than about Eichmann. He published drawings that he had made in Buenos Aires in 1960. They show Eichmann against the background of a travel guide to South America. Today, the man who let Eichmann slip through his hands lives alternately in Tel Aviv and New York. His new life consists of private views of art exhibits and talk shows.

Very different was the fate of Avraham Shalom. After the massacre in the Olympic Village in Munich, Eitan's deputy in the *Shin Bet* operations department advanced to become the new chief of the safety and security department of the internal service. His predecessor had been dismissed because of the Munich security débâcle. In 1981 he was appointed Director of *Shin Bet*. Among his spectacular operations during the ensuing years is the blow against the terrorist underground organisation of orthodox Jews.

The biggest scandal in the life of Avraham Shalom began on 12 April 1984. In the evening, four Palestinian youths took bus No. 300 from Tel Aviv to Ashkelon on the northern border of the Gaza Strip. They hijacked the bus, threatened the passengers with knives and hand grenades, and demanded the release of 500 compatriots. The vehicle was stopped in the Gaza Strip and surrounded by élite forces. Senior officers at the highest level came and negotiated with the culprits. Towards morning, the Army stormed the bus. Two of the kidnappers were shot at close range. The other two survived and were given into the custody of *Shin Bet* and the Army. Only hours later, they too were dead. The *New York Times* claimed they had been murdered.

An investigation committee accused *Shin Bet* and the police of having beaten the two Palestinians to death. Then the accusation was dropped again. It became more and more apparent that the leadership of the internal service was trying to cover up the deed. Finally a power struggle developed for Avraham Shalom's position. The scandal was now openly revealed. On 24 May 1986, State Attorney General Yitzhak Zamir announced his intention to prosecute Shalom. Israel's 'Watergate scandal' now gathered pace. On 6 June, Shalom resigned. He and three further officials were immediately pardoned by President Chaim Herzog, even though they had not even been indicted.

A new committee began investigations into the affair of bus No. 300. The result was shattering. The two Palestinians had been beaten to death in a VW bus on Avraham Shalom's orders. Shalom defended himself. He had only followed orders given by Prime Minister Shamir. Shamir recalls the conversation, but asserts it was not to be understood as 'permission ... to take prisoners, interrogate them and subsequently kill them'. Today, Avraham Shalom lives mainly in London and New York where he works in the private security business.

What became of the remainder of the *Mossad* team in Buenos Aires? Zeev Keren, who had been responsible for the cars and houses, lives in Israel on a pension from *Shin Bet*. Yaakov Gat, called Yankele, has also found employment in the private security business, where he works on logistic problems. Yitzhak Nesher lost touch with his former colleagues. Judith Nesiyahu said goodbye to *Mossad* long ago. She is married to a high-ranking functionary in the Labour Party. Shalom Dany and Efraim Ilani have died.

Efraim Hofstetter, of the Israeli police, who had met the blind Lothar Hermann and questioned him, began a second career in the diplomatic service. In 1971, then fifty-nine, he represented his country as Consul General in Istanbul. On 17 May he was kidnapped from his residence by four heavily armed left-wing extremists. Their organisation, the Turkish People's Freedom Army, demanded the release of imprisoned compatriots. The Turkish Government refused the deal, in agreement with Jerusalem. On 23 May, the Consul General was found dead. He had been executed by three shots in the head.

On 23 March 1961, informant Hermann again drew attention to himself. The blind man had a nervous breakdown, because he firmly believed that the Israelis had completely ignored his contribution to the successful Eichmann operation. He was taken to a police station. The old man was so confused that he claimed to be Josef Mengele. He was arrested. Next day the newspapers were already celebrating Mengele's capture. Only twenty-four hours later, the error was cleared up.

Aharoni recalls: 'I wanted to help him. On three separate occasions, I appealed to Isser to express our thanks to Hermann. Without Hermann, I reminded him, the whole operation would never have taken place. At this time the man was living in abject poverty. There was a rumour that his daughter wanted to move to the United States and that the parents would like to go with her. Isser always brusquely rejected my suggestion. He said there was no reason for a reward. There was surely a psychological reason behind Harel's motives. At the time, he was being fêted everywhere. He could hardly admit that there was someone else who also deserved recompense and thanks for the Eichmann operation. That was when our paths separated. I lost all respect for my former boss. Today I do not speak to him.'

Today, Rafi Eitan is still the link between the veterans of the Eichmann operation: 'Whoever wants something, comes to me! We are one big family,' he says proudly. 'We meet each other time and again.' He hesitates, reflects and then realises that the last joint meeting took place twenty-five years ago. The idea is now and then put forward to award a medal to the participants in the operation. The Government, however, always maintains that it is far too late.

Aharoni recalls: 'In 1970, I took early retirement for personal reasons. That only meant retiring from *Mossad*, because over the next fifteen years I became an active businessman. I lived and worked for several years each in

Hong Kong and Peking, in London and Frankfurt, as well as in Israel. In 1986, I retired to a country house in south-west England.

'Since then, there have been repeated occasions when Eichmann and the Nazi terror régime have returned into my life. In 1993, a letter arrived from Frankfurt/Oder. Seventeen-year-old René Bertel, from the *Friedrichs-Gymnasium*, very delicately approached the 'highly honoured Mr Aronheim'. On 1 July of the coming year the 300th anniversary of the school was to be celebrated. For this, the intention was to implement a project developed by the German course of the eleventh grade; a commemorative volume containing contributions by former students.

'"Of particular interest to me personally are your experiences as a Jew in the former *Deutsche Reich* and how you feel about these today. I hope that I have now not offended you in any way. But the reason I am so full of curiosity is that for the first time I now have the opportunity to contact a Jew. If you do not wish to write about this topic, I will not take this amiss..."

'I replied with a four-page letter, describing the increasingly intolerable life of Jews in the Third *Reich*, the lack of feeling, the coldness of the non-Jews. 'I believe the most important experience was the total lack of any experience at all. What I mean by this is very simple: during three years in school under the Nazi régime, it did not happen even once that one of my classmates or one of my teachers said to me: "We don't give a fig for all this Nazi propaganda. For us, you are the same Hermann you always were. Not a single person! Not even once! Either they enthusiastically joined in the cries of '*Juda verrecke*' ('Death to the Jews'), or they joined the ranks of the guilty by remaining passively silent.

'No thank you. The guest would prefer not to attend the anniversary celebration of his former *Gymnasium*. My time in school and my childhood in Frankfurt were connected with too many unhappy memories. It would be senseless to invoke all that again. So the celebration took place without me. My letter, however, was published and I received a number of very positive replies to it.

'In June 1995, I went to a meeting of a very special kind. My friend Gad Shimron, European correspondent of the Israeli newspaper *Maariv*, had arranged everything. Shimron came from Germany and brought a sympathetic, good-looking young man with him. We met in the Hilton at Heathrow.

'The younger man introduced himself: "Ricardo Eichmann."

'"Zvi Aharoni," I replied and stretched out my hand. Both of us were clearly tense. Almost apologetically, I broke the silence: "It is not easy when you meet someone, for the death of whose father you are responsible. You did not have a happy childhood. I am therefore particularly pleased to see that you have really made something of yourself. A professor of archaeology". I then told the young scientist that after the abduction of Adolf Eichmann, Rafi Eitan had tried to talk Isser Harel into some form of financial support for the Eichmann family, but had failed. Both Eitan, as well as myself, had felt this to be a moral obligation on the part of Israel. Harel had only shaken his head in disbelief and refused.

'The ice was now broken and I recounted the sequence of events at the time. I showed Ricardo pictures that had been taken – San Fernando, the house, the garden, Adolf Eichmann. Slowly and in minute detail, I described the kidnapping to him. The son listened silently. Occasionally, his face twitched.

'"I feel nothing towards my father. No emotions. I cannot find any words to describe the terrible things he did during the war. It is also a strange situation to meet a man who knows more about me and my family than most of my relatives and friends."

'When he returned home, Ricardo Eichmann had much to report: also to his sons, who were just six and eight years old. He does not want to repeat the mistakes of the past for which he blames his family. Ricardo and his children took advantage of the very next opportunity to visit the villa on the Wannsee, the site of the *Wannsee-Konferenz*. There is a large picture of Adolf Eichmann hanging on a wall there. Ricardo explained at length who grandpa had been and what he had done to people. And the two children from the youngest Eichmann generation were very sad and said that they could not love a grandpa like him.'

CHAPTER 12

Cue 'Auschwitzlüge'

'Even five decades after the war, the simple "Auschwitzlüge" is still not be found in the law codes as an offence in itself.'

Wilhelm Dietl

In the summer of 1994, the Hamburg periodical *Die Woche* published a survey on German perceptions of recent history. The FORSA Institute in Dortmund questioned a representative sample of 1114 citizens from the east and west of the republic on their stance towards the National Socialist past. The issues were: What lessons have the Germans drawn from the Nazi era? How do they view war and crime today? Is it time to draw a line?

Die Woche summarised the surprisingly positive result as follows: 'About two-thirds of those surveyed believe it is a good thing that Germany lost the war, and would not wish to live in Germany had Hitler won the war. Sixty-nine per cent regard the ending of the war as a liberation, only thirteen per cent as a defeat. The overwhelming majority, namely ninety-one per cent, reject the claim by the neo-Nazis that the mass murders during the Third Reich are only a propaganda lie by the victors. Only three per cent believe the fairytale of the *Auschwitzlüge*. And seventy-six per cent do not view these crimes as the work of only a small clique, but believe that large segments of the bureaucracy and the administration were also involved.'

Six years previously, in the autumn of 1988, the Cologne Institute for Empirical Psychology (IFEP) had surveyed 850 young people between sixteen and twenty-four years of age for the Hamburg magazine *Der Stern*. The topic then had also been the National Socialist past. The key question: 'Does your generation still have to feel burdened by the crimes of the Nazi era or is this only a problem of the older generation?' Eighty-eight per cent of the youngsters believed the following: 'While I do not feel personally responsible, these crimes are a part of German history. Everybody has to continue to face up to them, so that something like that will never happen again.'

The absolute majority of the German people thinks along these lines. With reunification, right-wing extremist activities increased markedly, but have since largely been halted through rigorous application of the law. Most of the right-wing organisations that could pose a threat to the inner stability of the republic are now prohibited. Their ideology, however, lives on, including the so-called *Auschwitzlüge*. This is the obstinate attempt to deny the mass murder of the Jews during the National Socialist *Reich*. An absurd situation, since those born later are refuting something that not even the accused at the Nuremberg Tribunal or Adolf Eichmann in Jerusalem denied. The war criminals only tried to shift the blame from themselves on to others.

The chief ideologues of the *Auschwitzlüge* include the French professor Paul Rassinier, who died in 1967 (*The Lie of Odysseus – What is Truth? The Jews and the Third Reich*), Emil Aretz (*Magic Formula of a Lie*), Thies Christophersen (*The Auschwitzlüge. An Experience Report*), Wilhelm Stäglich (*The Auschwitz Myth – Legend or Reality*), and Erich Kern (*The Tragedy of the Jews. Fate Between Propaganda and Truth*).

This squad of incorrigibles is trying to prove, either that there were no gas chambers at all, or that the number of Jews murdered was far lower. The American 'expert on executions', Fred Leuchter, is spreading the claim that there were only 'disinfection facilities' installed in the concentration camp at Auschwitz. The controversial English historian David Irving also proclaims that the gas chambers are merely a sham. In 1989, he said they were a 'brilliant invention by the British Office for Psychological Warfare' and in 1990 he described them as an artificially created tourist attraction.

In this context, the former National Chairman of the *Nationaldemokratische Partei Deutschlands* (German National Democratic Party, NPD), Günter Deckert, spoke derisively about the 'gas chamber myth'. He described the Holocaust as 'a collection of lies deliberately invented by the Jews following the Second World War for the purpose of exploiting and muzzling Germany to the advantage of the Jews'. The former teacher at a *Gymnasium*, Deckert was finally convicted after great endeavour, and only by means of a detour via the Federal Supreme Court. This latest precedent demonstrates that the German penal code with regard to *Volksverhetzung* (incitement of the people) is still not sufficiently accurately worded.

According to the actual state of the law, the *Auschwitzlüge* is a form of *Volksverhetzung* and an 'incitement to racial hatred'. It is punishable if the culprit identifies himself with Nazi racial ideology and claims the *Auschwitzlüge* to be an invention for the purpose of financial blackmail of the German nation. Simple denial of the murders in the gas chambers is already a borderline situation. The Federal Supreme Court does not yet recognise this as constituting *Volksverhetzung*. The right-wing extremists are normally only tried for libel. Even five decades after the war, the simple *Auschwitzlüge* is still not to be found in the law codes as an offence in itself.

BIBLIOGRAPHY
Recommended Reading

1. EICHMANN AND HIS TIMES

Ausschuß für Deutsche Einheit: Eichmann, Henker, Handlanger, Hintermänner: Eine Dokumentation (Committee for German Unity: Eichmann, Executioners, Henchmen, Men Behind the Scenes. A Documentation), Berlin, 1961

Beattie, John, Klaus Barbie. His Life and Career, London, 1984

Camarasa, Jorge, Odessa Al Sur. La Argentina Como Refugio de Nazis y Criminales de Guerra (Odessa in the South. Argentina as a Refuge for Nazis and War Criminals), Buenos Aires, 1995

Comité des Délégationes Juives, Die Lage der Juden in Deutschland 1933. Das Schwarzbuch, Tatsachen und Dokumente (The Situation of the Jews in Germany 1933. The Blackbook, Facts and Documents), Paris, 1934 and Frankfurt a. M., Berlin, 1983

Deutscher Bundestag, Referat Öffentlichkeitsarbeit (ed.), Fragen an die deutsche Geschichte. Ideen, Kräfte, Entscheidungen. Von 1800 bis zur Gegenwart (German Bundestag, Public Relations Office: Questions to German History, Ideas, Forces, Decisions. From 1800 to the Present), Bonn, 1993

Eichmann, Adolf, Ich, Adolf Eichmann (I, Adolf Eichmann) edited by Dr Rudolf Aschenauer, Leoni am Starnberger See, 1980

Gilbert, Martin, Endlösung: Die Vertreibung und Vernichtung der Juden. Ein Atlas (Final Solution: The Expulsion and Extermination of the Jews. An Atlas), Reinbek, 1982

Hausner, Gideon, Die Vernichtung der Juden. Das größte Verbrechen der Geschichte (The Extermination of the Jews. The Greatest Crime in History), Munich, 1979

Hilberg, Raul, Die Vernichtung der europäischen Juden (The Extermination of the European Jews), 3 vols, Berlin, 1982

Höhne, Heinz, Der Orden unter dem Totenkopf. Die Geschichte der SS (The Order under the Death's Head. The History of the SS), Munich, 1967

Joffroy, Pierre, Der Spion Gottes. Kurt Gerstein, ein SS-Offizier im Wider-

stand? (God's Spy. Kurt Gerstein, an SS Officer in the Resistance?),
Berlin, 1995

Kempner, Robert M.W., *Eichmann und seine Komplizen* (Eichmann and his
Accomplices), Zurich, 1961

Kogon, Eugen, *Der SS-Staat. Das System der deutschen Konzentrationslager*
(The SS State. The German Concentration Camp System), Munich, 1974

Märthesheimer, Peter and Frenzel, Ivo (ed.), *Im Kreuzfeuer: Der Fernsehfilm
Holocaust. Eine Nation ist betroffen* (Under Cross-fire. The Television
Film Holocaust. A Nation is Dismayed), Frankfurt a. M., 1979

Meding, Holger M., *Flucht vor Nürnberg, Deutsche und österreichische Ein-
wanderung in Argentinien 1945-1955* (Flight from Nuremberg, German
and Austrian Immigration in Argentina 1945–1955), Cologne, 1992

Posner, Gerald L. and Ware, John, *Mengele. The Complete Story*, New York,
1986

Rückerl, Adalbert (ed.), *NS-Vernichtungslager im Spiegel deutscher Straf-
prozesse* (NS Extermination Camps in the Light of German Criminal
Cases), Munich, 1977

Safrian, Hans, *Die Eichmann-Männer* (The Eichmann Men), Vienna, Zurich,
1993

Salazar, Sanchez G. and Reimann, E., *Barbie in Bolivien* (Barbie in Bolivia),
Berlin, 1989

Studt, Christoph (ed.), *Das Dritte Reich. Ein Lesebuch zur deutschen
Geschichte 1933-1945* (The Third Reich. A Reader of German History
1933–1945), Munich,1995

Wucher, Albert, *Eichmanns gab es viele* (There were many Eichmanns),
Munich, 1961

Zentner, Christian (ed.), *Adolf Hitlers Mein Kampf* (Adolf Hitler's *Mein
Kampf*), Munich, 1974

Zentner, Christian (ed.), *Internationaler Militärgerichtshof Nürnberg. Der
Nürnberger Prozess* (International Military Tribunal in Nuremberg. The
Nuremberg Trial) 24 vols, Reichenbach, 1994

2. THE HUNT FOR ADOLF EICHMANN

Black, Ian and Morris, Benny, *Mossad, Shin Bet, Aman. The History of the
Israeli Secret Services*, London, 1991

Harel, Isser, *The House on Garibaldi Street*, New York, 1975

Levy, Alan, *Die Akte Wiesenthal* (The Wiesenthal File), Vienna, 1995

Malchin, Peter Z., *Ich jagte Eichmann* (I Hunted Eichmann), Munich, 1991

Pearlman, Moshe, *Die Festnahme des Adolf Eichmann* (The Arrest of Adolf Eichmann), Frankfurt a. M., 1961

Raviv, Dan and Melman, Yossi, *The History of Mossad. Rise and Fall of the Israeli Secret Service*, London, 1989

Stein, Richard A., *Documents Against Words. Simon Wiesenthal's Conflict with the World Jewish Congress*, Rotterdam, 1992

Wiesenthal, Simon, *Doch die Mörder leben* (And Yet the Murderers Live), Munich, Zurich, 1967

Wiesenthal, Simon, *Recht, nicht Rache* (Justice, not Revenge), Frankfurt a. M., Berlin, 1988

Zuroff, Efraim, *Occupation: Nazi-Hunter. The Continuing Search for Perpetrators of the Holocaust*, Hoboken, 1994

3. THE EICHMANN TRIAL

Arendt, Hannah, *Eichmann in Jerusalem. A Report on the Banality of Evil*, New York, 1963

Council of Jews from Germany, *After the Eichmann Trial. On a Controversy about the Stance of the Jews*, Tel Aviv, 1963

Government Press Office, *The Trial of Adolf Eichmann. Opening Address by the Attorney-General Mr. Gideon Hausner*, Jerusalem, 1961

Hausner, Gideon, *Justice in Jerusalem*, New York, 1966

Lamm, Hans (ed.), *Der Eichmann-Prozess in der deutschen öffentlichen Meinung* (The Eichmann Trial in German Public Opinion), Frankfurt a. M., 1961

Lang, Jochen von, *Das Eichmann-Protokoll* (The Eichmann Minutes), Berlin, 1982

Lord Russell of Liverpool: *The Trial of Adolf Eichmann*, London, 1962

Mulisch, Harry, *Strafsache 40/61. Eine Reportage über den Eichmann-Prozess* (Criminal Case 40/61. A Report on the Eichmann Trial), Amsterdam, 1961, Munich, 1994, Berlin, 1995

Nellessen, Bernd, *Der Prozeß von Jerusalem* (The Trial in Jerusalem), Düsseldorf, 1964

Schmorak, Dov B., *Der Prozess Eichmann* (The Eichmann Trial), Vienna, 1964

Index